THE NEWSCASTERS

THE
NEWSCASTERS

Ron Powers

St. Martin's Press New York

Library of Congress Cataloging in Publication Data

Powers, Ron.
  The Newscasters.

  Includes Index.
  1. Television Broadcasting of News-United States.
I. Title.
PN4888.T4P6   384.55'4'0973   76-62789
ISBN 0-312-57207-7

This book is for my father and mother,
Paul and Elvadine Powers

ACKNOWLEDGEMENTS

Many people, both inside and outside broadcasting, were helpful in the preparation of this book. In addition to those quoted in the text, the author is particularly grateful for the advice and assistance of the following:

Fred Friendly, Edward R. Murrow professor of communications, Columbia University; Marvin Barrett, editor, The Fifth Alfred I. DuPont-Columbia University Survey of Broadcast Journalism; Nicholas Johnson, chairman, National Citizens Committee for Broadcasting; Edwin Diamond, author, commentator and co-director, Massachusetts Institute of Technology News Study Group; Stephanie Edwards, broadcaster; Mike Wallace, CBS; Les Brown, television reporter, *New York Times;* Gary Deeb, television critic, *Chicago Tribune;* Frank Swertlow, television critic, *Chicago Daily News;* Robert Lemon, broadcaster and educator; Marsha Morgan, *Playboy* magazine; Opal Hoffman, aunt and typist, and Honoree Fleming, a scientist who understands, communicates and practices research in its most worthy form.

CONTENTS

FACES AND PLACES

The biggest heist of the 1970's never made it on the five o'clock news.

The biggest heist of the 1970's *was* the five o'clock news.

The salesmen took it. They took it away from the journalists, slowly, patiently, gradually, and with such finesse that nobody noticed until it was too late.

By the 1970s, an extravagant proportion of television news—local news in particular—answered less to the description of "journalism" than to that of "show business." This transformation, carried out by sales-oriented station managers in an unbounded quest for profits, bore the profoundest implications in the way Americans were to receive information and perceive political choices. Many local newscasts ceased serving the public (at best, they served the public only incidentally) and bequeathed their primary allegiance to the advertisers. No longer did a station manager judge a news program on the basis of how diligently it informed citizens of economic events and social developments, or acted as a watchdog on government. The fashionable criterion for judging the sleek, antiseptic news "package" became the size of the audience it could attract to view the main event—the commercial. Local television news, in fact, scarcely bothered to maintain the fiction of addressing "citizens" at all; it ingratiated itself instead to members of some vague society called "the 18-to-49 age group"—the purchasing bloc of Americans most coveted by sponsors.

John Coleman and Joel Daly in Chicago, Tom Ellis and Tom

Snyder in New York, John Hambrinck in Los Angeles, Bill Bonds in Detroit — these were the new symbols of the new, processed, cybernetic news. Anchormen, weathermen, and reporters all, each represented a radical discontinuity with journalistic tradition. Each was a curious hybrid of personal magnetism, looks, showmanship and — in some cases — newsman. Each, to the degree that he was successful, was a bigger audience "draw" than the news he reported or read. Each had been selected in the first place according to a standard unique in video journalism: his presumed ability to personify a shared viewer fantasy, a collective need.

But the usurpation of television news reached a far deeper level than that of anchormen's personalities. It attained the status of a covert and insidious reversal of the very journalistic process itself. Instead of striving to impart information *to* the viewers, the salesmen-managers of television stations were engaged in a tacit conspiracy to extract information *from* the viewers — information that would serve the managers in their efforts to maximize audience size and thereby establish their respective newscasts as the top-dollar advertising draw in the market.

What did people *want* (not need, but *want*) under the rubric of "news"? What pleased them most? Amused them? Gratified them, charmed them, or provided them with the sort of vicarious cheap thrills that kept them mesmerized during prime-time entertainment? What colors did they like? What faces, voices? Conversely, what did viewers *not* want to know? What sort of news displeased them, threatened them, bored them, impelled them to switch *away* from a disturbing confrontation with harsh reality and into the lulling glades of television torpor?

The managers, the salesmen, would find out. There were ways. New ways. New Chaldeans had arrived in the global village. The managers sought them out. Diffidently, at first — speculatively — then with a gathering whoop of abandon as their innate superstitions took hold, the managers flocked like leisure-suited catechumens to that most orphic and esoteric witch doctor of the corporate tribe, the consultant. Just as nature abhors a vacuum, unnatural television adores a panacea. The consultant beckoned with a jeweled finger; he invoked the sweet, mysterious patois of behaviorist psychology and then preached the ringing, pure gospel of profit swift and certain. Done, said the managers. They had their astrologer, and his sign was the dollar. Armed with question-naires, with the rudiments of Gestalt—and, in some cases, with electrodes—the consultant set about to spy on the viewing au-diences for the managers, to pry into behavior patterns, to pilfer the unconscious if necessary; but above all, to find out which stim-uli (faces, voices, colors, names, jokes, bedtime stories, charades, or, God help us, *ideas*) would serve as the best bait to lure the viewer before the Client's Channel.

It was a uniquely American dance, this torrid tribal twirl be-tween manager and consultant. But in this case, it was something more. When market research (the consultant's divining rod) in-vaded the TV newsroom, it threatened to change the course, if not the very definition, of American journalism.

For it was an inescapable fact of advertising competition that as television news went, so went the newspapers. For the last de-cade, American dailies had weakened under television's drain of the advertising dollar. The demise of more than one newspaper (the Boston *Herald-Traveler*, Chicago *Today*) was attributed partly to TV's stranglehold on revenues.

If American newspapers (which already had been tending to-ward market research for years) were to survive the threat of an-nihilation, they would survive partly by emulating television news. Hence the lemming-like trend to "People" features in newspapers in the mid-seventies; "People" was (as opposed to *were*) discovered by the consultant to be a major growth area for TV audiences, and soon no station manager or city editor could open his mouth with-out "Pee-pull" escaping it like a paternoster.

The station managers soon devised a high-sounding justifica-tion for their burglary of the viewers' minds. They said they were giving the Pee-pull What They Want.

People did not *want* complicated, disturbing newscasts any more, the managers told themselves and each other. The Vietnam War was over. Watergate was over. People were "sick" of unpleas-ant news. The new "mood of the country," they discovered to their delight, was no longer "issue-oriented" but "People-ori-ented." The very term "Pee-pull," to denote a news genre, became oracular; it was spoken in hushed italics; it bore the tin-tinnabulation of cash-register bells.

People in the News. Faces and Places. Personalities. These

became the new staples of the local newscast, with the items themselves being delivered by People with beautiful Faces in wondrous Places (the futuristic, color-coordinated new sets), People who were themselves Personalities. People who were members of News Teams, who wore identical tailored blazers (or smart designer blouses and scarves); or, in some cases, People who dressed conspicuously apart from the rest of the Team and thus were certified as Personalities apart. People who grinned wryly at one another; who traded banter about their personal lives (golf games) at the commercial break; who, by their very dress and manner and sense of fulsome consumer-well-being, spoke a new national language of comfort and assurance, of a peace that passeth for understanding.

To be sure, social and governmental stories were still being reported on the local newscasts. In fact, few if any of the traditional *categories* of news had been eliminated. What had changed was the degree of emphasis, the amount of thoroughness, the method of presentation within those categories. The television crews were unfailingly present at political press conferences, at ceremonial appearances, at political party dinners, presentations, dedications, and other official events. Sometimes, during one of these soirees, an enterprising reporter might work in a "tough" question: "Mr. Mayor, what *about* that proposed Crosstown Expressway?"

And certainly, the cybernetic newscasts carried summaries of the *results* of official government action: new taxes, new budgets, new ordinances, new measures to control crime, stop drugs, create jobs.

What was emphasized in all this was the *personality* of the newsmaker—his style, his degree of histrionics before the camera, his performance as a figure in opposition to another personality.

What was lacking was a sense of the abstractions of government, of the way government impinged on the private life in the absence of the galvanic personality—a sense of forces and dynamics in city life.

Bill Kurtis, of CBS-owned WBBM in Chicago, is an anomaly among the new breed of anchormen-showmen. Educated in the law (he passed his examinations for the Kansas bar) and as a journalist, Kurtis has covered more major trials than any other electronic newsman in America: the Chicago Seven, Angela Davis, Daniel Ellsberg, Richard Speck, Charles Manson. In the summer of 1974, at a personal cost of $1,700, Kurtis flew to Saigon to photograph and report the story of children who would not be involved in the massive orphan-lift preceding the fall of Vietnam.

Kurtis is troubled about the lack of attention to difficult, abstract stories on local television news. He spoke of his concern one spring morning in his tiny, cluttered office inside WBBM's barnlike broadcast complex.

"I see a fork in the road," he said, "and we are heading in the wrong direction in television news. There are a lot of things that dictate to us that we stay with the superficial. The direction is not toward substance in local television news, but to a more superficial coverage.

"We're living in decaying cities. We have seen our metropolises rise and decay. We have seen a population migrate from the rural areas to the big cities, and we are now seeing the cities disintegrate. This is a pattern that is not going to turn around for 25 years.

"I think there are myriad stories that could be done that document the depth of an inner city, and at the same time suggest alternatives. What is going to bring a family back from the suburbs into Chicago? How are people going to live together? What is going to happen to the South Side and West Side, where dope is being pushed, where we have more vacant buildings than after the bombing of London? What is happening there? What is the pattern of growth?

"Look," continued Kurtis, a tone of frustration in his voice, "here is the story I would like to see covered. Why isn't open housing a fact in Cicero and Berwyn [two predominantly white Chicago suburbs]? Why have federal prosecutors, as well as local, all steered clear of that? We all know why: because it would be committing World War III. But there's got to be a time when we come to grips with that."

Kurtis shrugged. "But you see, by their very definition, stories like that are not 'visual.' They don't revolve around one or two personalities. It takes so much talent and time to visualize a story like that on television. We do visual stories best. Newspapers do in-depth stories best—investigative stories best."

One reason Bill Kurtis (who correctly prides himself on being a reporter) did not have time to put together a story such as the one he outlined was that, in the early weeks of 1976, he was variously preoccupied with such vital assignments as riding along the highway with a truck driver, investigating the social appeal of the soap opera, and covering the phenomenon of runaway wives.

Local television news did not fall victim to the salesmen-managers overnight, of course. TV news's vulnerability to ratings considerations is endemic to a medium designed primarily to move goods. The "Camel News Caravan" designation that graced John Cameron Swayze's reports in the early days is testament to that truth.

The tyranny of advertiser interests escalated in the late sixties largely because of TV news's booming popularity; in that sense, the TV newscast was a victim of its own success. The suddenly "visual" nature of the news—footage from the Vietnam War, student demonstrations, ghetto riots, the Democratic National Convention in Chicago—all converged to attract nightly viewers in unprecedented numbers. This sea-change in audience size took the TV newscast out of the category of something that *had* to be done (to please the Federal Communications Commission) and into the heady realm of profitable programming. Maximized profits were an inevitable next step in an industry that recognizes no badge of achievement *except* maximized profits. Newscasts grew from 15 minutes in the old days, to half-hours in the early sixties, to hour blocs in the late sixties, to the sophisticated two-hour national and local packages on many network-owned stations today. Along with that growth in air time came a growth in audience-building expertise.

Station managers today are fond of pointing to the very bulk of the contemporary newscast as evidence that the station is not in the news game just for the money. They are correct in arguing that a local newscast is an expensive operation, much more so than plugging into a network game show. (Overlooked in this argument is the fact that the local station had *better* do news, or risk having its license successfully challenged.)

And it cannot be denied that superior news operations exist in television. Some station managers are enlightened; they are

concerned about the news and are willing to stake their reputa-
tions on integrity and thoroughness as well as profits. Electronic
journalism is by no means the exclusive province of the second-
rate journalist, the empty-minded pretty face. The profession
is attracting some of the ablest young reportorial talents in
the country.

Those truths, however, can and do exist alongside the unavoidable evidence that TV journalism in this country — local TV
journalism, in particular — is drifting into the sphere of entertainment. Its propellant is cybernetics, the comparative study of the
human nervous system and the human brain, toward the end of
determining what gratifies, as opposed to what is useful or necessary.

American television has entered the era of cybernetic news.

VAMPING IT

"Hello again, everybody, on the readout from 'News Center 4' here at the top of the hour on this Tuesday night ... many people out of work here in New York, the unemployment rate up over 11 per cent in January, we'll have details on why...."

Tom Snyder is in his shirtsleeves.

"... Big protest here in town, thousands of people on the street, protesting the city's plans to close John Jay College of Criminal Justice. Prison authorities visited Riker's Island for the first time since the uprising there about three months ago...."

What is Tom Snyder doing in his *shirtsleeves*?

"... There could be a new hotel in Manhattan at a vary famous old location. And tonight, Part Two of the Sex Connection: sexual fantasies the topic for this evening. Chuck?"

The fact mesmerizes. It is a trivial fact, an annoying fact — here is Tom Snyder, the greatest local newscaster of them all, his brows knit in terrible concentration, informing us in his quivering staccato voice about unemployment and protest groups and prison authorities, and somehow one's attention cannot wrench itself from the absurd preoccupation about Tom Snyder being in his shirtsleeves.

It is 5:59 P.M. in New York. WNBC's gargantuan early-evening newscast, "News Center 4," is lumbering toward the halfway mark of its nightly cycle. For the first hour Chuck Scarborough was at the anchor desk: Scarborough the embodiment of Rational Man, correct and handsome beneath his Robert Redford wheatwave; Scarborough, pin-striped and respectful, his very name vaguely connoting an ambitious suburb; Scarborough the son in every mother's dream.

That was from five to six. Now the universe has changed, the universe in front of the TV sets. In the hour that Scarborough has been on the air, there has been a population explosion in videoland. Scarborough read headlines to an audience weighted toward the upper ages and lower incomes. But even as he read, an elegant army was moving through Manhattan: an army of consumers, young and affluent and hip. Out of the offices at five, down the elevators, into the streets, into the taxis and buses and commuter trains and car pools, across town, through the traffic, toward their own brownstones and high-rises.

Toward a vodka martini and the evening news on television.

It is this army to which Tom Snyder is playing, every bit as insouciant as a Las Vegas headliner with his tuxedo tie dangling open around his neck.

These people are the high rollers. And to them, Tom is vamping the news.

SCARBOROUGH: Thomas, last night we, we, uh, took people a bit unawares with our Part One of that, and we got a few phone calls complaining about it, so . . .

SNYDER (*irritably*): We had *several* phone calls.

SCARBOROUGH: Yes. Perhaps we should warn the people.

SNYDER (*turning to the camera*): Last night there was explicit *sexual material* in that report, or piece. And I suppose I'm allowed to go in and see it before we go on the air, but nobody *says* why don't you go in and look at it so you can *do* something, so I don't know *what's* going on tonight.

SCARBOROUGH: I presume there's more of the same, and at least you can get the kids out of the room if you don't want them to see it.

Something else is at work here. This is the "overlap" period of the newscast; the changing of the guard, the moment at 5:59 P.M. when Scarborough hands the symbolic reins of "News Center 4" over to Snyder. The conversation is ceremonial. But something more than that is at work. Scarborough, detached and orderly in his dark pin-stripe business suit, is relinquishing control to a seeming borderline hysteric— a nervous-voiced, vaguely angry man in his shirtsleeves, a smoldering individual who by all appearances has just arrived in the studio and who is preoccupied by some private pique concerning the newscast's content.

Quickly, the ambiance of "News Center 4" has changed from a relatively serious, subdued newscast (although the first three stories on this particular evening, and five of the first ten, were about violent crime) to something approaching a theatrical event. At 5:59 the "News Center 4" atmosphere has been charged with a brooding energy, a sense of random urgency garnished with sexual promise.

SNYDER: You know, it's a funny thing, and we could probably spend the rest of the hour just *talking* about this and let people come in and talk about it with us. And I understand how people don't want their children to see naked bodies on television; I-I-I *guess* I understand that, a person's home is their castle. *(Pause)* But yet they go down to Forty-second Street and see it *there*, and they complain about seeing it *here*, and last night we had a picture which I thought was a little extreme, a guy in a car with five bullet holes in his *head*—and, and nobody complained about that, but they complained about seeing a woman's *breasts* on television.

SCARBOROUGH: Well, it's . . .

SNYDER *(snappishly):* It's *confusing!*

SCARBOROUGH: I think we should just give 'em the option, that's all. They have the option of going to Forty-second Street.

SNYDER: Exactly. Anyway, it comes on at 6:45 and, uh—that's it. It's called Sex Fantasies.

In 1976, "News Center 4" was quite likely the best local newscast on television: the New York *Times* of TV news. As the flagship station of NBC, Channel 4 could command tremendous resources of network-quality reporters, writers, camera crews, news editors, and anchormen. Indeed, after it hit the airwaves in May 1974 with its revolutionary two-hour magazine format, the show won two consecutive New York Emmy awards—while achieving a 113 per cent increase in adult viewers for WNBC news.

As for Tom Snyder, he was a TV journalist of unquestioned credentials, the definitive electronic newsman, the modern specie of an evolutionary chain that stretched back to the primeval forests of Douglas Edwards and John Cameron Swayze: a nationally known interviewer (host of NBC's "Tomorrow" show), a skilled reporter (the skills honed through 17 years of apprenticeship in a scatter-quilt of American cities), and a personality of almost mythical reputation.

So what was Snyder doing on this evening at the helm of august and venerable "News Center 4," decked out in conspicuous relief to his austerely suited colleagues and muttering distractedly about sex fantasies?

The answer is that Snyder at "News Center 4" was doing what every other local TV newsman in the country was doing, only he was doing it better.

He was doing journalism as show biz.

If Edward R. Murrow, the patron saint of TV news, had returned to life in 1976 and traversed the nation, searching for refinements of his legacy, here are some of the strange and wondrous sights he would have seen:

—At WLS in Chicago, the ABC-owned station, there is a filmed report by the station's weatherman, John Coleman. Coleman is standing beside a highway in North Dakota. He is holding an envelope toward the camera. He is saying, "In this envelope are a group of never-before-published pictures of flying saucers. Are these the real thing? Or . . . are these hoaxes?"

—At KNXT in Los Angeles, the CBS-owned station, a woman reporter in a wet suit plunges awkwardly into a tank of water. She begins playing with a large porpoise.

—At KTTV in Los Angeles, an independent, co-anchormen Chuck Ashman and Charles Rowe are reading the night's lead stories. The lead stories include an item about a bill in the Tennessee legislature advocating a state fossil and a misprint in the Azusa *Herald* announcing the appointment of Mary Hartman to the town planning commission.

— At WMAL in Washington, a woman reporter named Betsy Ashton is announcing a story on Howard Hughes's will. She is sitting in a cemetery.

— At WMAL's competitor, the *Post-Newsweek* station WTOP, the "Eyewitness News" team is temporarily unable to continue. It is collectively trying to recover from a case of the giggles engendered by the mispronunciation, by one of them, of "Silver Springs," Maryland.

— At KSTP in Minneapolis, NBC-affiliated, the comedienne Judy Carne pops into the newsroom during the newscast and begins playing with a sportscaster Tom Rather's ears.

On a subsequent newscast at KSTP, Dave Gilbert, the station's "action" reporter, is covering a demonstration of canoe safety for high-school students on one of Minneapolis' city lakes. Gilbert wittily capsizes his own canoe; then, in an attempt to pull himself from the water, he overturns the canoe with the KSTP camera and film crew.

— At WKYC in Cleveland, the NBC-owned station, reporter Del Donahue is broadcasting from inside a lion's cage. The "angle" is that Donahue is "learning how" to train a lion. Donahue sits down upon the supine lion's haunches. The beast, who lacks a sense of humor, springs up and begins to maul Donahue, who suffered cuts requiring 60 stitches before he is pulled to safety by the real trainer. Journalism is served in the end, however. WKYC's camera records the entire grisly episode, and it is shown on several NBC stations — as a news event.

Murrow would have seen rank upon rank of "news teams" in matching blazers and coiffures like so many squadrons of "Up With People," teenagers, all fixed with standardized wry smiles behind their "Star Trek" desks. He would see news teams that begin their evening's duty by strutting on camera en masse (at WABC in New York, they sort of *cascade* onto the set, like the Angelic Messengers taking the stage for Part Three of the *Dybbuk Variations*).

He would have been puzzled by full-page newspaper ads that trumpet a news team as though it were a new kind of low-tar cigarette, and by TV "promo" commercials that show anchorman, weatherman, sportscaster, and principal reporters riding around in cowboy suits on white horses or passing inspection dressed up like doughboys. (Los Angeles' KABC has a reported yearly budget of $1.4 million for this type of advertising alone.)

What the hell, Murrow might understandably have asked, has all this got to do with *news?*

He would have seen news, all right — in a manner of speaking. (And the manner of speaking would have been strange to Murrow's ears indeed). TV journalists in 1976 not only entertained, they covered "serious" news as well.

That is, it would be safe to say that on any given nightly TV newscast in 1976, a viewer would be exposed to the three or four most important stories that graced the front pages of his local newspaper. Most large-city TV news departments offered, in addition, a noble-sounding catalogue of secondary news services: consumer tips; perhaps a mini-documentary, in several parts, on some civic issue; an "action" reporter who was a conspicuous participant in the stories he covered; often a minority advocate, handsome/beautiful and vaguely ethnic, along the lines of Geraldo Rivera; an "ombudsman" reporter who checked out complaints made against local businesses and services.

But there was something missing at the core. Amidst all the self-consciousness, the preening, the ingratiation and the bonhommie, Murrow might have noticed that in very few cases was there a sense of *mission* about the TV newscasts: a sense of continuity in the life of the city (or "market") covered; a palpable willingness to perform the vigorous, adversary, check-on-government, intervening role that American journalism has traditionally performed.

There was little feeling of real partnership with the viewer, only a vague, disguised condescension. There was little evidence that any of the coiffed anchorpersons or "action" reporters or "ombudsmen" on the air shared — or were even aware of — the Jeffersonian notion than an informed public will make its own best decisions if given the hard facts on which to judge.

To put it into practical terms: had Murrow stuck around a station, chosen at random, for six or eight weeks (or months or years), chances are good that he would not have seen one piece of journalism, initiated by that station, that sent a corrupt politician to jail. Or that resulted in widespread and lasting structural reform. Or that forced a change in official policy. Or that prepared

citizens for an impending crisis (as in inflation, municipal bank-
ruptcy, educational funding, environmental shortages, union-
labor negotiations).

He would, however, have witnessed unending reports on sex
fantasies. And runaway wives. And UFO's. And celebrities. And
fires. And murders. And accidents.

And, oh yes, the weather and sports.

MOONSCAPES

Tom Snyder is television's real Six Million Dollar Man.

He is the prototype personality for the cybernetic era of TV news. He is, in fact, television's child come of age. His boyish face—the huge eyes soulful beneath an exaggerated page-boy swirl of graying hair—has peered into the red eye of the television camera for exactly half his 40 years. Snyder is among the first contingent of TV news personalities who had grown up exclusively in the electronic medium. Unlike Walter Cronkite (his antithesis in style) or Mike Wallace or John Chancellor or Dan Rather, Snyder has never worked a day in the print press.

He has, however, built a reputation as a reliable journalist during a 17-year odyssey that began in his native Milwaukee (he attended Marquette University) and continued through Savannah, Atlanta, Los Angeles, Philadelphia, and L.A. again—as anchorman, in 1970, of KNBC's nightly newscast.

Few people have questioned Snyder's abilities as a newsman, but there are lots of newsmen, many of them in Cedar Rapids. What propelled Snyder past fascinated colleagues—and mesmerized viewers—was his style.

Harrumphs Fred Friendly, Murrow's old producer and a staunch critic of broadcast journalism's New Ways: "That program ["News Center 4"] really got made by Snyder. Snyder has this enormous animal vitality, like Mike Wallace. He could just count to 30 and the audience would stay with him . . . but he's pretty good. He's not yet a serious journalist, and it's a pretty interesting thing whether he ever intends to be a serious journalist . . . but he's pretty good."

Pretty good. And pretty damned maddeningly successful.
TV newsmen in Los Angeles like to chuckle about a certain L.A.
anchorman, still on the air there, who has tried unconsciously to
ape the elusive Snyder mystique. Rumor has it that the poor fellow has gone so far as to place a "pin spot"—a miniature beam of
light—directly beneath his eyes, to give them a Snyder-like glitter
on camera. (It was easier when the guy was unconsciously imitat-
ing NBC White House Correspondent Tom Brokaw. All he had
to do then was make *W*'s of his *L*'s)

While in his second L.A. stint, Snyder was selected to be the
host of NBC's new post-midnight talk show, "Tomorrow." This
assignment thrust him beyond the restraints of merely local reputation; he was now a national celebrity. The distinction was significant. For in the very act of becoming a celebrity, Tom Snyder had
conspicuously embraced two worlds that had, in terms of lip service, at least, been kept strictly separate: the worlds of journalism
and show business.

It did not take Snyder long to establish himself as television's
completely modular man. He is utterly adaptable to any situation
beneath the klieg lights. He seems to understand himself instinc-
tively as a television presence; his reactions are usually impec-
cable.

On the "Tomorrow" show, Snyder converses with an eclectic
assortment of entertainers, authors, seers, prostitutes, terminally
ill patients, scholars, advocates, and political ideologues. His personality dominates the show. Hunched and intense, the dark
brows merging, Snyder provokes and challenges and goads his
guests; it is never uncertain where his sentiments lie.

When the occasion demands, however, he can lay aside the
shtick and do brilliant interviews—as he did in 1973 when "Tomorrow" took its cameras to Saigon for conversations with South
Vietnamese military officials there.

On the KNBC newscasts, meanwhile, Snyder was modular-
within-modular: now the outrageous, happy-talking roue, almost
literally jabbing an elbow into the weatherwoman's ribs; now the
crisp, detached newscaster; now the incensed advocate; now the
ingratiating boy. Always somehow larger than the news he read.
And always a force in the ratings.

Such a broad and effortless range of personae could hardly
escape the notice of those who were refining and polishing the cy-

bernetic newscast. Like the acolyte wanderer in Hermann Hesse's *Magister Ludi*, Snyder was about to ascend near the fulfillment of his destiny: "News Center 4."

If Tom Snyder was the perfect man for the cybernetic era, "News Center 4" was his perfect habitat. In early 1974, WNBC was a distant third in the early-evening local news race in New York. Its hour-long newscast drew an average nightly audience of 333,000 adult viewers—compared to 937,000 for WCBS, the New York leader, and 697,000 for WABC.

Seventeen months later, with a revolutionary two-hour program in operation and Scarborough-Snyder sharing the anchor, WNBC was Number One, with 708,000 viewers, to WCBS's 696,000 and WABC's 610,000.

What happened?

Snyder—to an extent.

But there was more to the story than that. In creating "News Center 4" WNBC had belatedly joined the burgeoning rush toward the promised land of cybernetics: the use of extensive and sophisticated audience research to divine the audience's psychological motivations for watching TV news.

Before unveiling "News Center 4", WNBC—called "the world's richest television station" by *Variety*'s Bill Greeley—spent no less than 18 months enmeshed in audience research. Lee Hanna, then NBC News vice president, was quoted as telling his staff that it was "the most comprehensive and expensive research operation in the history of the world."

What form did the research take? Edwin Diamond gives some provocative insights in his useful 1975 book, *The Tin Kazoo.* Reported Diamond:

> Emmanuel "Manny" Demby, the audience research consultant for "News Center 4," has been using a questionnaire technique he calls "psychographics" to get at the connection, if any, between the personalities of viewers and elements of the news. Demby often uses a "test facility"—a tastefully furnished room at the offices of Demby's Motivational Programmers, Inc., at 770 Lexington Avenue in New York. There, Demby and his NBC clients can observe, through one-way glass, a roomful of unsuspecting people as they watch "News Center 4."

"Psychographics." "Motivational Programmers." Rooms with one-way glass. It was a strange and other-worldly land, that promised land of cybernetics—a moonscape of terms, devices, and practices that seemed culled from science fiction. There was more: "psychometrics" and "Q factors" and electrodes that could be attached to the finger tips of sample audiences to determine "galvanic skin responses" to certain stimuli (which took the form of sample news stories); teams of parapsychiatric counselors that would fan out across the country to give on-the-job Gestalt therapy to beleaguered news teams. . . .

All in the name of journalism.

As Diamond summed it up: "In many stations, television news had become too important to be left to the newspeople."

What the testing did for WNBC was to produce a relatively noble enterprise. A news-oriented program housed in a $300,000 set, top pay for on-air talent (a reported $100,000 for Scarborough as of August 1975; an estimated $500,000 for Snyder, which included compensation for "Tomorrow"); and a staff of 200— what Diamond called "the largest group anywhere putting out a news program, national or local."

The overall program budget: up to $12 million a year.

Was NBC's cybernetic-research venture some sort of Orwellian monstrosity, a sick parody of the eternal impulse to decode, for monetary gain, the unspoken, subliminal needs of others? Not when compared to the efforts of Channel 4's competitors and of other stations around the country.

WNBC entered the cybernetic sweepstakes rather late in the game, and the results were mostly benign. In the hands of other broadcast news entities, cybernetic news took on equal aspects of the hopelessly comic and the chillingly totalitarian.

The very act of broadcasting news on television was for years similar in motivation to the act of marrying the pregnant girl.

It is very difficult to lose money running a VHF television station—so difficult, in fact, that no one has yet succeeded in doing it, although the industry has attracted many men whose intellectual capacities would seem to stake them with a better-then-even chance.

Lord Thomson of Fleet, the international communications mogul, once cast a baleful eye at American commercial television and remarked: "A television license is a license to print money." Alexander Kendrick, Murrow's biographer, despairing of the medium's inclination toward excellence, lamented that "it is not required for television to be a marketplace of ideas . . . only a marketplace."

And the one dark corner of the marketplace — one of the few areas of TV in which it was possible to lose money in the early days — was the news.

News is, at best, an unnatural function of television. Far from being conceived as an instrument of dissent or as a critical watchdog of government, as were newspapers, American TV owes its very livelihood to the status quo. Licensed by the federal government, it hardly dares to be insurrectionary. Financed and controlled largely by the country's most powerful conglomerates, with a mandate to reward advertisers, it hardly dares to risk alienating its audiences with bad tidings.

Television's first mission is not to inform. It is not even to entertain. It is to move goods, to round up viewers for the main event — the commercial.

So why did TV ever bother with the news in the first place? Several reasons.

First, there was a handful of good men and true in the pioneer era who simply believed that television had a clear obligation to present newscasts, as radio had done. These included Murrow and Friendly, of course, but also such men as Robert Kintner of NBC and Robert Lemon, a statesmanlike broadcaster who organized a model for local-station news at WMAQ, the NBC outlet in Chicago.

A second reason was radio itself. The CBS overseas crew had lent broadcast journalism a great deal of glamour during World War II and had legitimized the art. As television derived from radio in so many other ways, so did it derive in this one.

Third, there was that small matter of the Federal Communications Commission, which issued (and could revoke) broadcast licenses. The FCC expected a certain amount of programming "in the public interest, convenience and necessity" in return for allowing a station to suckle at the fabulously lucrative airwave teat.

At both the network and the local level, TV news is clearly a stepchild of radio. As Martin Mayer pointed out in his book *About Television:*

> The 15-minute nightly news that all the networks broadcast in the 1950's and early 1960's was essentially a radio service with occasional films. In the absence of videotape, film from out of town had to be flown in (network news motorcycles racing from the New York airports were a familiar sight) or sent twice over the wire to New York at extravagant line charges. . . . When the propagandists for television acclaimed the medium's capacity to communicate reality, what they were talking about was the studio-originated press conference or interview show, the televised Senate hearing, and the documentary, the nonfiction film produced at Hollywood ratios of 10 feet shot for every foot used, with Ed Murrow telling the viewer what it was all about.

Mayer, along with many other observers of American broadcasting, believes that TV's Great Leap Forward in news owed its impetus to TV's Great Stumble Backward, the quiz-show scandals of the late fifties.

When the roof fell in on the quiz shows, Mayer points out, news shows were minuscule ingredients of the network schedules. In response to the public outrage over the quiz fixes, the Eisenhower Administration put the arm on the three networks to produce each week at least one hour-long public-affairs show that did not conflict with any similar program at the same time.

Mayer again:

> The resulting burst of inexpensive and ill-prepared public-affairs programs was important mostly in terms of personnel . . . the key matter was quantity rather than quality: the news divisions had to be beefed up considerably to carry the weight. And the public-affairs shows did not begin to pay their way: typically, they had to be sold at prices that covered little more than the cost of air time alone. Corporate executives noted that ratings and sales were better on the evening news; if the 15-minute format could be doubled, the larger staffs could be more profitably employed. In 1963, within two weeks of each other, both CBS and NBC went to a half-hour news program.

Meanwhile, the local news was hatching itself as a very ugly duckling indeed.

Robert Lemon, now retired, recalled the early days of broadcasting after a round of golf one afternoon in suburban Chicago:
"Throughout the fifties, the local news on TV was a throwaway.
Stations had literally no control over any of their programs, news
included. Programs were sponsor-created in those days. In 80 to
90 per cent of the major markets, one sponsor owned the newscast
entirely, and called all the shots. I mean all. Who was the anchorman, what was the appearance of the show—and content. Especially content.

"The greatest offender was Standard Oil, which franchised
local newscasts in several cities.

"So the news didn't have any stature; it was whorishly done.
Station managers didn't like it because it was expensive—all those
crews, cameras, writers, anchormen. It was so much cheaper to
have a sponsor come in and sell you a program, fully produced."

But Lemon and others believed in the news, believed in its
sanctity and the need for its independence. "My intention," said
Lemon, "when I got to WMAQ, was to make the news profitable—
and to free it from outside control."

Little did Lemon and his contemporaries dream just how
profitable the news was destined to be—or into whose manicured
hands the control was destined to shift.

TOM SWIFT AND HIS ELECTRIC POLL-TAKER

Despite its futuristic aspects, market research is hardly a new phenomenon in American business. Along with its companion systems of political polling and public-opinion sampling, market research reaches more than 150 years back into the country's history.

In July of 1824 (according to Jack J. Honomichl, writing in the April 19, 1976, *Advertising Age*), the Harrisburg *Pennsylvanian* printed a report of a straw vote taken at Wilmington, Delaware, "without discrimination of parties." In that pre-Voter Profile Analysis poll, Andrew Jackson received 335 votes; John Quincy Adams, 169; Henry Clay, 19; and William H. Crawford, 9. (The Harrisburg *Pennsylvanian* was the Chicago *Tribune* of its time: John Quincy Adams, playing Truman to Jackson's Thomas Dewey, was elected President.)

Other evidences of market research surfaced in 1879, when N.W. Ayer & Son surveyed state officials around the country on grain production, and thus wrapped up a nifty agricultural-machinery account with the Nichols-Shepard Company; and in 1895, when one Harlow Gale of the University of Minnesota mailed out questionnaires to obtain public opinion on advertising.

The science—and in its purest state, market research is a scientifically valid tool indeed — began to take hold in American commerce around 1910, when several businesses were formed for the purpose. The following year, reports Honomichl, R. O. Eastman, who was then advertising manager for the Kellogg Company in Battle Creek, Michigan, organized a joint postcard survey to determine magazine readership. This undertaking inspired Mr. Eastman to begin his own company, the Eastman Research Bureau, whose first clients included *Cosmopolitan* and the *Christian Herald.* A bit later an organization known as the General Electric Company joined the fold. GE designed a consumer survey to determine whether people liked its "Mazda" trademark. The everhopeful Chicago *Tribune* plunged into the field in 1916, with a door-to-door survey of consumer purchasing habits in Chicago.

The business-happy 1920's, that decade of foredoomed Babbitt-like ebullience, saw the founding of some of the dynasties in market research and opinion polling today: men such as Dr. Daniel Starch, Dr. George Gallup and Arthur C. Nielsen were toying with their methods and staking out their territory. Starch first used the "recognition" method for measuring readership of advertisements and editorial content in papers and magazines in 1922. Gallup, whose name was to become synonymous with opinion sampling, entered the field through advertising readership measurements in 1923; his Gallup Poll was first published in 35 newspapers in 1935.

There is an irony in the presence of A. C. Nielsen in the list of antecedents for today's TV news consultant. After entering the field in 1922, the Nielsen Company provided the science of market research with some of its most important innovations, and ultimately became a national byword for the measurement of broadcast audiences.

And yet market research for television programming — including news — is one area that A. C. Nielsen scrupulously eschews.

The company tells the networks and local stations how many people are watching a given program, and how that audience is characterized by such traits as age, sex, race, education and income levels. There is no attempt by Nielsen to "analyze" this data, nor to draw conclusions as to what sort of programming is likely to attract audiences, nor to advise its television clients on how to improve their ratings. Nielsen differs from such firms as Frank N. Magid Associates in that it simply counts and sorts the audience; it does not attempt to read their minds.

Nielsen's breakthrough in broadcast audience measurement was achieved through a device called the Audimeter, developed in 1936 by two professors at the Massachusetts Institute of Technology, Robert F. Elder and Louis Woodruff. It took six years of experiments and improvements with the Audimeter—during which time the Nielsen Company was often on shaky financial ground indeed—before the invention was introduced as a commercial service for network radio. By 1950, the Audimeter was such a success that Nielsen sold the service to network television; the radio arm was discontinued in 1964.

The Audimeter (proper name: the Storage Instantaneous Audimeter) is a small, unobstrusive electronic box that rests in the closets, basements and cabinets of 1,170 households around the United States. (Nielsen selects the households based on a gigantic survey operation that starts with U.S. Census listings of all the households in the country; from this raw data, a "sample universe" of all America's cities, towns, farms, neighborhoods, and housing units evolves. Each household in this "sample universe," having agreed to cooperate with Nielsen, provides information on its TV-watching habits for a period of five years.) As members of a Nielsen household turns the set on and off and switch channels, their viewing patterns are recorded in the Audimeter's electronic memory. Each Audimeter is connected to a special telephone line used only by Nielsen. At least twice a day, a Central Office computer dials up each home unit and retrieves the stored information. This instantaneous capability enables Nielsen to provide its fabled "overnights," or morning-after ratings, in major cities.

The Audimeter thrust Nielsen ahead of its audience-survey competitors, such as Hooper and the American Research Bureau, because the machine eliminated for the first time the uncertainties of memory and the temptations of deceit. However, to this day, Nielsen augments its Audimeter service with diaries in 2,100 additional households. The diary supplements the Audimeter by telling Nielsen not only what programs were watched and for how long, but also who in the family was watching, by age and sex. Ever vigilant in its search to eliminate human error through the application of control systems, Nielsen attempts to offset the inherent fallibility of diaries in several ways: its recruiters visit the households several times; demographic information is obtained in person; there is a systematic 33 per cent sample turnover each year—a turnover so demographically accurate that it takes into account families in newly-constructed houses.

What emerges from this computerized mulch of American patterns of mesmerism is an intelligence-gathering operation perhaps unexampled in modern technology. Nielsen can arm its clients with such infinitesimal data as:

—The number of households tuned to each network program during the average *minute* of a telecast—an estimate based literally on the metered measurement of every minute of the telecast.

—The percentage of all U.S. television households using TV by half-hour segments. (The figure is strategically important for broadcasters, since it identifies the available audience for programs that compete with one another during the given time period.)

—The share of audience. This concept is a Nielsen signature. It first appeared in the 1920's as "share of market," an item which businessmen have spent more money to pinpoint than any other single piece of intelligence in the marketing-information field. Audience "share" is based on the assumption that not every set in the U.S. is in use at once. Thus the "share" concept makes it possible to compare the ability of programs to attract the households *using* TV during their respective time periods, even when TV usage is at different levels at these different times.

The care and comprehension of Nielsen survey techniques suggest a degree of exactitude almost beyond the attenuation of human error and, in fact, the Nielsen methods are recognized as clinically sound when judged by the yardstick of statistical science. (Nielsen's closest competitor, the American Research Bureau, has not attained the national stature of Nielsen, and is primarily a comparative service for local stations in major cities.)

But no theory of probability has yet been able to overcome the variable of human free will, and so the precise degree of accuracy of Nielsen's TV audience projections will always remain a mystery. Some critics have pointed out that Nielsen has other, more practical, limitations, not necessarily a fault of its own structure.

Because television advertisers (and hence, television pro-

grammers) are not interested in attracting the "fringes" of television viewership—that is, the very rich, the very poor, the very
young, the foreign-language immigrants, and others whose buying patterns are not in the mainstream of American commerce—
these catagories are not proportionately represented in the Nielsen sample. The broadcasting establishment is Nielsen's client; the
client can and does, in ways both subtle and direct, influence the
perimenters of the market area to be surveyed. The very fact that
Nielsen's Audimeters and diaries are found in *households* (as opposed to college dormitories, saloons, hospitals, prisons, and other
aberrant environments for watching television) indicates a bias,
for example.

Imperfect as they are, however, Nielsen's techniques represent a quantum leap above those of the researchers-consultants
who regularly, and in increasing numbers, presume to tell television *what* to program. The one consultant whose visionary genius
eclipses Nielsen's plodding, methodical efficiency—the one
thinker whose extraordinary perception beggars the absurd pos-
turings of those self-important "authorities" who have created the
cybernetic newscast—is not available to the narrow province of
television news. His clients are governments, educational programs, corporations. His name is relevant here because he invented the concept of consultancy as corporate America knows it;
he is, although many news consultants may *not* know it, their progenitor. He is the Viennese-born philosopher, writer, and post-
industrial prophet, Peter Drucker.

It is impossible, in the space of a few paragraphs, to adequately convey Peter Drucker's impact on American management
systems, or the scope of change he has wrought on business and
industry through his devastatingly simple approach to consultancy. Suffice to say here that Drucker invented the *concept* of
"management" as distinct from general business efficiency, decision-making and executive discipline. John J. Tarrant, in his definitive study *Drucker: The Man Who Invented Corporate Society* (Cah-
ners Books, Inc.), asserts:

> The manager of today may never have met Peter Drucker,
> never heard him speak, never worked with him as a consultant. He
> may have read some of Drucker's books and articles. But even if he

has never come into contact with Drucker's work in any form, the businessman's life, day-in-day-out, year-in-year-out, is profoundly affected by Peter Drucker. What Drucker dreamed of thirty years ago, the manager now takes for granted.

Why be concerned, in this examination of journalistic practice, with the influence of a man who devotes his own attention to business, to "management"? Because television news *is* a business, in that it is perceived as a profit tool by network presidents and by the career salesmen-turned-station-managers who govern its form and content. And yet, except in a few enlightened instances, the problems of television news have never been treated as *structural* (or management) problems, only as cosmetic ones. "One of the greatest changes," remarks Drucker in Tarrant's work, "has been the growing consciousness of the importance of structure." He adds, "I have learned to be very conservative. Reorganization is surgery. One doesn't just cut." A cursory glance at the wholesale firings—of anchorman, news director, reporters, assignment editors—that frequently accompany a dip in station ratings is evidence enough that most TV stations are innocent of Drucker's warning. (The ordeal of CBS-owned KNXT in Los Angeles, to be described later, is an excellent example of this innocence.)

There are other facets of Drucker's insight that commend themselves—vainly, so far—to television news. Drucker is the high priest of "management by objectives," of the demand that organizational roles be clearly defined. He has also remarked that "the average businessman, when asked what a business is, is likely to answer: 'An organization to make a profit.' And the average economist is likely to give the same answer. But this answer is not only false; it is irrelevant." But television news departments are by and large negligent in devising coherent expressions of what their goals are (the one exception to that negligence is, significantly, the profit motive); they are far more interested in employing research-consultants to outguess the *public's* definition of news.

Drucker, in many other ways, is in direct opposition to the style and methodology of news consultants who will be described in this book. Nearly all of them, for instance, make a great argument (and present a large bill) for the preliminary audience research that, supposedly, leads them to their recommendations. Tarrant quotes Chris Argyris, of the Harvard University Graduate School of Education:

Some social scientists may fault Peter for not being more of an empirical researcher. I do not, for if he were, I wonder if he could have made the conceptual path-clearing contributions that he has made. If I were to fault Peter, it would be that he never seemed to realize that embedded in his "nonscientific" consulting-based methods of inquiry were the seeds of a new methodology for social science — one that it needs desperately if it is to become genuinely acceptable.

Most broadcast consultants have staffs, the largest one employing more than 100 people. Drucker works alone. Most consultants pride themselves on their strict secular rationalism — what they are pleased to call their "pragmatic" tough-mindedness. Drucker, writes Tarrant, finds himself giving much thought to the confrontation between God and man in today's society. Most broadcast consultants are men of narrow backgrounds; an alarming percentage of them are career broadcasters themselves, and others are products of utilitarian educations. Drucker, a multinationalist, has written about American and European history, philosophy, education, religion, and the arts.

Clearly, Peter Drucker is a man apart from his fellows in the field. But his monumental achievements, beginning with his legendary assignment with General Motors in the mid-1940's (in which he defined the corporation in America as a self-renewing, permanent institution, placed it in a superior position to the transitory stockholder, and generally honed his characterization of Industrial Man) and continuing through his commentaries on multinational corporations and his concept of the "global shopping center," suggest that he personifies a standard by which others in that field may be judged.

As we shall see, that arm of the broadcast industry mandated to keep America informed about itself scarcely requires its own consultants to approach that standard.

"LEAST
OBJECTIONABLE"

By the mid-sixties, local newscasts were coming out of the Stone Age. They were building audiences, looking more professional, and becoming assets—rather than liabilities—to their stations.

One major reason was the explosive nature of the news itself. The Vietnam War, urban riots, political assassinations, student protests, the civil rights movement, a general landscape of confrontation that made for exciting "visuals" and theatrical reportage—all these helped create an enormous new audience for television news.

Another reason had to do with default. As the networks grew in power, they absorbed programming creation from their affiliates. By paying stations rebates for accepting a network feed (and then sharing in the commercial revenue), the networks made it more profitable for stations to relay national programs than to create their own.

Soon the local newscast was the *only* original programming most stations did on a regular basis, outside the obligatory Sunday-morning and post-midnight "public service" throwaways.

Suddenly the newscast was no longer just a writeoff. It performed two vital competitive services, neither of which had anything to do with journalism. First, it served as the station's "signature," its collective personality (and as the major local attraction for commercial time-buyers). Second, the early-evening newscast took on an enormous show-business obligation: assembling a large audience to be delivered into the parent network's prime-time schedule.

This second function was a by-product of the more rarefied levels of strategic television theory. In the 1960's, an unorthodox but brilliant thinker named Paul Klein, then an audience research executive for NBC, formulated a concept that he called "Least Objectionable Programming." The theory was so simple, so clean in its apparent logic, that it gained immediate acceptance in the industry, where it became universally known by its initials.

L.O.P. argued that people did not watch *programs*, they watched *television.* Therefore, the task facing a given network (or station) was not to get the viewer to turn her set on so much as it was to attract the viewer to the desired channel. Klein believed that some human law of inertia rendered a viewer passive in her chair once she had tuned in to a given channel and that a viewer tended to switch channels only when inspired by negative stimuli: when the program she was watching aroused her anger, inflamed her prejudices, offended her morality, challenged her political beliefs. (The use of the feminine pronoun here is not just a bow to feminist sensibilities. It has long been an article of faith among broadcasters that women, not men, control the viewing choices in the household—an assumption that, in itself, yields interesting aspects of sexism.)

Therefore, the trick to retaining audiences was twofold and simple: build them up early and don't offend them. The early-evening local newscast figured prominently in both elements of this theory.

Thus, without ever quite intending it, television station managers began turning their principal liability into an advantage. Local news became part of L.O.P. By 1965, the day of the local newscast as a "profit center" was at hand.

Three years later, the first cybernetic newscast was to follow.

The natural attractiveness of the medium was reflected in many audience surveys. By the late 1960's, Roper polls were beginning to show that upward of 64 per cent of Americans relied on television as their "primary" source of news.

And the fifth Alfred I. DuPont *Survey of Broadcast Journalism,* published by Columbia University in 1975, had this to say about TV news's "prestige":

In April 1974, *U.S. News & World Report* asked 500 U.S. "leaders" to rate organizations and institutions "according to the amount of influence . . . for decisions or actions affecting the nation as a whole." TV came in first with a score of 7.2 on a scale of 1 to 10. The White House tied the Supreme Court for second place, and newspapers came next.

. . . In a special study of public institutions done by Louis Harris for the Senate Subcommittee on Intergovernmental Relations, TV news was found to have made by far the greatest gains in public confidence since 1965—overtaking the military, organized religion, the Supreme Court, the U.S. Senate, the House of Representatives, and the executive branch of the federal government.

There was another factor in the impact and appeal of television news, one that added an unwelcome ethical consideration to the commercially-oriented medium: Americans, in increasing numbers, were *obliged* to watch television for their information. They were forgetting how to read.

23 MILLION CALLED ILLITERATE

Thus ran the headlines on Oct. 29, 1975.

The U.S. Office of Education had just released the results of a four-year study which indicated that more than 23 million U.S. adults were functionally illiterate—unable to read help-wanted ads or make the most economical purchases.

The Associated Press quoted the report as saying: "It is surprising, perhaps even shocking, to suggest that approximately *one of five Americans* is incompetent or functions with difficulty and that about *half of the adult population* is merely functional and not at all proficient in necessary skills and knowledges."

Earlier studies, by the National Center for Health Statistics, had indicated the problem was not confined to adults. One million American youths, aged 12 to 17, were found to be illiterate—almost 5 per cent of that age group's total.

"It offers new evidence," wrote Eric Wentworth of the Washington *Post,* "that the United States has a serious literacy problem despite the more than $40 billion spent yearly on public school operations."

And where are the illiterate most likely to turn for information? To the beguiling device that flickers for nearly seven hours a

day in the average American household; the device most often
listed as the "primary" source; the device with the "Number One
amount of influence"; the device that had made "the greatest
gains in public confidence"; the device that, by 1976, was tapping
unparalleled resources of behavioristic science to offer amusing,
ingratiating, titillating, "least objectionable," and otherwise nones-
sential "news" as a bait to the army of affluent viewers, to hook
them for the main event—the commercial.

RHINESTONE COWBOYS

We take you now to the single most profitable television news operation in the United States—WLS, Channel 7, in Chicago, Illinois. WLS, an ABC-owned station, has been the far-and-away leader in local news ratings since 1970, drawing an average nightly audience of 1.1 million. In comparison, the Chicago *Tribune,* the city's largest-circulation newspaper, reaches 747,715 readers daily. In fact, the combined circulation of Chicago's three major downtown newspapers is 1,682,245. Obviously, WLS is the single most influential news outlet in Chicago—and, because of its wide ratings lead over its competitors, among the wealthiest stations in the country.

(WNBC in New York may have a larger cash flow than WLS, but its expenses are far greater. Channel 7 keeps its disbursement line slim by maintaining the smallest news staff in Chicago and by maintaining a nearly religious do-nothing attitude toward prime-time public affairs. In 1975 WLS pre-empted the regular ABC prime-time gold mine exactly once for a local special, as compared to 12 times for WBBM and four times for WMAQ.)

WLS realizes a net profit of $15 million a year—compared to $5 million each for CBS-owned WBBM and independent WGN, and $3 million for NBC-owned WMAQ.

And how well does Channel 7 "Eyewitness News" serve the informational needs of its viewers in a city distinguished for its political corruption, learning disabilities in its public schools, health-care scandals, ghetto alienation, and patterns of crime?

Here is a good example. Here is Channel 7's John Coleman

standing by in North Dakota with some more on his "never-be-fore-published pictures of flying saucers":

COLEMAN: *(thrusting pictures toward camera):* I want you to take a look at 'em. Look as closely as you can and make up your own mind. And listen to what J. Allen Hynek, the Director of the Center for UFO Studies, and Philip J. Klass, UFO skeptic and debunker, have to say about pictures of flying saucers.

KLASS: Every still picture that has been shown that I have seen—a still picture—that shows a solid, craftlike object, is a hoax. Uh—the reason that it is so easy to—to make a hoax photo—uh, is that all one needs is a little imagination. One can carve out a little model out of plastic, you can take a hubcap, you can suspend it from a thin thread. Then you defocus the camera a little bit, so the eye cannot see this thin thread. And then you have a beautiful UFO—uh, picture.

HYNEK: I'm quite sure in my own mind that not all of them are Frisbees or hubcaps or these things, sure, that is the thing that is done by some pranksters and (sic) will go out and try that. But we have them, the same sorts of things from all sorts of countries. When you get the same kind of thing from Peru, from Australia, from Japan, from Brazil, from Canada, as well as the United States, and under very strange circumstances, in very rough country sometimes, I just don't think those are all Frisbees.

COLEMAN *(wheeling toward the camera and speaking in his best This-Is-London voice):* You have now seen some good, clear pictures of flying saucers. The best that there are. We don't know whether these pictures are the real thing or hoaxes. We can never get a good clear story to go with the good clear picture.

Tomorrow, I'm going to give you another look at these pictures. And you'll hear what our Air Force has to say. After all, if nuts-and-bolts flying saucers are in our atmosphere, shouldn't we detect them with our spy satellites and radar? That story about UFO's tomorrow, when our series continues.

WLS has taken cybernetic news far beyond any major station in the country, even beyond the limits of its sister station in New York, WABC (which has fashioned some pretty weird newscasts in its own right).

WLS is the original Happy Talk station. In 1976, its basic news team—anchormen Joel Daly and Fahey Flynn, weatherman Coleman, and sportscaster Bill Frink—were the same men who introduced the format to the airwaves in 1968. (The team was put together by Dick O'Leary, then the station manager and subsequently rewarded with the presidency, ABC-owned television stations.)

Happy Talk and cybernetic news should not be confused. They are not interchangeable terms, although Happy Talk is compatible with the behavioristic assumptions of the cybernetic newscast. The term "Happy Talk" was coined by Morry Roth, the respected Chicago broadcast correspondent for _Variety_, to describe the aura of exaggerated joviality and elbow-jabbing comradeship evinced by the Flynn-Daly-Frink-Coleman team night after night. Once it had proved itself as a salable gimmick in Chicago, Happy Talk quickly spread across the country, imitated by grinning, lantern-jawed news teams from New York to San Francisco, and most stops in between. (WXII in Winston-Salem, North Carolina, was an outstanding exponent for a while, with its news team dressed "like refugees from the Sunday morning gospel hour in matching lemon yellow blazers," according to the Winston-Salem _Journal and Sentinel_.)

"Happy Talk" is virtually the signature of ABC-owned stations around the country. They have brought the technique to its fullest flower. In fact, New York's flagship ABC station, WABC, owns the dark distinction of having broadcast the ultimate "Happy Talk" gambit—an ill-chosen utterance by veteran weatherman Tex Antoine on Nov. 24, 1976, that ended a broadcasting career begun in 1944.

Anchorman Bill Beutel had just read a news item about an alleged rape attack on an eight-year-old girl. Roger Grimsby then came on the air and introduced Antoine and his weathercast.

Antoine's first words, presumably spoken in the lighthearted spirit that flavors all Eyewitness newscasts, were of such blatantly bad taste that they even exceeded ABC's permissive notions of propriety—a spectacular achievement in itself.

Quoth Antoine:

"With rape so predominant in the news lately, it is well to remember the words of Confucius: 'If rape is inevitable, lie back and enjoy it.'"

Later that night, WABC apologized to its viewers for what it called Antoine's "inexcusable lapse of judgment." Antoine was suspended until Dec. 20 of 1976; when he returned, he was allowed to work in the WABC weather department, but was prohibited from appearing on the air.

Happy Talk owes much of its identity to the bantering remarks made among anchormen, reporters, weathermen, and sportscasters during transitions from topic to topic. But the concept has a broader scope. It defines a newscast that is weighted toward the trivial—curiosity-stories of the type that Fred Friendly refers to as the "two-headed calf"—and away from the abstract, the disturbing, the vital, or what Friendly calls the "complicated-dull."

Coleman again, with another segment in his ten-part *(ten-part!)* North-Dakota–based series on UFO's:

COLEMAN: Something significant happened at this spot on Interstate 94 on the early morning of August 26, 1975. At three-thirty in the morning, Sandy Larson, her daughter Jackie, and a friend Terry left Fargo, North Dakota, headed westward along this Interstate. What happened next, when they reached this point about 39 miles west of Fargo, is Sandy Larson's story.

SANDY LARSON *(a middle-aged blonde woman shown standing next to Coleman, vaguely confused, her hair blowing in the wind):* Well, first we heard a big noise, a rumble it was, louder than any thunder imaginable. . . .

COLEMAN: But was it louder than that truck that just went by?

LARSON: Very definitely.

COLEMAN: Could it—uh, what kinda noise? Like an explosion or a jet roar?

LARSON: More like thunder. 'N' 'nen the sky lit up an' eight or ten glowing objects came down out of the sky . . . they were round, orange, glowing balls. [At this point, Ms. Larson's voice began to tremble.]

COLEMAN: Were they—were they frightening?

LARSON: Very definitely. Then we realized there were taillights in front of us. So we pulled up alongside of 'em, and I rolled the window down, and I said, "Didjou see that?" And the guy said, "Yeah". . . .

Enough.

Is it fair to single out John Coleman's North Dakota expedition as an example of the level of his station's newscast? One could, on the other hand, point to the headline stories read by Daly and Flynn (a dignified broadcast veteran who has contributed most of Channel 7's limited journalistic prestige) or to the "in-depth" stories developed by members of the WLS reporting staff. And one will. One will.

What makes Coleman's flying-saucer-Frisbee fandango interesting is its insight into the station's priorities. All news outlets do light feature stories. They are plentiful in newspapers, in *Time* and *Newsweek*. But they seldom constitute a major drain of money and personnel on the outlet's news-gathering resources.

And there is an even greater fallacy inherent in comparing "soft" material in a newscast with light features or circulation gimmicks in a newspaper.

This comparison implies that an entire newspaper should be judged against an hour (or two-hour) newscast. But the judgment should in fairness be measured on the basis of total newspaper content against the station's total broadcast day, the sum of all its offerings: news, entertainment, commercials. It is instantly apparent that the newscast is a minuscule fragment of a daily outpouring that includes game shows, soap operas, sports events, movies, "The Bionic Woman," "Starsky and Hutch," "S.W.A.T.," "Charlie's Angels," "Happy Days" . . . and up to five hours' worth of commercials.

Back to Coleman.

When he was not combing the Dakotas for flying-saucer enlightenment or tripping off to the Caribbean for a five-part "report" on the Bermuda Triangle (as he did a few weeks later) or making regular appearances on the ABC network's "Good Morning, America," Coleman was the WLS "Eyewitness News" weatherman.

As such, he was the Number One personality in WLS's Happy Talk mythos; the Prime Card, the bright wrapping on the news-cum-entertainment package that Channel 7 had successfully hustled for eight years. Newscasts in the Midwest are built around the weatherman-jester to a much greater degree than on either coast. And WLS misses not a single trick in merchandising its meal ticket.

The weathercast comes midway through the production, and is the emotional climax of the show. Periodically throughout the opening minutes, the anchorman works the audience like a carnival advance man, hinting, teasing, tossing off a one-liner here and there to build up a state of mirthful anticipation.

When Coleman takes the stage, it is ham's holiday, with gaudy cartoon visuals and chroma-key sleight-of-hand that require hours of careful preparation. (Chroma-key is an electronic process that allows a director, using two cameras, to superimpose a foreground image—say, Coleman—against an unrelated background field—say, a cartoon igloo.) At WLS, the weathercast can run a whopping three and one-half minutes (this in an era when "a minute-ten" is the rule for any story short of World War III), with Coleman doing a star turn that would boggle the crowd at Reno Sweeney.

Even the regulation opening of the Channel 7 "Eyewitness News" leaves no doubt as to the show's headliner. It is Coleman, and Coleman alone, who is allowed to wander nonchalantly onto the "Eyewitness News" set under the opening credits; the others are already seated and beaming. Coleman strolls into view from somewhere among Us—from among the cameras—and with elaborate casualness attaches his neck microphone as he takes up a standing position at far Stage Right, next to the sportscaster.

Although we cannot yet hear the "Eyewitness News" team, we see Coleman's mouth moving; we see the sportscaster grin. And we know that for the duration of the newscast, no matter how grim the headlines, no matter how bloody the footage, no matter how moodily soul-searching Joel Daly's commentary—we know that nothing is really wrong in Chicago or in the Republic.

Coleman is smiling. Later, Coleman will make us laugh. There are no structural flaws in our universe. A climate of assurance has been smoothed about us, like a warm blanket.

And, in gratitude, assured and off the hook, relieved of the world's worries by comfortable Coleman and the "Eyewitness News," we will tune in again. And again.

JOEL DALY: . . . And in California, first it was no rain, then it was too much rain. John McDonald gets some help trying to dig his car out of a mud-swamped garage near Los Angeles. This is not the kind of picture that the Chamber of Commerce likes us to see, John.

COLEMAN: No, Joel, but I'm very proud. Because, let's see, it was Friday morning I was on the network, I predicted mudslides for the Los Angeles area.

DALY: And you're gonna take—

COLEMAN *(loudly):* I don't care how bad it is, just so it's the way I predicted! You know what I mean?

If John Coleman is the complete buffoon on camera (he paraded about the Channel 7 weather set with a large yellow "Peace" sign the night that U.S. involvement formally ended in Vietnam; he stood on his head during a forecast as he promised he would do if the weather got below 40 degrees, or something), off-screen he is a different person entirely. Now he is Pagliacci, the misunderstood poet of meteorology, the sober-sided intellectual who must don the trappings of the fool in order to make himself noticed by the rabble.

There is a certain condescension here, if you care to take notice of it, a condescension that redounds throughout the assumptions of cybernetic news.

Consider these excerpts from an interview I conducted with Coleman for the Chicago *Sun-Times* a few years ago. Is it hard, I asked professorial Coleman, to get into the mood for video Coleman?

"I'll be candid with you," said Coleman. "I don't know how to lie. It's work. The 'me' you're talking to now is more the 'me' than that guy on television. When I came into the Chicago market, I looked at the competition. And I chose the role that I felt would have the best chance of succeeding."

Coleman sighed. He is a plumpish middle-aged man (one rap that nobody could make stick against the Channel 7 team was that they were beautiful), with sad eyes arranged around a generous beak, whence derives his slightly nasal basso profundo.

"I would say," Coleman continued, "that the weatherman is much maligned from all sides. He is greatly misunderstood by almost everybody but the public.

"You become a comic character. Now—with this image in the community's mind, you're constantly trying to rise above it, yet you know you can't be perfect; that you're going to have those em-barassing days and weeks, so you mustn't be pompous about your-self."

And how does Coleman feel about Happy Talk?

"If you really studied it," he said, "you would realize that it's not a discredit to journalism. And maybe, in fact, it is a real step forward in journalism. I personally feel that's so. Let's start with the fact that almost half a million more people watch the Channel 7 news every night now than they did in 1966. I don't care how good a news service is, it's only as good as its communication job accomplished.

"And unless you give them [the viewers] a framework of hu-manity, the perspective that day-to-day life will go on, that people are still drinking beer and laughing, I think you've done a dis-service to the community."

That is where one usually winds up when speaking with a member of Happy Talk news team. The Orwellian inversion of values: Happy Talk is not just a slightly gamy fact of competitive life in broadcasting; Happy talk is good for you. Happy Talk puts more people in front of the TV set so they can receive the impor-tant news ("You can't save souls in an empty church"). And, if somehow the "important" (read: "disturbing") news does not ever get delivered to these augmented hordes, or is not delivered in the depth and scope it has traditionally deserved — why, then, an equally important service has been rendered to the community. People are still drinking beer. Laughing. The "framework" has been established. Life is going on.

Oh, perhaps it is not going on as pleasantly as it might, be-cause the laughing beer-drinkers have delivered another dema-gogue into public office (in-depth political reporting is com-plicated and dull and often disturbing); or because they are, suddenly and without warning, in the midst of an economic crisis (financial reporting tempts yawns, and nips at deep-seated uneasi-ness); or because their neighborhoods are under siege by mem-bers of an enemy race (race stories are best covered at the point of picketing and rock-throwing; the "visuals" are much more ex-citing, and no one has to think much about the abstract, unpleas-ant root causes); or because, being good television-trained con-sumers, they have not examined many of the alternatives to drinking beer.

There are interesting similarities between Happy Talk news's sense of mission as articulated by Coleman, and U.S. public schools' goals as perceived by the radical education critic, Jonathan Kozol.

Kozol believes that "the first goal and primary function of the U.S. public school is not to educate good people, but good citizens . . . manageable voters, manipulatable consumers and, if need be, in the case of war or crisis, willing killers."

In *The Night Is Dark and I Am Far From Home,* Kozol goes on:

> The first objective and the most consistent consequence of public school is the perpetration of a U.S. value system: one that dominates both how we think and how we feel about those people who do *not* live in this land, or else who *do,* but live here in those Third World colonies which are the non-white ghettos. The goal is self-protection in the face of activating guilt and shame . . . The surfeit, over-fullness, over-richness we enjoy, exist somehow upon a plateau of untouched and non-malignant privilege.

Granted, TV news lacks a malign ideology of the sort that Kozol perceives in the public schools. The effect is essentially the same.

In their frenzy to invest their news team with a hard-core lowbrow persona, the WLS promotional department in 1976 tried every trick except opening the newscast with Aaron Copland's "Fanfare for the Common Man." (They probably would have done *that* had they not thought it too highbrow.)

What the Channel 7 image-makers did attempt was the hillbillization of Joel Daly. It was a difficult task. Daly, the anchorman and Coleman's straight man, had — like Coleman — delusions of profundity. A gentle-mannered soul, accessible and easy to like personally, Daly on-screen was a study in schizophrenia. He dutifully carried out his Dr. Interlocutor role with Coleman, but he never really seemed comfortable in the part.

A more reliable clue to the Daly self-image came at the close of every newscast. This was the segment reserved for Joel's "Commentary," and it was generally a pietistic blend of O. Henry, Dr. Norman Vincent Peale and Erich Segal, delivered in stately cadences and accompanied by a tilted-head, sad-eyed expression on Daly's honest Howdy Doody face.

Daly was a *magna cum laude* graduate of Yale University, the possessor of a $100,000-a-year salary, a familiar personage nationwide on ABC as occasional anchorman for the network's

"Weekend News" out of New York—hardly the kind of guy you would imagine in Levis, puffing a Lucky Strike and humming, "I Turned 21 In Prison Doin' Life Without Parole."

And yet this is exactly the fiction that WLS sought to bestow upon their amiable, compliant anchorman-intellectual.

Full-page advertisements began appearing in Chicago newspapers. They featured handsomely-wrought pen-and-ink drawings of Daly the Plain Cuss: Daly—in a country-western jacket, string tie, and hand-tooled cowboy boots, with a guitar resting on his knee—grinning out at the reader like Porter Wagoner. Daly in work jeans, behind the wheel of a semi-trailer truck. "TONIGHT JOEL DALY RIDES WITH THE LAST AMERICAN COWBOY." Daly, in a T-shirt, balancing a can of pop on his thigh, the can cunningly labeled "Seven."

The apex came on Sunday, February 1, 1976. The occasion was a country music concert at Chicago's Arie Crown Theater. Chicago *Sun-Times* columnist Bob Greene was present and told the story in his Tuesday column:

> . . . Midway through the concert, the master of ceremonies—one Stan Scott—broke into the program and announced that a special guest would be coming onto the stage.
>
> And with that, from behind a curtain, strode a tall man wearing a western suit and cowboy boots.
>
> It was not, as first glance might have indicated, a Tennessee singing star or a rodeo cowboy.
>
> It was, instead, Joel Daly, the Channel 7 news anchorman.
>
> Now, Channel 7 has always prided itself as the folksy "Happy Talk" station in its quest for higher and higher ratings, but as far as I could tell, this was the first time that a television journalist had ever appeared on a country music concert stage to entertain the fans in person. It was tantamount to seeing Walter Cronkite on "Hee Haw."
>
> The thousands of people in the audience whooped and cried as if it were Merle Haggard instead of a news reporter. Dozens of men and women rushed to the front of the stage with Instamatic cameras and flashed bulbs in Daly's direction.

And then, Greene reported, "a silence settled over the house" as Daly began to read a poem he had composed about how it feels to be a hillbilly:

A hillbilly is not just one who lives in the hills,
Who drinks from the stills
Or works in the mills.

A hillbilly is not just one whose neck is red,
Whose tail is lead
Or is by a shotgun wed.

No, a hillbilly isn't just a mountaineer ready to feud,
A hillbilly isn't merely a person,
It's an attitude.

Daly's poem went on to extol the alembic advantages of hillbilly love, hillbilly joy, hillbilly grief, hillbilly laughter ("the key to relief"), hillbilly tears, hillbilly loneliness. As the Arie Crown rafters echoed his oratory, Channel 7's Yale *magna-cum*-hillbilly brought the transfixed crowd to a celebratory pitch of Whitmanesque brotherhood:

So call me a hillbilly;
Make me part of that crowd.
At least I know when music is good and not just loud.

And if my poem sounds corny and just a little bit silly,
What the heck do you expect?
I'm just a hillbilly.

The very day on which the Daly column was published, Bob Greene received a memo, delivered by messenger, from John Briska, WLS's manager of press information.

Was the memo castigating? Did it reprimand Greene for unwarranted and out-of-context ridicule of a fine television newsman? Did it petulantly riposte that print journalists had been known to do some pretty foolish things too? Did it threaten a meeting with the *Sun-Times* editor?

No. Here, in its entirety, was what Briska's memo said:

BOB: Went good and turned out same way. Many thanks. Hope we can keep you in touch to other goddies [*sic*], especially now that you have more to write.
Best,
John Briska, Manager Press Info.

It would be pleasant to report that the travesty stopped there, that everyone concerned came to his senses and put an end to the foolishness. That is not the case.

Buoyed by his superstar reception at the Arie Crown Theater and by his critical acclaim in the press, Joel Daly made a recording of "The Hillbilly." It was aired on some of the Chicago country-western stations, one of which reported in November that it had risen to Number 23 on the charts.

There is more still. On the flip side of "The Hillbilly," Daly made his commercial yodeling debut. The tune in question, written by Daly himself, was titled, "The Difference in Me Is You."

That particular side of the record received considerably less air play than "The Hillbilly." Nevertheless, it is an indisputable footnote to the saga of electronic journalism that Joel Daly, of WLS-TV's "Eyewitness News" team, became history's first anchor-yodeler.

A crucial ingredient in the value system taught in U.S. public schools, believes Kozol, is a sense of impotence. The pupil must feel that he is powerless to effect change—to take an intervening, ethical stand—because of the overwhelming vastness of the social forces at work.

Kozol quotes John Kenneth Galbraith as saying, "It is the essence of planning that public behavior be made predictable," and asserts:

> What the teacher "teaches" is by no means chiefly in the words he speaks. It is at least in part what he *is*, in what he *does*, in what he seems to *wish to be*. The secret curriculum is the teacher's own lived values and convictions, in the lineaments of his expression and in the biography of passion or self-exile which is written in his eyes . . .
>
> By denial of conviction, he does not teach *nothing*. He still teaches *something*. He teaches, at the very least, a precedent for non-conviction.

Thus we have television's "teacher," John Coleman (and many others like him), the man who "doesn't know how to lie," choosing a didactic TV "role" that belies his own, self-confessed true nature for the sake of persuading viewers nightly that things are generally okay, that there are no deep structural flaws in the society they live in, that laughing and drinking beer are the accepted responses to the American community in the seventies.

None of this is to suggest that local television news stations (and their station managers) were systematized, conscious, and ideological agents of the counterrevolutionary forces in America. They were not. They were businessmen, good citizens, probably a bit more "civic-minded" than their management contemporaries at, say, Xerox or IBM or Exxon.

But in their pursuit of a competitive edge—and in their resultant and largely innocent embrace of cybernetic techniques for audience manipulation—they had managed to form a lock step pattern with public education goals as Kozol sees them.

Network news in 1976 was still relatively free from the stylized complacency, the hustling and the euphemism of the local stations. This relative freedom owed much to the character and vision of the network personnel: CBS's Richard Salant (news director), Walter Cronkite (who had managing-editor status at CBS News), Mike Wallace, documentary-maker Perry Wolff, Dan Rather and others; NBC's news director Richard Wald, John Chancellor, and David Brinkley. (At ABC, the visionaries were not quite so visible.)

Most of these men had been around in the formulative days of network news; their background was in reporting, not business, and their very longevity had legitimized their resistance to the newer and fashionable ideas.

But the duration of their influence seemed in doubt. By 1976, cybernetic news was already solidly established at one network and was feeling its way toward the others.

STEPCHILD
ON THE MAKE

Alone among the three major television networks, ABC is a stepchild. It is the smallest network. And until the 1975–76 prime-time season, it had been the weakest in the ratings.

To understand these three facts, which are interrelated, is to understand why ABC became the first television network to hire outside consultants for large-scale advice on the appearance and, to a degree, the content of its "Evening News" show. (Both Frank N. Magid Associates and McHugh & Hoffman Inc. were on the network payroll in the 1970's.) And it is to understand why ABC's owned and affiliated stations, most notably WABC in New York and WLS in Chicago, were in the vanguard of the razzle-dazzle newscast style of the late 1960's, the style that came to be known as Happy Talk.

ABC was born of excess and grew up in deprivation. The network evolved from the National Broadcasting Company; until 1947 it was NBC Radio's Blue Network. To forestall a monopolistic threat (it is strange indeed to consider that mighty CBS was, through its first quarter-century, a weak and vulnerable challenger to NBC) the government ordered NBC to release its Blue division; it was allowed to retain the Red, which is the NBC of today.

In 1952, ABC was purchased by the Paramount Theatres chain. By this time, CBS and NBC had established themselves as America's pre-eminent broadcasting empires, and, between the two of them, had acquired the largest and most powerful local outlets as affiliates or owned stations.

This pre-eminence shared by CBS and NBC put ABC at a grave competitive disadvantage from the outset. Large, well-known urban stations generate large audiences, and it is on the basis of audience rating points that network revenues are set. Through the years, ABC has trailed its two older rivals, not only in ratings competition in cities where the three networks were head-to-head, but also in the crucial category of total affiliate stations. You can't get ratings unless you turn on a transmitter, and in cities with fewer than three TV stations, ABC often did not have a transmitter to turn on. "Catch-up" became the operative ethic at ABC.

There was a further obstacle to the youngest network's struggle toward parity: the broadcasting inexperience of ABC's early chieftains. When Paramount Theatres took over the network, Leonard Goldenson, a career theater man, became president of the complex. His executive vice president was Simon B. Siegel, also a product of theater management. As Les Brown points out in his book *Television: The Business Behind the Box,* Goldenson and Siegel "were not intuitively broadcasters. Their approach to the business was to keep an eye on what CBS was doing."

As the 1960's progressed and ABC's leadership passed to younger, more competitive hands, ABC's catch-up absorption intensified. The network acquired a certain opportunistic penchant: a willingness to gamble, when the odds seemed favorable, for a quick solution to competitive problems. This tendency gave ABC a mercurial aspect that was, by turns, the hope and the bane of the industry.

On the one hand, it led the youngest network into brilliant bursts of experimentation: the airing of professional football on Monday nights in 1970; a late-night news-entertainment umbrella form, "Wide World of Entertainment"; the bold "Close Up" series of investigative journalism. On the other, it prodded ABC into expedient programming philosophies, often with embarrassing and self-destructive results: the ill-conceived spate of "relevant" entertainment shows around 1970; the general *content* of "Wide World"; the monumentally lurid melodrama based on Marilyn Monroe's life, as interpreted by Connie Stevens; the demise of

"Close Up"; the palpable loathing with which ABC regarded talk-
show host Dick Cavett, and Cavett's attendant slide into oblivion.
   Les Brown sums up ABC's vicissitudes most accurately:

> In network society, ABC is the parvenu, wealthy as a com-
> pany through its vast chain of motion picture theaters and its own-
> ership of television and radio stations in the largest markets, but as
> a television network somewhat out of its class. ABC is the climber,
> and it has been a hard climb. It is hard to catch up with network
> leaders who are entrenched, hard to beat them at the game they
> invented, hard to convey a public impression of respectability with-
> out a history of it, and hard to win the full cooperation and support
> of affiliated stations which, through the lean years, have operated
> from short-range goals.

   ABC's opportunistic instincts found expression in many
ways. Among the most conspicuous was its strident self-portrayal
as the Network of the Young. Until NBC's administrative bum-
blings and CBS's lassitude finally allowed ABC to "win" the
1975–76 prime-time entertainment programming race, the network had seldom been able to coax the required numbers of
viewers away from its two grownup rivals. Perhaps as the result of
some feverish delirium born of perennial frustration, ABC began
to tantalize itself with the notion that there was a huge, untapped
multitude of potential television viewers "out there somewhere."
This horde, the fantasy had it, was impossibly attractive to advertisers. Brand-conscious. Affluent. Trendy. And young.
   In the late 1960's, when the "youth culture" was rampant in
the land, ABC, with the touching absorption of some gigantic
Elmer Fudd, set about to construct a series of gaudy "youth-ori-
ented" programs — electronic wabbit-twaps in which to snare all
those prodigal Bugs Bunnies. It was dimly apparent even to the
Gucci-slippered minions of the ABC executive suites that something of a revolution was being perpetrated by those selfsame
bunnies, a revolution that rejected the very consumer culture of
which network television was a life-support system. It doesn't matter, the minions told themselves; they'll all come to their senses in
a few years. And when they do — when they put down their Viet-
cong flags and get around, finally, to shopping for pantyhose and
Hamburger Helper and cat chow — they'll remember that we are
the Network of the Young.

So ABC began its attempt to ingratiate itself to the young consumers and consumers-to-be "out there." Some of the programming results were on target; "Mod Squad" was the under-25 hit of the late sixties. Most were just plain dreadful: transparent, painfully transparent, in their tendency to give lip service to radical values, then pull back at the last minute to reveal their (moderately) long-haired, (sort of) disaffected young heroes and heroines to be closet Defenders of the System. In this category fell such groaners as "The Young Lawyers," "Matt Lincoln," and perhaps the all-time champion of hypocritical television fare, "The Young Rebels." This last piece of gaucherie, which premiered in the troubled autumn of 1970 and died quietly some weeks after, concerned the fortunes of a bunch of Revolutionary War "activists" who worked for the American cause behind enemy lines. The implicit parallels to the radical youth movement were all but announced on idiot cards at the beginning of each episode.

Les Brown is excellent on the topic of such programming — excellent partly because his insights do not apply to the entertainment sphere alone:

> Far from satsifying the viewers who wished for a more significant fiction from the medium, television's version of socially consequential programming was only a betrayal of the commercial industry's *inability to deal honestly with life and of its ingrained commitment to a dead-center point of view.* [Emphasis added.] Whatever the social question, its resolution in the melodrama pointed up a single video truth: the existing order was always right.
>
> Fault-finding youth was conceded its points: there were wickedness, injustice, and unreason, but they were the sins of individuals and not of the system. The scriptwriters echoed some of the anger of the young, but their stories invariably went on to demonstrate that they were captives of their un-ripe passions and misled by sinister individuals among them who played on their passions. Implicit in virtually every story was the message that teen-age and post-teen rebels eventually would recognize the error of their ways and take their proper places within the system.

It is true that ABC was not alone in its covetous pitch to the emerging consumer-youths "out there." NBC and CBS were seeking essentially the same audience—although not to ABC's extreme of self-caricature. It is also true that the notion of a large, untapped, and affluent group of viewers was, to some degree, valid: ABC, by its Network of the Young crusade, *did* augment its audience size and demographics. (The network was often guilty of overestimating that new audience's size and gullibility, however — as witness its catastrophic experiences with "AM America," that ready-mix challenger to the "Today" show, and, later, "Saturday Night Live With Howard Cosell."

The point of describing ABC's instinct for opportunism in prime-time programming is to illuminate a tendency that is universal within the network. ABC wants viewers — a lot of them, young ones, now — and it doesn't particularly care how they are rounded up. That mentality is true in entertainment. And it is true, in some quarters at least, in the news.

"When you have a Patty Hearst thing, a Symbionese Liberation Army shootout, an attempted assassination of the President, you have an influx of younger viewers around the country. These normally go to the ABC station. It's the format of the show. It's a younger-oriented look."

The speaker is Ron Gleason. Gleason is director of research and development for ABC News. He is talking to me by telephone about ABC News's philosophy, but he is distracted at the moment. He is distracted because there is a helicopter flying around the ABC building at 1330 Avenue of the Americas in New York. Gleason is in communication with the helicopter, which is circling the ABC building to shoot footage for promotional spots on the network, advertising the Harry Reasoner-Barbara Walters evening newscast.

"These are very mobile people who have other activities," Gleason is saying about ABC's young, presumably shootout-happy news audience. "When something does happen [and, by "something," Gleason makes it clear that he means bloodshed or disaster], they're more likely to go to ABC. They're our audience."

Gleason's background is instructive. For years, he was employed by ABC's owned station in San Francisco, KGO — a station whose call letters, one employee told CBS's Mike Wallace in a burst of reproachful irony, stood for "Kickers, Guts, and Orgasms." She was referring to the station's "tabloid" penchant for news items dealing with fire, crime, sex, accidents, and tear-jerkers.

Now Gleason is in charge of the parent network news division's research department, the division entrusted with the responsibility of finding out which people watch the "ABC Evening News," how old they are, what their buying patterns are, and what they seem to want. Gleason's concept of the news—as a commodity that attracts a certain bracket of America's consumer force—reflects his orientation toward the arena of sales, marketing, and promotion. Such men abound at the networks and their owned-station divisions, and at affiliate stations everywhere. Their influence is enormous. ABC is certainly not alone in the employment of men with a sales-related background in its news division. The pre-eminence of the salesman in TV news is a fundamental circumstance of electronic journalism, which, after all, exists within a medium whose *raison d' etre* is to advertise. At ABC, however, the sales ethic appears to have somewhat greater sway. A business organization that has had to play catch-up all its life against larger, wealthier, more experienced competitors, tends to pull out the stops in every sector of competition.

Av Westin understands the realities of TV ratings competition. A thin-faced, professorial man in his early forties, natty in his dark-rimmed glasses and dark, correct suits, Westin scored brilliant critical successes in ABC's news division before his departure early in 1976. As executive producer of the "Evening News" from 1969 to 1973, Westin was responsibile for sharply refining the network's news objectives and for introducing a sophisticated system of visuals behind the anchorman. As vice president of documentaries until January 1975, Westin developed ABC's award-winning "Close Up" series of tough, pertinent investigative reports. He left the network after losing a series of organizational battles to keep "Close Up" on the air at full strength, when it became clear that he did not share the philosophies of ABC's new news chief, William Sheehan.

"I believe," Westin told me not long after his resignation, "that all of us in the TV news business have from time to time been seduced by the ratings game. The worst thing that ever happened to network news, in my opinion, was in 1975, when the prime-time ratings race finally tightened up.

"At that point CBS, which had always been Number One, and ABC, which had always been Number Three, moved toward the middle. When that happened, both networks became less willing to pre-empt programs for public affairs or to put on regularly scheduled information programs.

"CBS had been way out in front all through the years, and in keeping with its noble public image, occasionally pre-empted an entertainment show to do a 'CBS Reports.' ABC, on the other hand, was so far behind that we felt nothing we did was going to make any difference anyway. So we pre-empted because we knew we'd get the brownie points with the FCC, and we'd get the reviews. NBC remained sort of in the middle, maintaining a steady course, neither increasing nor decreasing its public-affairs programming.

"All right. Now it's 1975 and the ratings race has become so close that CBS says, 'Wait a minute. We're not going to take a ten-point drop to put in "CBS Reports." ' And ABC says, 'We're so close that *we* are not going to take a ten-point drop by pre-empting "La Verne and Shirley," because we may win it.'

"The point is, television is a profit-making business, first and foremost. Let me make a newspaper analogy for a moment. The newspaper publisher and the newspaper journalist always have an adversary relationship. And if they don't, something is wrong. The publisher of a newspaper wants to reduce the news hole to put in more supermarket ads. The journalists wants that space for news.

"Now, the same relationship should exist, but *does not yet exist,* in broadcast journalism. And this is because television is essentially an entertainment-advertising medium. Its 'spin-off' is news. The newspaper is essentially a news medium, and its spin-off is entertainment. So as soon as you get into a conflict of news as opposed to entertainment, the TV 'publisher'—that is, the station manager—is going to try to find ways of increasing his circulation at the cost of the quality. He is not really dedicated to quality."

Westin, in his evaluation of quality as opposed to profits, was not speaking primarily about the regularly scheduled evening newscasts, but of the closely-related public-affairs programming, which includes documentaries and news specials. At all three networks, the news divisions are separate from the entertainment divisions. The news divisions *create* public-affairs programs, but the decision of when or whether to schedule them in place of entertainment shows rests at the level of network presidents.

The degree of a television network's overall commitment to informational programming is thus arbitrary. The nightly newscasts are fixed in the schedule, but beyond that, the frequency of informational programming is strictly a factor of profit and loss. And, as Westin pointed out, the pull is inexorably toward the middle, toward a modicum of public affairs programs that will cause minimal damage to the bottom line. With the demise of ABC's "Close Up" in 1975, CBS remained the only network to offer a weekly public-affairs show ("60 Minutes") anywhere near prime time.

As for documentaries themselves, by 1976 they were approaching extinction. Only 15 were aired on CBS, 13 on NBC and eight on ABC. (The previous year, CBS had broadcast 28, ABC 18 and NBC 15.)

ABC's abiding priority of the last ten years, its catch-up approach to building large audiences fast, was bound to have an effect on the news. The wonder of the whole enterprise was that the *network* news remained relatively immune to adulteration.

Prime-time network news *specials* suffered to a considerable degree, as Av Westin argued. But where ABC's commercializing had its most telling effect was at the owned-station level. Here, that effect resounded throughout American local-station TV journalism.

Each network, by federal regulation, is allowed to own five stations in the United States. (Beyond those, the networks distribute their programming through arrangement with as many independently owned, "affiliate" stations as they can line up.) ABC owns stations in New York, Chicago, Los Angeles, Detroit, and San Francisco. The manager of an owned station reports, not to some single owner or board president in the station's city, but to the owned-stations division of ABC Television in New York.

The station managers tend to reflect the thinking of the parent network, having in most cases been salesmen for the network: their orientation is toward the New York office and its business

considerations, and only secondarily to the informational needs of
the local community. Thus, when ABC intensified its competition
in prime-time programming, the new mood of aggression carried
through all divisions of the network, including owned stations.
And the foremost competitive product at the owned stations was
the local news.

It is true that ABC's local stations (principally, Chicago and
New York)—not the network—discovered the techniques of cybernetic news. They, not the network, were the first to embrace
the wholesale use of consultants. They, not the network, were the
first to reap huge profits from the ratings successes of Happy Talk
and its related forms. In that sense, the catch-up techniques, as
they applied to news, trickled *upward* from ABC's owned stations
to the parent network. (McHugh & Hoffman were retained by the
network news division in October of 1968; Magid was not hired
on a network basis until 1973.) However, in the sense that the
owned stations were administered by the New York office in the
first place—and that their managers were largely honed in New
York sales—it is fair to say that cybernetic news was a child of
ABC's overall network competitive needs. And as its questionable
influence spread first to other local stations and finally to the
"ABC Evening News" itself, it was apparent that cybernetic news
was ABC's version of *Rosemary's Baby*.

Although news consultants—Frank Magid in particular—
have left an imprint on the "ABC Evening News," the effects by
late 1976 had been largely cosmetic (a new, paneled set, new visuals). True, some critics discerned a softening of "secondary" news
items, such as light features and personality profiles. Still, the basic ABC News agenda differed little from those at CBS and NBC.
Network newscasts had their weak points in 1976, but cybernetic
techniques were not yet among them.

Even the Alfred I. DuPont-Columbia University *Survey of
Broadcast Journalism,* pre-eminent in the criticism of TV news, gave
the networks high marks in its 1975 edition: "Despite claims to the
contrary, we find the general level of balance and fairness in network news commendable, and we rise to its defense. The programs deal with matters of daily import and are never trivialized
or cosmetized." (Harry Reasoner's interior decorators arrived after the DuPont survey was published; nonetheless, the evaluation
was basically on target.)

Why is the network news as serious-minded as it is? Logic seems stacked against the possibility. There is nothing sacred about a network news division. It is one of many parts of a network's corporate structure, and corporations exist to make money. David Halberstam writes that CBS, under founder and board chairman William S. Paley, has made money with a vengeance unexampled in broadcasting: "A smaller company in contrast to RCA-NBC, [CBS] has been incomparably profitable. At times during the 1960's it accounted for 75 per cent of the total profit in broadcasting, and generally, over the last 15 years, has beaten NBC in profit on a rough scale of 8 to 5 or 9 to 6, with ABC showing profit only in the last three years." Halberstam asserts that CBS's net profits after taxes have steadily risen, from $47.5 million in 1964, to $108.5 million in 1974.[1]

Yet the news divisions of the networks are not profit-makers. Budget breakdowns within a network's divisions are guarded secrets, but it is generally agreed that although the evening newscasts *themselves* generate big revenues, the profits are plowed back into such loss-leading enterprises as convention coverage, space shots, election-night marathons, and news specials.

News-division costs are gigantic almost beyond comprehension. CBS's network news budget alone has been estimated at upward of $80,000,000 a year. This includes the costs of high-salaried anchormen and correspondents, electronic equipment, and worldwide news bureaus.

If all this expense, energy, and anguish do not generate profits to the corporation, why do the networks bother?

Adding to the paradox is the matter of the networks as corporations. The most useful kind of news tends to be insurrectionary: exposés of official malfeasance, corrupt diversion of taxpayers' funds, scandal, illegal use of power in both the public and private sectors. As corporations, the networks have a self-interest in maintaining the status quo, the appearance of a calm and orderly business-political universe. As corporate kin, how does CBS News report a payola scandal at Columbia Records, or ABC report the motion-picture industry's vested-interest lobby against cable television? As entities of the government (through the Federal Communications Commission's licensing power), how do the networks report a Watergate, especially under the eye of a malign

[1] "CBS: The Power & the Profits," *The Atlantic Monthly,* January 1976.

administration that is demonstrably willing to use its license-re-moval power as a club?

Not too well. Television news has had its moments as an ad-versary "press" in terms of criticizing government, starting with Edward R. Murrow's McCarthy broadcast in 1954 and continuing through Walter Cronkite's commentaries on Vietnam policy in the late 1960's and CBS's documentaries "The Selling of the Pen-tagon" and "Justice in America" in 1970. The moments have been few. As a watchdog on corporate power, TV network news has been, at best, myopic.

Given these limitations — some of which are shared by news-papers as well — network newscasts labor diligently to give the viewer a reliable, if encapsulated, nightly summary of the world around him. Why is this so?

Three answers suggest themselves:

Tradition. For this word, read: "Murrow." His imprint on tele-vision news is impossible to overstate, despite the fact that he was primarily a radio man. The history of network news is in many ways the history of CBS News, and the legacy of CBS News is World War II. As CBS Radio's European director beginning in 1937, it was Murrow's duty to put together a foreign correspon-dent staff, and, as David Halberstam indicates, he chose the best and the brightest:

> The CBS men hired by Murrow became what one colleague, not entirely admiringly, called a special kind of philosopher-king-intellectual-statesman-journalist. They included such men as Charles Collingwood, Eric Sevareid, Howard K. Smith, William L. Shirer. After the war, this coterie held together as a radio news elite. When television came into being, they lent it an early stamp of journalistic legitimacy. Murrow never became a television "news-man" in the strict sense of covering hard news or anchoring a news-cast. But his "See It Now" series of documentaries, produced su-perbly by Fred Friendly, provided a standard of toughness, pertinence and intellect that the medium found hard to ignore.[2]

Meanwhile, another founding father of TV news was fortui-tously working his way toward CBS from another direction. Wal-ter Cronkite covered the war for United Press. His were the old-fashioned instincts and values of print journalism, which included

[2] Ibid

a strong sense of what constituted important news and a stronger reverence for objectivity. Like Murrow, Cronkite influenced the early direction of TV news along traditionally accepted lines. The continued presence of men such as Cronkite, Sevareid, and Smith through 25 years of television news was in itself a kind of guarantee against dissolution.

Self-interest. Because government and broadcasters are so often in conflict, it is easy to forget that TV news owes its existence partly to the nobler visions of government. The Communications Act of 1934, which sets forth the powers of the Federal Communications Commission, provides restraints against the pure profit motives of the businessmen-station owners. The Act articulates the concept of serving the "public interest" as a fundamental price for owning a license.

Edward Jay Epstein, in *News From Nowhere* (Random House, 1973), provides a good definition of "public interest":

> The concept of the public interest which emerged in FCC and Court decisions rests on three central assumptions about the role of a communications medium in a free society. First, it is assumed as "axiomatic" that the "basic purpose" of broadcasting is, in the words of the Commission, "the development of an informed public opinion through the public dissemination of news and ideas concerning the vital public issues of the day." The "foundation stone of the American system of broadcasting" is then the "right of the public to be informed, rather than any right on the part of the government, any broadcast licenses or any individual member of the public to broadcast his own views on any matter." The broadcasting of news and information on matters of public importance is thus presumed to be an indispensable element in fulfilling the "public interest."

Thus, television networks are more or less stuck with doing news, whether they like it or not. Since the network news is largely concerned with the affairs of national government (and is therefore closely scrutinized *by* government, including influential senators, congressmen, and administration aides) it makes sense to present the news with a patina of sobriety, dignity, and detachment.

Identity. Until ten years ago, the three networks each had a distinct personality. NBC was the network of variety; it was Milton

Berle, Bob Hope, Dinah Shore, Jack Paar. CBS put itself on the map, competitively, by raiding NBC in the late 1940's of much of its talent, including Jack Benny and Red Skelton; it subsequently became the network of comedy, and later (with Jackie Gleason) of situation comedy. ABC slowly evolved into something of an alternative network, unpredictable, provocative, and it attained a certain identification with sports.

But in the last decade, the old star system began to fade; the Hopes and Skeltons became vestigial. Entertainment fare grew standardized, a product of the same centralized formula factories: Universal, Screen Gems, and the like. With the advent around 1970 of Norman Lear and Mary Tyler Moore Productions, CBS was able to change that mold somewhat, but even then, the distinctions were marginal—and quickly imitated on the other networks.

So it was that the *news* divisions filled the void as the networks' identifying signatures. Cronkite, Chancellor, Brinkley, Reasoner, Walters—each became, in his or her way, something of a symbol for a network's collective persona. And the news these people reported had to look responsible; it had to exude a certain feeling of integrity and earnest professionalism. It was each network's coat of arms.

FOLLOW THAT HELICOPTER!

Whatever their organizational reasons for keeping a good, gray, straight face, the network news chieftains have certainly mastered the rhetoric of the intrepid, detached news-hawk.

"I really don't know and I'm not interested," snaps CBS News president Richard Salant when asked what sorts of people watch his product. "I take a very flat elitist position. Our job is to give people not what they want, but what we decide they ought to have. That depends on our accumulated news judgment of what they need."

If CBS News does audience research, it keeps mum about it. "We don't have any," is Salant's terse reply to the question. Asked why research and consultancy are so ingrained in local-station news organizations (including CBS's five owned stations), Salant is equally unbending: "It's a simple explanation. Too many people who are operating these stations don't have confidence in the news judgment of the news director, so they desperately turn elsewhere. It is a refusal to accept my philosophy that you do what you ought to do."

ABC's vice president for news programs is 38-year-old Bill Lord, who replaced Av Westin in February 1976. Lord is a career newsman; he was ABC's Washington bureau chief before his promotion. Like Salant, Lord professes little patience for those who would program the news according to audience demographics or to presumed tastes.

Lord fairly snorted when I asked him, during a telephone

59

conversation, whether he agreed with Ron Gleason's characterization of ABC News as having a "younger-oriented look."

"It seems to me," said Lord, chosing his words evenly, "that
what we're putting on is for all age brackets. Gleason has no authority to say what he said. I think the use of the news consultant
must be very limited. Yes, we have them at ABC. Their influence
is diminishing, and I intend to continue to see that influence de-
minish. We are at a new juncture here. I want to expand the definition of the word 'news.' I want to go into consumer reporting on
a regular basis. I want to use specific news features that go into a
particular locality in the United States. I want the news more involved at the viewer level. Never before have people needed or
wanted to understand complex issues more than they do today. I
mean long-term inflation, the energy crisis, unemployment. This
is my concept of news."

When Bill Lord speaks of expanding the definition of the
word "news," he is on treacherous semantic ground. So far, there
has been no *basic* definition of "news" on which to expand. Man
may bite dog, President may subvert Constitution; in the end, only
the subjective judgment of the news-gatherer (Salant's "flat elitist
position") determines which, if either, is fit to print.

It is safe to say, however, that American journalism has always derived from a central assumption that elected officials need
careful watching. The modern newspaper sprang from the broad-
sides and handbills of Revolutionary times, those sanguinely sub-
versive tracts that excoriated the Crown, damned the dreaded tax,
and championed common sense. Diluted though it is with horo-
scopes, "Dear Abby," recipe swap shops, and iron-on decal campaigns, today's newspaper still manages to fulfill a vestigial measure of that ombudsman role—as Woodward and Bernstein
demonstrated in their solitude in 1973. Agnew was right: the
press *is* "elected by no one." That is the point.

Network television news attempts, however imperfectly, to
duplicate that central responsibility of the newspaper—and to
supplement it, as do the papers, with other traditionally accepted
categories: war coverage, crime stories, disasters, natural "acts of
God," economic news, human-interest features.

How the networks go about assembling their 23 minutes of
news each night is a complex process involving chains of com-

mand that circle the world and that are organized into sometimes overlapping, but minutely defined, divisions of labor.

CBS News's organizational flow is a useful index of how the three networks operate.

Before Walter Cronkite loosens his tie and bends over his copy with a blue pencil each weeknight a half-hour before air time, the "story" may have passed, in various forms, through a dozen pairs of hands.

Ron Bonn and John Lane are the two men who whip each night's amorphous mass of information into something called the "Evening News." They are co-producers of the show. Their production chores are split down the middle: Lane organizes the content of each upcoming newscast, while Bonn oversees the planning of future story projects and the editing of ongoing material, such as coverage of a political campaign.

Below Bonn and Lane are eight associate producers, who work out of CBS's massive news barn on West Fifty-seventh St. During last fall's campaigns, one of them was permanently assigned to Jimmy Carter (the Washington bureau looked after President Ford). Others were involved in related political-coverage projects. In addition, CBS maintains one associate producer each in Los Angeles and Washington.

CBS owns stations in New York, Chicago, Los Angeles, Philadelphia, and St. Louis. It maintains bureaus in the first three of those cities, and in Atlanta and Washington. An additional bureau is planned somewhere in Texas. (ABC is likewise looking toward the Sun Belt as an emerging source of national news; it will expand to the Southwest sometime in 1977.) Each of these bureaus is staffed with correspondents and film crews who are responsible for news in a broad coverage area around the city. (Pecking orders being what they are, though, CBS—like the other networks—will send its "stars" from New York and Washington, the Roger Mudds and Dan Rathers, to the bureau cities during major scheduled events such as primaries and election campaigns.)

CBS's worldwide bureaus are in London, Moscow, Bonn, Rome, Paris, Tel Aviv, Cairo, Beirut, Hong Kong, Rio de Janeiro, and Tokyo. An additional bureau will open soon somewhere in Africa. Each foreign bureau includes a correspondent and a film crew.

Back in New York, all domestic stories are directed by the assignment editor, Peter Sturtevant. He commands the movement of film crews and correspondents; bureau managers around the country report to him.

When CBS news film (and, increasingly, videotape) arrives at the "Evening News" offices, it is attacked by several of the eight film-tape editors assigned to the program. On important stories, these editors may travel with the crews, editing film or tape at the source. Each story is deliberately "overshot." An editor's assignment is to get the footage down to coherent length and to choose footage that best conforms to the correspondent's story line.

Meanwhile, three writers are busy producing the final copy — other than the voice-overs sent in by the correspondents themselves — that will find its way to Cronkite's hands. One writer specializes in foreign news, one in domestic. The third is what Bonn calls an "all-else" writer; a sort of all-round verbal handyman.

At CBS, Cronkite — the "managing editor" of the "Evening News" — has editorial discretion over the copy. Cronkite also has the right to involve himself in the selection of stories, but in practice that duty usually falls to Lane.

Although a tremendous amount of footage is shot each day for CBS News and only a small fraction gets on the evening newscast, the rest is not wasted. Like its competitors, CBS is budget-minded. Besides the "Evening News," which is the news division's "A" market, there are other outlets: the hour-long "CBS Morning News" with Hughes Rudd each weekday morning, an hour and a half of weekend news, and CBS's own news syndication service.

"Once you get through all that," says Bonn, "it's like you've been through a packing house. You've used up everything but the squeal."

From the distant perspective of an organizational chart, a network's news flow seems almost too dignified, correct, and preordained to be real. In practice, that is hardly the case. For all their dark-suited sobriety on-screen, network correspondents can act like characters out of *The Front Page* when they are on the beat. The "scoop" may be passé in print journalism (having given way to the more elegant "exclusive") but it thrives in TV news, where competent correspondents keep score on one another — and go to outrageous lengths to run up the score.

I found myself in the middle of such a *corpo-a-corpo* in the summer of 1974, during the last days of Richard Nixon's presidency. This particular contest happened to be a three-cornered game involving CBS's Rather, NBC's Tom Brokaw, and presidential press secretary Ron Ziegler — who wanted *both* men to lose.

I had accompanied Rather to the press headquarters near San Clemente for a magazine interview. On the last day of that visit, a Friday, Ziegler called a news conference to announce the resignation of Nixon's chief economic adviser, Herbert Stein. The resignation was the latest in a week-long series of embarrassing developments for the administration, and Ziegler knew that if the story could somehow be kept off the networks' Friday evening newscasts, its impact would be softened. With the savvy that marked the Nixon regime's understanding of electronic media, Ziegler was aware that the news audience dropped sharply on weekends. He also knew the White House correspondents' daily deadlines. At 3:00 P.M., Los Angeles time, it would be 6:00 P.M. in New York — one-half hour from air time for the evening news.

The press conference was called for 1:00 P.M., in press headquarters, a large cabana on stilts that overlooked the Pacific Ocean beach. One P.M. passed, with a roomful of reporters and cameras, and no Ziegler. No Stein. Rather fidgeted. One-thirty came and went. Brokaw's jaw tightened. Two o'clock arrived, and two-fifteen. Rather squeezed his way through the crowded aisle and whispered to his cameraman. The cameraman nodded.

At two-thirty, Ziegler and Stein entered the press room and took the low stage in front of the camera lights. Ziegler, for the first time that week, appeared immensely pleased with himself; he had a tight, private smile for Rather and Brokaw. The cameras began to record Stein's lengthy apologia for the collapse of his economic recommendations.

After about 15 seconds of this, I felt Rather's elbow in my ribs. "Get ready," he murmured to me. "We're leaving." He made his way again through the crowd of reporters to the camera area. He snatched the spool of videotape from the CBS camera and beckoned to me. Along with Bernard Kalb, another CBS correspondent, we made our way to the rear door of the press room and down the back steps of the cabana.

I wondered what insanity Rather had in mind. The nearest transmission site for videotape to New York was at the CBS bureau in Los Angeles—some 60 miles up the coast. It all seemed rather vainglorious.

We bundled into a four-door car which was waiting in the parking lot, complete with driver. The engine was running. Rather took the front seat by the window. The car screeched out onto the blacktop highway, north toward Los Angeles, with Rather, his head hanging out the window, yelling, "Clear right! Clear right!"

About a mile from the cabana, the car wheeled off the main highway and onto a mountain road. We roared up the mountain road. Rather, his left arm draped over the seat, was looking smug. At the top of the mountain a helicopter waited. I began to feel like a character in a James Bond movie. We piled out of the car and into the helicopter, which rose and flapped up the California coast, toward Los Angeles.

During the flight Rather relaxed enough to play the role of rubbernecking tourist. "That area down below us," he said, pointing to a gleaming harbor, "that's where H. R. Haldeman lives."

We landed on the roof of the CBS building in Los Angeles. Rather dashed out of the helicopter and ran to the makeup room. Two minutes later he emerged and took his place behind the desk of a small studio before a single camera.

At three-fifteen—15 minutes before air time in New York—Rather fed his account of the Herbert Stein resignation, complete with videotape, to the "CBS Evening News." It made the newscast.

Later, as I boarded the jet that would take Rather back to New York, where he would anchor the "CBS Weekend News," I realized that Ziegler had not been Rather's only opponent for the Herbert Stein story.

Across the aisle from us sat Tom Brokaw. He had his own helicopter.

Dan Rather's triumph against time and Ron Ziegler rekindled some of the old dash and glamour of American news-hawking. But there are critics who would point to the incident as an example of network news's limitations. The end result of Rather's (and Brokaw's) careful advance planning, split-second timing and considerable energy, after all, was the airing of a staged, ceremonial event. Rather did not—could not—go behind the scenes. As conscientious and resourceful as he is, he did not—could not—*predict* Stein's resignation, or offer viewers an inside account of the discussions and processes that led up to it. What CBS and NBC news produced, finally, was the symbolic and ceremonial result of political choices that took place beyond the range of the cameras' scrutiny.

To extend the example a bit further: though Dan Rather and his competitors became nationally recognized journalistic "stars" as Watergate developed, though they became identified in the public mind with the reportage of Watergate, they—the White House "regulars"—did not break the original story. Nor did they pursue the main thread of that original story into the developing saga of corruption, illegal surveillance, and Constitutional abuse. Watergate coverage followed a consistent pattern from first to last: uncovering and development of facts by the print press (and for "print press," read: "Woodward and Bernstein of the Washington Post," because the rest of the nation's newspapers largely sat on their hands) and *amplification* of these facts by TV news. Certainly the networks contributed some original material to Watergate, but it was, in the main, ancillary.

When I asked Rather why he and his colleagues—some of whom had been around the White House since Nixon's first inauguration—had not broken Watergate; his response was characteristically forthright.

"I still ask myself that question every day," he said. "We had plenty of inklings. It was around, sure. We saw it in the attitude of Haldeman and John Ehrlichman. Charles Colson. We knew in a vague, general way, if not specifically, that they had brought to the White House a new attitude; that they didn't operate in the way previous staffs had operated. When Agnew began the early attacks on the press in late 1969, we know this was part of a carefully orchestrated campaign within the White House itself. Sometimes you don't want to believe what you know in your own mind and heart is true. I know it ought not to be that way, but it is.

"We were lazy. We didn't follow up as we should have. *I* was lazy. And consequently, we didn't get the story of a lifetime."

Rather paused to think for several moments, and then continued in his clipped Texan's delivery: "There were, though, some more practical reasons. The story was broken by two Washington *Post* reporters who were basically police reporters. The Watergate break-in itself, which was the crack that threw the door open, was a local story that required local contacts to break. We didn't have those, since we are a national news organization.

"But I still can't and don't excuse myself and my colleagues at the White House. We should have been smarter. We should have gotten onto it. When the *Post*, through its local contacts, began to break the story, our lack of follow-up was glaring. The break-in was the lead item on our Saturday evening newscast. But we didn't follow up, and we quickly got very far behind the *Post*. The problem then became one of bringing in information on our own. We couldn't find a single source."

That Dan Rather and his colleagues were "lazy" in reporting Watergate is unlikely. Rather struck closer to the heart of TV news's dilemma when he pointed out that CBS, NBC, and ABC are *national* news services. A different way of stating this is to say that TV news is set up to report and record the *expected* behavior of national *newsmakers:* the ceremonial comings and goings of politicians and their formal opposition. Conspiracies, payoffs, and forgeries do not take place in the White House press room. Yet that is where the cameras and the correspondents must perforce station themselves in order to assimilate the numbing quantity of daily briefings, statements, and official "handouts" that constitute the bulk of Washington news. To cultivate a network of sources, as Woodward and Bernstein did, would be to court dismissal as a Washington correspondent, since the daily ceremonial news would have to be left uncovered.

Perhaps the classic study of network news's interior organizational imperatives was produced by Edward Jay Epstein in his book *News From Nowhere*. Epstein argues that TV networks do present a limited and distorted picture of world reality—not because of some ideological bent or professional ineptitude, but because of the nature of the beast: encumbered by its own bulky electronic apparatus, cramped by budgets, aware of government's stern eye, TV news tends to be self-censoring, stereotyped in its subject mat-

ter, unrealistically tied to available news pictures, under-re-
searched, predictable, and simplistic.

In Epstein's words, the self-limiting process works this way:

> Network news . . . is forced by the cumbersome business of
> setting up cameras and shuttling camera crews between stories to
> seek out the *expected* event—that is, one announced sufficiently in
> advance for a film crew and equipment to be dispatched to the
> scene . . . Assignment editors, producers and executives focus their
> search for news on the stories that can be depended on to materi-
> alize as "news stories" because, as one NBC assignment editor ex-
> plained, "We regularly only have nine or ten crews a day assigned
> to domestic news, and we need a minimum of nine or ten stories to
> feed the news shows." This leads to coverage of "routinized
> events," as the assignment editor put it, such as press conferences,
> Senate hearings, and speeches by important newsmakers, which
> are usually conveniently located and "wired for television". . . .

Thus the networks, insulated though they are from the crass
considerations of cybernetic news, must live with built-in shackles
that prevent them from digging beneath the surface of predictable events and acting as true ombudsmen for the viewers.

And thus there exists a vacuum in electronic journalism.
Somewhere between Washington and other capitals (the networks' territory) and City Hall (theoretically the purview of the local station) exists an invisible realm of political and corporate
power, decision-making and policy-setting, economic theorizing
and personal ethics that simply does not get monitored on a day-
to-day basis by television news.

Since all elected representatives come to Washington *from*
somewhere in America, and since corporation presidents and fin-
anciers operate not on some national Olympus but in city buildings with addresses and telephone numbers, it would seem that
local television news departments could take up some of this reportorial slack—could act the role of the Washington *Post,* not to
uncover a Watergate, perhaps, but to increase the accountability
of powerful men and women whose ultimate influence is funneled
to Washington.

It would seem that way. But the local newscasts have other
things to do.

EYEWITLESS NEWS

On April 7, 1976, I turned into the six o'clock "Eyewitness News" on Channel 7, the ABC-owned station in Chicago. The evening was chosen at random. Here is an item-by-item account of the stories that were broadcast in the ensuing hour.

The newscast's lead story, the equivalent to a newspaper's banner headline story, dealt with a manhunt by Chicago police for a murder suspect. There was lengthy on-the-scene film footage of policemen dashing along sidewalks to surround a South Side school building where the suspect was reported to be hiding. There were quick-cut close-ups of cops wearing sunglasses and brandishing shotguns. The Channel 7 cameras panned along the excited faces of neighborhood crowds who had gathered to watch. Then the action cut to the story's "climactic" moment: close-up footage of a suspect being forcibly escorted from the school building by two policemen, in a scene reminiscent of Al Pacino in *Dog Day Afternoon.*

At the conclusion of all this drama and excitement, the Channel 7 "Eyewitness News" reporter provided the story's true denouement: the suspect was not the real murderer. He was an innocent man. The real murderer was not at the school building, after all — something that the "Eyewitness News" producers knew, of course, before they put the footage on the air. The lead story had amounted to a few minutes of meaningless titillation.

Co-anchor Nancy Becker read an item stating that Chicago Mayor Richard J. Daley had introduced a "prostitute ordinance" in the City Council. Behind her appeared an orange drawing of a woman in an elaborately flowered hat.

Anchorman Joel Daly narrated a report that FBI agents had

secured indictments against 12 persons dealing in stolen goods. There was a film clip of a United States Attorney holding up a captured automatic weapon.

Reporter Rosemarie Gulley, in the field, interviewed a small boy who had overheard a telephone conversation among crooks at a grocery store and had turned the crooks in. Beneath the boy's face was superimposed the legend "Kid Hero." Ms. Gulley concluded that the boy's performance demonstrated that "little people can be big people."

There was a report on a controversy involving the chairman of the Chicago area's Regional Transportation Authority and suburban RTA board members, who wanted the chairman thrown out. In separate film clips—taken at news conferences—the chairman and the suburban group's spokesman were shown making disparaging remarks about one another.

A field reporter narrated a lengthy on-the-scene story, with a heavy larding of "wry" humor, on the failure of the Michigan Avenue bridge to rise and allow a small sailboat to proceed down the Chicago River. There were numerous shots of pedestrians along the bridge rail, and of the lines of stalled traffic. There was a long, concluding shot of the small sailboat turning in a circle.

Weatherman John Coleman strutted on camera. Behind him was a chroma-key shot of a forsythia bush. The camerawork made it appear as though Coleman were standing beside the bush. Coleman expressed comic wonderment that the forsythia bush was taller than his head. He pretended to cut a branch from the bush, and by sleight of camera a real cutting appeared in his hand. Coleman presented the cutting to Nancy Becker, who shook her head in wry amusement. Then Coleman proceeded with the weather forecast, standing before a backdrop that included a cartoon drawing of a clown.

This segment—from the opening, bogus "manhunt" footage to Coleman's forsythia-clipping performance—consumed 15 minutes of the hour-long newscast. There followed the first commercial break.

After the break, Coleman completed his forecast. A bit of Happy Talk ensued, in which anchorman Daly (in the role of Dr. Interlocutor) allowed as how he didn't care about the weather; he had already planned his next trip to New York. Coleman (Mr. Bones) rolled his eyes skyward and silently beseeched the heavens to deliver him from this madness. The rest of the "Eyewitness News" team whooped it up at this uproarious exchange.

Daly then read off a series of brief items: an old-time Chicago train station had burned down; an early-morning explosion had "ripped through" a building; work crews had righted an over-turned truck on an expressway (there were film clips of work crews "righting" the overturned truck); a roadway was closed while firemen washed gasoline off. Commercial break.

Feature reporter Frank Mathie was next. He did an on-location "standup" from the South Shore YMCA, about an instructor who teaches children to swim by tossing them into the deep end of the pool.

Daly then introduced sportscaster Mike Nolan (a recent addition to the "Eyewitness News" team) who, in turn, introduced a film report from Augusta, Georgia, concerning the Masters Golf Tournament. In the report, an ABC newsman asked a golfer whether he was going to get the ball up higher before the tournament started, or if he had got it up as high as he wanted it. The golfer commented favorably on the blooming of the flowers about the golf course.

Back in Chicago, said Nolan, City Hall was saluting the state basketball champions. There was a filmed vignette of Mayor Daley presenting a trophy.

"Action 7" reporter Bob Petty was up next. Petty interviewed a man described as an "auto buff." "Action 7" is, putatively, WLS's consumer-ombudsman feature.

There was another commercial break. Frank Mathie returned to the screen in his role as Channel 7's "Gee, I'd Like to Try That" reporter. Mathie—who had been seen in the various roles of housewife, bartender, country-western singer, and so on— was now trying out for stage manager of the Evanston Concert Ballet. In a film clip, the *real* stage manager, Nancy Sawyer, showed Mathie how to call for light cues. The clip concluded with Mathie calling for light cues and ending up in total darkness. Mathie's punchline: "This is Frank Mathie, Channel 7 'Eyewitness News'—*I think!*"

The camera returned to Coleman, who was doing a pirouette, with his hands clasped high above his head. Coleman lisped to no one in particular: "Did you notice? Topless ballet in my home town! What's this world coming to?"

Not even the WLS "Eyewitness News" team—normally re-

sponsive to a degree bordering on the feral — could think of a re-
joinder to that remark, so Coleman continued with yet another
weather report, which included some information on a "stellar
eclipse."

"Is there anything in the stars for *me?*" Mike Nolan leaned
forward to ask, with a suggestive wink at Coleman. Nolan, curly-
haired and the possessor of a prognathous jaw, had quickly been
cast as the "Eyewitness News" team's resident roué. Coleman and
Daly responded to Nolan's question with wry shakes of their
heads, accompanied by knowing chuckles. Nancy Becker looked
away; she was the long-suffering (but amused) feminist foil in sce-
narios such as this one — sort of a latter-day Jane Wyman.

Joel Daly recapped the results of the Wisconsin and New
York presidential primaries.

To properly appreciate what happened next on America's
most profitable television news program, a little background is in
order.

As mentioned, the newscast in question occurred on April 7,
1976. At that time, the presidential campaign of Democratic candidate Jimmy Carter had already begun to be the object of controversy. Newspaper and magazine articles were critically exam-
ining Carter's consistency in his public pronouncements on civil
rights, welfare, public housing, and other touchy domestic issues.

In fact, the March issue of *Harper's* had published what
proved to be the litmus of this developing skepticism: an article,
by Steven Brill, titled "Jimmy Carter's Pathetic Lies." In the ensuing public debate over the accuracy of the article, it became
clear that the supposedly humble Man of the People had built a
coolly effective public-relations machine to perpetuate a public
image (down-home, ingenuous, a romantic outsider) that was substantially at odds with the private man (a sophisticated, aggressive
politician savvy to power).

As Carter's campaign surged forward from victory to victory
in the early months of 1976, the need for a clear accounting of his
policies became increasingly apparent. How did he answer the
contradictions listed in Brill's article? What did he have to say
about his own staff's orchestrated effort to discredit Brill as journalist and thereby discredit the allegations Brill had made? What
were the points of departure between his stands on, say, farm
price supports, and those of Henry Jackson?

On April 7, the day after Carter won Wisconsin, Channel 7

sent its veteran "political editor," Hugh Hill, along with a camera crew, to probe the former Georgia governor's *Weltanschauung*.

Hill caught up with Carter at the Milwaukee airport. In true *Front Page* tradition, Hill buttonholed the great man. Viewers of the "Eyewitness News" saw their nightly source of political wisdom and insight, trenchcoated and looking serious indeed, right there on TV with a prospective future President. It was a grand and dramatic moment.

Hill had the opportunity for one question. Though brief, it constituted a veritable textbook on "Eyewitness News" assumptions, values, and priorities.

"At this point, Governor," demanded Hill, "after you've won in Wisconsin, is there anybody who can beat you?"

Carter opened his mouth to answer, then paused a beat as if in disbelief. This question was not just a "soft ball," of the type Carter often received from the electronic press. This one was a medicine ball.

What was he expected to answer? "Yes, I expect to be defeated on the first ballot by Hubert Humphrey"?

Carter studied Hill with amusement in his glittering blue eyes. Then he smiled his as-advertised smile and explained into Hill's hand-held microphone, as patiently as though he were a father answering a child's query as to why the sky is blue, that it was too early to tell, but that he was definitely ahead.

Back in the Channel 7 "Eyewitness News" studio, there were more items: a radio personality was dead; the Wall Street Dow Jones averages; a quote from a suburban town president.

Rosemarie Gulley did a brief report, with film footage, about a program to combat drug abuse in Chicago elementary schools.

"Stay tuned now," concluded Joel Daly, "for 'The Bionic Woman.'"

Daly, who prided himself on irony, undoubtedly missed the exquisite irony of his suggestion. What better lead-in to "The Bionic Woman" than the Bionic Newscast? The hour just concluded in the name of journalism was in fact a glistening example of cybernetic news.

In every important area, on this night as on most nights, the WLS "Eyewitness News" team had followed a meticulous and familiar blueprint for audience-building, in which journalism played a secondary role at best.

The blueprint, as we will discover, is almost infinitely thorough: it offers procedural recommendations for virtually every second of an electronic newscast. A few of its major requirements are instructive as they relate to the newscast just described:

—A high story count, with a short amount of time devoted to each story. Including John Coleman's various weather appearances, the sports items and the features, Channel 7 covered 24 stories in that hour. Subtracting 16 minutes for commercials and another two or three for the opening, for transitions, and for clipping forsythia bushes, the average time allotted to each story was something under two minutes.

But his average was misleading. Weather and sports consumed a disproportionately large amount of time, as did the opening "murder suspect" piece. These elements reduce the average story time to little more than one minute.

—The use of "visuals," preferably film footage, wherever possible. Film footage creates "audience interest" and adds "color and vitality" to a TV newscast. This explains why WLS used as its lead "story" a film-accompanied report that was long on visual excitement—cops and crowds—but utterly devoid of hard news value (nothing happened).

—A "team atmosphere" among the principal news personalities, emphasizing warmth and friendliness. The incidents described in the newscast are self-explanatory.

—Use of an "action" reporter to create a feeling of the station's "involvement" with the community. Bob Petty's interview with the "auto buff" was a poor example of his ombudsman role, but Frank Mathie, acting as a surrogate viewer in his "Gee, I'd Like to Try That" series, personified a refinement of the technique.

—Simple stories; an effort to stay away from the "stiff and formal" approach; a style that is easy to understand. Hugh Hill's "interview" with Jimmy Carter is a classic embodiment of that principle, as well as of most of the others described above.

In all, the April 7, 1976, early-evening newscast on WLS was distinguished less by what it *told* viewers than by what it *appeared* to tell them.

WLS appeared to deliver information about (among other

things) a major criminal search in the area, a mayoral assault on
prostitution, a transportation crisis, the duties of a stage manager
at a suburban ballet (responding to the well-known shortage of information on that subject), and the thoughts of a presidential candidate.

In fact, WLS did almost nothing of the sort.

It did not deliver information about a major criminal search
(assuming such information would be of any use to a viewer); it
showed disconnected film footage of police and crowds in one
specific neighborhood. Moreover, the pointlessness of the film
was concealed until the end.

It delivered limited information on Mayor Daley's prostitute
ordinance. But in doing so, WLS overlooked Daley's companion
proposal, one which was soon to eclipse the prostitute legislation
in civic debate: an ordinance aimed at movies that would ban not
only obscenity and nudity, but also filmic violence such as "cut-
tings, stabbings, floggings, eye gouging, brutal kicking, and dis-
memberment." This controversial proposal was to be described by
Variety as a potential national "model" for legislating violent films.
Perhaps the prostitute ordinance lent itself more easily to a strik-
ing "visual."

In its transportation-crisis story, WLS built its emphasis
around pictures of personalities in conflict: the RTA chairman
against the suburban board members. Missing was an explanation
of the abstract issues that forced the confrontation.

The suburban ballet "stage manager" story was really the
story of likable Frank Mathie, the viewers' surrogate, proving
himself once again a klutz.

And in the Hugh Hill-Jimmy Carter vignette, what counted
was not so much what Carter said — Hill could as well have asked
him about the pennant chances of the Milwaukee Brewers — as the
visual imprint of Channel 7's Hill *being there*, on the scene, on the
case, alongside celebrity Jimmy. Again: the *sense* of Channel 7's involvement without the substance.

The newscast amounted to a good deal of self-aggrandize-
ment for the Channel 7 "Eyewitness News" product, and little in
the way of useful information — little sense of community, of ongoing, integrated issues and concerns, of attempts to dig beneath
the surface for more enduring truths and subtle shadings. It was a
big, succulent but empty calorie of a newscast — a Quarter-
Pounder of the airwaves.

But perhaps WLS had a plausible excuse. Perhaps it was just a bad day for news.

An examination of the following morning's edition of the Chicago *Tribune* indicates that this was not the case.

The April 8 *Tribune* did not mention the manhunt "story" that WLS had led with—not surprising, since there *was* no story apart from Channel 7's home movies. The *Tribune* did give front-page display to two items on the WLS newscast: the report on FBI agents' obtaining the 12 indictments against persons dealing in stolen goods was the banner headline, and the RTA transportation feud was prominently displayed.

Inside, the *Trib* gave a fuller and more coherent account of Mayor Daley's anti-prostitution ordinance (actually, as the newspaper made clear, a move against massage parlors) and explained the national significance of the mayor's attempt to legislate violent films.

There were no items on Kid Heroes or bridges that would not rise or swimming instructors who tossed kids into the deep end of the pool. There were, however, some other stories that were missed by Chicagoans who depended on the WLS "Eyewitness News" for all their information.

Among these stories were:

—A detailed analysis of suburban Oak Park's controversial school reorganization plan, which had significant racial implications in that it would (1) create two new junior high schools out of existing grade schools, causing pupils who had attended those schools to enroll outside their immediate neighborhoods, and (2) redistribute the suburb's black pupils for greater racial balance.

—A report that taxpayers in the eight-county Chicago area paid more federal income tax per taxpayer in 1974 than did taxpayers in any other of the nation's 30 biggest metropolitan areas—the thrust being that the older productive American cities are being shortchanged, if not swindled, by the flow of federal income taxes.

—A prediction from the paper's environment editor, Casey Bukro, that Illinois would become the twenty-third state in 1976 to challenge the growth of nuclear power in the United States. Bukro reported that a state representative planned to introduce a bill calling for a five-year moratorium on nuclear-power-plant construction.

—A piece, by "blue collar" columnist Mike LaVelle, that detailed the efforts of the Amalgamated Clothing Workers of America to organize bank employees in the Chicago area. LaVelle reported that a Labor Department study of the Chicago area had revealed "glaring evidence of discrimination" against women in banking jobs: women held 99 per cent of bank clerical jobs, as against only 1.7 per cent of computer-related jobs; and their average weekly salary was $118.27, compared with $199.39 for the mostly-male computer operators.

None of these stories was particularly "colorful" or "vital." None lent itself to illustration by "visuals" — certainly not film footage. None could be adequately reported in a minute and 30 seconds. None could be enhanced through a "team atmosphere" among reporters or by an emphasis on "warmth" and "friendliness."

What the stories had in common was a connection with the ongoing, everyday concerns of the people in the *Tribune*'s coverage area. Without being ultimately spectacular or dramatic or "effective" in the sense of uncovering scandal and sending rascals to jail, the stories nevertheless had utilitarian value. They were reference points, indicators of the way things were, should anyone care to try and change them (or to manage more equably within the status quo).

Does anybody care?

John Coleman — if one judges from his remarks earlier — thinks not; thinks that people would rather laugh and drink beer than involve themselves in America's social processes. His attitude seems to prevail throughout the electronic broadcasting establishment.

That attitude represents an amazing extreme of fatuity. One thinks back upon the era that was the crucible of local television news, the late 1960's, when America was being rent apart by people from all sectors of what television is pleased to call "the 18-to-49 age group": by blacks, by middle-class laboring whites, by radical students, by police, by priests and nuns, by Vietnam War veterans, by urban housewives — by all the caring Americans who formed what Garry Wills has called "a confluence of poisons," people whose cares were inexpressible to an indifferent medium and who at length found expression through violence, through marches and picketing and slogans and screams of hatred (hitting at last upon an idiom that interested the TV cameras) — people who, in their final scheme of priorities, could not give a good sweet damn whether the Michigan Avenue bridge stayed up or down.

Fred Friendly has had some experience with caring. After helping define the nobler calling on television news as Edward R. Murrow's producer in the early 1950's, Friendly got out of the business in a huff of bitterness. He resigned his position as president of CBS News in 1967 after higher-ups deleted coverage of Vietnam War debates in the Senate Foreign Relations Committee in favor of an *I Love Lucy* rerun.

Now the Murrow professor of communications at Columbia University, Friendly — still a keen observer of the American broadcast scene — turns the question of "caring" around: "Are *they* really interested?" asks Friendly, meaning the TV news personalities themselves. "Is that what they think of when they get up in the morning — do they *care* about their city? That's something that the great newspapermen of history have all had in common. I mean, you go back to Tom Paine. Or you go back to H. L. Mencken, for all his cynicism. Or Walter Lippmann. Or Mike Royko. They *cared desperately* ...

"I don't think these guys care about anything. Except how their hair looks."

And Michael J. Arlen, the brilliant broadcast critic of *The New Yorker,* expressed it this way in a January 1975 essay:

> Admittedly, it used to be a truism that the public wasn't "interested" in [abstract news], and doubtless that's still so to a degree. Neither was the public "interested" in Europe in the early nineteen-thirties, or in Southeast Asia in the middle nineteen-sixties, or in the complexities of the Arab world for much of this century. The public, one is told, prefers football games, craves entertainment, and is obsessively concerned with its own neighborhoods — and all that is true.
>
> But, on a deeper level, this is the same public that sent grain to Lenin's Russia, and died on French and Italian beaches, and airlifted supplies to West Berlin, and trudged through Philippine, Malayan and then Vietnamese jungles — and at all times it has counted on *others* to provide it not just with snippets of information but with a coherent picture of its real connection to the larger world.

But caring is one of the few variables that is not factored into the blueprint for the cybernetic newscast. A close look at some of the blueprint-makers may provide some clues as to why this is so.

BLUEPRINT

'It is not surprising ... that research indicates ratings rise when the broadcaster is successful in exposing the listener to what he wants to hear, in the very personal way he wants to hear it. In terms of news, this means ratings are improved not when listeners are told what they should know, but what they want to hear."

In that quotation is the essence of the blueprint.

The passage if from a "Summary of Findings" made by Frank N. Magid Associates of Marion, Iowa, for radio station WMAQ in Chicago. In 1974, Magid was hired by WMAQ at a cost of $25,000 to survey the "attitudes and opinions toward radio in the Chicago area." Bypassing what listeners "should know" in favor of "what they want to hear" in the news was one of his prime recommendations. It is his veritable signature.

Although the quotation was taken from a radio-station survey, not a television one, it is consistent with the philosophy Magid has imparted to more than 100 TV news departments since he began consulting for broadcasters in 1970. In 1976, Magid was the pre-eminent broadcast news consultant in the United States. He was Number One because his stations moved up in the ratings, not because of good-journalism plaques that appeared in their lobbies.

In fact, after Magid's people had visited Channel 8, the CBS affiliate in San Diego, in autumn 1973, the station manager had been moved to tack up this burst of newsroom Babbittry:

*"Remember, the vast majority of our viewers hold blue-collar jobs.
The vast majority of our viewers never went to college. The vast majority of
our viewers have never been on an airplane. The vast majority of our
viewers have never seen a copy of the* New York Times. *The vast majority
of our viewers do not read the same books and magazines that you read ...
in fact, many of them never read anything ..."*[1]

Ergo, keep it short, keep it simple, show them lots of pictures,
make them giggle, throw in plenty of stuff about crime and flying
saucers and sex fantasies. They are, after all, children. Alongside
this brand of paternalism, the British colonialists in New Guinea
treated their minions as equals in Socratic debate.

Frank N. Magid Associates was one of perhaps ten major
broadcast-news consulting groups in 1976. (The pool was on the
verge of rapid expansion, however: the year saw several former
network and local-station news executives poised to dive into the
lucrative waters.)

Besides Magid and Emmanuel Demby, the most prominent
news consultants were McHugh & Hoffman Inc. of McLean, Virginia, the pioneers in the field; Melvin A. Goldberg, Inc., Communications, of New York; Rierson Broadcast Consultants of New
York; an emerging San Francisco–based organization, newly
formed, known cryptically as Entertainment Response Analysts;
and an even more esoteric firm in Philadelphia called the Athyn
Group.

Of the last two, more later.

Goldberg, Inc., served as consultant for a few major stations,
including WTOP in Washington and KWY in Philadelphia. Rierson worked for stations in Washington, New York, and Charlotte,
North Carolina. Demby's Motivational Programmers, Inc., con-
centrated mainly on News Center 4.

But clearly, the Big Two in news consultancy—and the principal architects of the cybernetic newscast—were the fiercely competitive Magid and McHugh & Hoffman. In 1976 these adver-
saries found themselves sharing the ultimate power trophy: all
five of ABC's owned stations retained *both* firms so that no com-

[1] The fifth Alfred I. DuPont-Columbia University *Survey of Broadcast Journalism,* Apollo
Editions, 1975.

petitor in any of the cities would have the benefit of either's strategic wisdom. Not that it was that hard to get a bearing on the thrust of a given station's marching orders; they were not exactly distinguished by their subtlety, and all a war-game-happy competitor had to do was flick on Channel 7 and begin counting UFO stories and charting the weatherman's choreography. But television executives have always been a little like Balkan archdukes, and a rating-point advantage on a New York newscast *is* worth a cool million—so what's $50,000 protection money?
What does a station get for its money?

From Magid and McHugh & Hoffman, it gets a systematic survey of audience "attitudes and opinions" in the station's coverage area. (Magid's staff of more than 100 does its own interviewing of sample audiences; McHugh-Hoffman, with a permanent staff of only four men and five women, farms out the research chores to private firms.)

The data is then analyzed—Magid's firm feeds it through an IBM 1130 computer in its futuristic plant in an Iowa meadow—and presented to the station manager in an impressive bound volume. A typical Magic summary may run 500 pages; it is bound in black with gold trim, and its crisp white pages yield substantial-looking tables and charts of "attitudes and opinions" as a Linn County corn field yields roasting ears. At $25,000 the copy, the volume makes an imposing coffee table display in the station manager's office.

Such a summary, though, is about as appetizing to the average broadcast executive's reading tastes as *The Gulag Archipelago*. ("Uh, that's all very well, Mr. Magid, your boys sure did a bang-up job on this here study, but truth to tell, like the man says, I was sort of hoping that the Secret to Business Nirvana here could be boiled down a little bit; I mean, we like to do things in a minute-ten around here. . . .")

Obligingly, Magid has anticipated this request. There is a second bound volume. It usually arrives about ten days after the first. It is slim, about the width of an anchorman's attention span.

It contains a tightly condensed version of the thick volume—the brass tacks.

Most news consultants cheerfully admit that their mandate is mercantile, not journalistic: they are hired to move broadcast news operations ahead of competitors in the ratings. Nothing wrong in that, they point out. The consultant's self-described role is that of a combination elocution coach and cosmetician: he advises on the production values of a newscast, the attractiveness of the set, the "atmosphere" among the "personalities," the lucidity of the writing. He may comment on the appearance of this anchorman or that sportscaster. He may—on the basis of his surveys of "attitudes and opinions"—suggest some broad ranges of interest among the viewing audience; he may act as a sort of fine-tuned Nielsen service, telling exactly who's out there, how old, how well educated, how affluent, with what cares and what concerns. His handsome bound volumes may contain snatches of vox-pop interviews with viewers—"My folks changed to Channel 7, and I got to like it better." "I just recently became interested in baseball in the last year, and Channel 9 has a better line of information on local baseball." "Channel 2 goofed up the news with poor continuity."—and tables showing "Identification of Channel on Which Preferred News Team Appears."

But never, *never,* say the consultants, do we get involved in the journalistic process itself. Never do we intrude into the area of content.

That criticism—that they are involved in the area of news content—rankles consultants the most. Running a close second is the charge that their recommendations are identifiably similar from market to market, no matter who the client or how extensive the audience research—that they sell, in the words of one station's news chief, "franchised news—like McDonald's."

Confronted with the question of content involvement during an interview with me, Frank Magid replied: "Well, let's just look at that. Let's look at it from a very practical point of view. In the first place, even though we have a rather large staff, it is absolutely impossible for us to be present in the newsroom on a daily basis in all the client stations that we serve.

"The decisions, as I think all of our client news-directors will tell you, are made by them, as to what is going to be incorporated in the news each night. So let *alone* the fact that it is patently false. In terms of just thinking of it logically, the fact that we are not present every day and the fact that the decisions that have to be made day in and day out are made by the news director there—I think that belies what has been said."

It was an interesting response, elliptic and carefully worded as a politician's—but it contains evasions. For one thing, it is not the *news director* who is a consultant's client. The news director (who normally is a trained journalist) is merely a salaried employee of a TV news department—like the news team itself. Rarely does a news director have managerial discretion. It is the *station manager* who hires consultants. And station managers are, in the overwhelming majority of U.S. stations, salesmen. Having risen through the business ranks of the broadcast hierarchy, they are demonstrably the most aggressive and competitive of their breed, and they have been rewarded with the ultimate bonus: management of a TV station. They are career businessmen suddenly entrusted with immense journalistic discretion, for which they frequently lack both temperament and training. They seek direction from fellow businessmen—the consultants.

There is a second evasion in Magid's reply about involvement in content: true, he and his staff *cannot* be in their clients' newsrooms on a daily basis. But their "Summaries" and "Overviews" can be. And are.

And their "Summaries" and "Overviews" contain such maxims as, "In terms of news, this means ratings are improved not when listeners are told what they *should* know, but what they want to hear."

Such a sentence is dedicated to the very definition of content.

There are good reasons why the consultants wish to keep a nominal barrier between themselves and journalistic decisions. One of the best was articulated by Dr. David LeRoy, director of the Communication Research Center at Florida State University. There is a possible intrusion, believes Dr. LeRoy, "upon the programming responsibility of the licensee in meeting his obligations and responsibilities under the 1934 Communications Act and its subsequent amendments. In these days of license renewal challenges, any material that suggests a delegation of the licensee's programming responsibility to an outside contractor should be eschewed. It should be made clear at all times that the outside firm's responsibility is to advise and inform, and not to dictate personnel, program, or other changes. Further, specific comments about how the news should be collected, edited, and presented, as well as what stories should or should not be covered, must be avoided by the consulting firm."[2]

To see how scrupulously consultants respect the sanctity of content, it is necessary to look only as far as the WMAQ Radio survey prepared by Frank Magid:

"Many journalists make the error of assuming that good factual reporting alone will involve typical 'concerned' citizens. The truth is that there aren't too many 'concerned' listeners out there . . .

"First, we suggest that the writer avoid starting a newscast with a stark fact. Begin instead with an evocative line which will catch the ear of the listener, arouse his curiosity, and begin to 'pull' him into the newscast . . .

"For example, instead of beginning with the words, 'Ralph Botts has been fined $10,000 for his part in an alleged . . .,' you might begin with, 'Is the FBI nosing in on Chicago?' or, 'He'll have to cough it up . . .' or, '*Ten thousand dollars* and the poor guy is penniless . . .'

"The whole idea is to set the listener up so that he becomes interested and must listen for more."

The listener as junkie. It is a touching and noble point of view. Leaving aside the question of whether "Ralph Botts's" $10,000 fine would have anything to do with the FBI "nosing in on Chicago" (a seemingly prodigious leap of logic, but then we're dealing in hypothesis), let us flip a page or two and find some other examples of how Mr. Magid's employees restrict themselves to cosmetics and piously avoid involvement in news content.

Under the heading "Use of Recorded 'Beepers'," we find this advice (a "beeper" is a segment of tape-recorded telephone conversation): "It is important that 'beepers,' whether they be actualities or voicers, also have a very *personal* orientation. Actualities, for example, should not be taken from a disinterested 'reporting' party, they should be taken from an enraged parent, a scared child, a marching picketer."

It makes sense. Enraged parents and scared children are, on the face of it, far better equipped to put a highly emotional event into perspective than a disinterested reporter. Besides, they sound so much more entertaining to the listener-junkie (who is likely to reach a shaky hand for the dial at the first disinterested syllable).

[2] *Ibid.*

But there is even headier strategy to come. Hammering home the point of "personal involvement" as the key to marketable news stories, the Magid analyst indulges himself in a euphoric pipe dream: "For example, at one point in the newschecks we monitored, there was a rather lengthy actuality of an attorney explaining all the detail of rape trial procedures. Instead of this institutional, bureaucratic approach to the issues, imagine getting an actuality from someone who had been through the rigors of an actual rape trial."

Yes, imagine! One can almost see the Magid analyst, face flushed, rubbing his hands with excitement as he surrenders himself to his rape-trial-rigor reverie.

And yet a question asserts itself here: *How does such an approach serve journalism?*

A rape victim may indeed provide instructive conversation regarding rape-trial procedure. Then again, she may yield to the understandable impulses of bitter outburst, self-pity, histrionics. (And if the "enraged parent-scared child" exhortation is any clue, we can be sure which option the radio reporter will root for and encourage.) She may not be articulate. She may not *know* what happened to her in the courtroom.

On the other hand a lawyer, burdened though he or she may be with an "institutional, bureaucratic" temperament, just may shed some valuable light on what women may expect in the volatile and humiliating arena of the rape trial. It is not entirely beside the point that, within the last five years, women's paralegal groups have been forming in several major cities to try to disseminate advice and guidelines for rape victims. One can only guess at the frustration of these groups should they look to a "personal"-oriented station for a conduit.

Not that it would matter much, in the end, whether the interviewed rape victim spoke with calm reason or went into frothing verbal seizures. The very next paragraph of recommendations makes it clear that a sustained idea is not the point of the exercise anyway: "Both actualities and voicers should be kept fairly short. Some very effective actualities can be delivered in *ten seconds* [italics mine], or a series of two or three five-second actualities might be tied together with copy in a very powerful way."

Edward R. Murrow was lucky he got out when he did. It used to take him the better part of ten seconds to say, "This . . . is London."

News consultants have been at least a peripheral part of the broadcast scene since 1962, when Philip McHugh and Peter Hoffman formed their partnership in Birmingham, Michigan. McHugh (now the company's president) had been a radio newsman–network program director at CBS in 1946 — and later an advertising executive at Campbell-Ewald in Detroit. Hoffman (the vice president) had been with Campbell-Ewald since 1954, specializing in research.

When the two men joined forces, their aims were innocuous enough. News in itself was but an incidental element in their inquiries. The men had it in mind to advise TV and radio stations in a broad range of categories — their entire daily output, which in those days still included several locally-originated entertainment shows: music, variety, and children's programs.

Only as the years went on and local stations surrendered more and more program origination to the networks did McHugh and Hoffman find themselves gradually limited to the newscast as the target of their advice.

Thus, the emergence of the "news consultant," the specialist in broadcast journalism, was an accident of evolution.

In 1968, McHugh and Hoffman got their main chance. WABC in New York was reorganizing its TV news department under a *wunderkind* out of Pittsburgh, Al Primo. The nervous ABC top brass summoned McHugh and Hoffman to oversee Primo's efforts.

Magid entered the field in 1970. The former professor of social psychology at the University of Iowa was no stranger to market research; he had been providing it to broadcasters for 12 years, in the form of raw data.

With Magid's ascendancy as full-fledged broadcast news *adviser,* cybernetic news had come of age.

The resulting transformation of TV news in the early 1970's was electrifying. Boom times were in, the greatest boom in local-station history. A National Association of Broadcasters survey of 383 stations showed that average TV stations profits for 1973 had zoomed 19.4 per cent over 1972. The lists of clients for Magid and McHugh-Hoffman lengthened. Other consulting groups entered the field.

Meanwhile, a sense that something was awry in electronic journalism had begun to spread among critical observers of the media. TV-radio columnists, whose normal subject matter for TV reviews is prime-time entertainment, devoted increasing space to chiding local anchormen for their insouciant style—for Happy Talk.

That the newspaper critics were diverted by Happy Talk from the more substantive issues of cybernetic news is not hard to understand. For one thing, the presence of news consultants was a relatively well-kept secret outside the industry for several years after their 1968 breakthrough. News consultants' "summary" books are still regarded as confidential and are extremely difficult to obtain. For another, to attempt analysis of a TV newscast's content requires time and thoroughness. A daily critic would have had to spend precious time transcribing tapes and making meticulous comparisons with the content of daily newspapers, news magazines, *and* the general sense of the city as the critic perceived it. His editor, in the meanwhile, would have been pressuring him to concentrate on sit-com reviews and "personality" interviews with starlets. Editors and publishers in this country have limited expectations of daily TV columns—a sad comment on print journalism itself.

Nevertheless, by 1974, content analyses were being produced—and they indicated that television news, until so recently the foundling of television, the sober-sided exercise of license protection under the eyes of the FCC, had become a three-ring circus (news, weather, sports), with the cash registers clinking like cymbals.

In May 1974 the American Association of University Women (AAUW) monitored half-hour news programs at 262 local TV stations across the country. Among their findings were these:[3]

— Newscasts had an average of fifteen commercials, totaling an average of eight minutes per half-hour. (The National Association of Broadcasters Code allowed a maximum of 16 commercial minutes to the hour outside prime time.)

— Forty-three per cent of the stations exceeded the NAB guidelines; one station had a staggering 15 minutes and 45 seconds of ads in its half-hour newscast.

[3] *Ibid.*

—An average of five and one-half interruptions per half-hour was reported for commercials.

Clearly, the local newscast had transformed itself from loss leader to profit center. The rest of the findings showed why:

—Weather portions of local news programs averaged two and one-half minutes per half-hour. Sports averaged three minutes, leaving an average of exactly 16 and one-half minutes per half-hour for news items, transitions, openings and closings, light features, and the ever-popular Happy Talk, of which the following example is prime:

JOEL DALY: Well, what kind of cat-and-mouse games do you have for us in the weather, John?

JOHN COLEMAN: I'd be willing to discuss the weather, Joel, if I knew that nursery rhyme. "Ding, dong, dell . . ."

DALY: "Pussy's in the well."

COLEMAN: Go on.

DALY: I don't remember the other . . .

COLEMAN: I never heard that nursery rhyme, did you, Mike?

DALY: Sure. Oh, that's a famous one.

MIKE NOLAN: Oh, yeah, I heard it.

DALY: That's right. "Who put him in?"

COLEMAN: Who?

DALY: Little . . . Johnny . . . *Coleman! (general laughter)*

COLEMAN: Aw, now, cut that out. Well—I'm sure we're not experts on nursery rhymes, but I am reasonably well informed meteorologically at this moment, and a one-word comment would be, YAH-HOOOOOO! . . .

The AAUW survey concluded that a trend to more short items was reported at 32 per cent of the local stations; more funny items were reported at 31 per cent, and human interest stories were increasing at 56 per cent of the stations.

By 1975, the news consultants finally met their all-out nemesis. He was Marvin Barrett, the director of the Alfred I. DuPont-Columbia University Survey and Awards in Broadcast Journalism. In the fifth edition of the survey, titled "Moments of Truth?", Barrett devoted an entire chapter to a low-keyed but devastating case against the emergence of news consultants. (This in a year in which the major survey items included coverage of Watergate and the energy crisis, and the relationship of government and broadcasters.)

Barrett's chapter on news consultants was titled "The Trojan Horse," derived from a remark by Ralph Renick, who was then vice president for news at WTVJ in Miami and a man disenchanted with cybernetic news.

After Renick had convinced his station to terminate the services of Magid, he told the DuPont survey:

> They are really a Trojan horse. They roll it in and suddenly the enemy troops are in your camp. Too often the service is put to political use to permit management to get control of the news when the news director is in conflict with management ... These agencies have taken hold of many stations and virtually dictated news policy "in absentia," by the use of their research techniques. Too often stations with consultants end up trying to present news only as the research results suggest the people want. But lost in this concept is that a professional journalist should have the ability and news judgment to determine what is important and significant.

Renick's remarks were among those of 1,500 broadcast-news directors who responded to a questionnaire Barrett had sent out across the country. Renick was not necessarily typical; Barrett also printed responses praising the consultants. The following came from a news director in the Southwest:

> I feel fine with the recommendations and our ratings have increased considerably. However, some members of our staff feel that they have somehow prostituted themselves. They are (amazingly enough) more concerned about having their peers pat them on the back for their great principles than telling the viewing public what is happening in their own area of interest. Some members of the staff think we are here to teach rather than inform and that we should decide what is important for the public to know about rather than finding out what the public is truly concerned about and telling them about that.

It was Barrett who commissioned the AAUW survey, and it was Barrett who published, for the first time, a sample of how coolly the consultants operated within a news department, how thorough was the blueprint.

In "The Trojan Horse," Barrett reproduced a "Summary of Recommendations" that Magid had made for Renick's station, WTVJ, in 1971. With names of station personnel deleted, the summary suggested:

1. Replace _____.
2. Tandem format on both early and late news.
3. Replace _____ with certified meteorologist.
4. Replace _____.
5. Include opinion with sportscast, but not as separate segment.
6. Develop team atmosphere through conversational interchange, perhaps at head of show but certainly in transitions. Develop atmosphere which will produce genuine spontaneity.
7. Change title on both early and late newscast. Same title for both. ("The World Tonight" or something similar.)
8. Use voice-over credits for promotion preceding newscasts (particularly late evening), including at least one headline and standard.
9. Develop production opening for both newscasts. (Similar but not identical.) A production close should also be produced. Audio emphasis in open and close on complete coverage.
10. Lead anchorman should introduce himself at the top of the show.
11. New, distinctive set allowing personalities to be shown sitting together.
12. Participation format, rather than sponsored reports. (Already in effect.)
13. Tease upcoming stories before commercial break.
14. Use bumper slides before commercials. (Already in effect.)
15. Headlines at top of show presented by the personality involved.
16. "Kicker" at conclusion.
17. More stories should be covered; a number of stories should be shortened.
18. More use of voice-over explanation of film stories with background sound from the scene.
19. Use field reporter as extensively as possible.
20. Use of some national news in early newscast.
21. Make every effort to avoid duplication of early newscast by late newscast.
22. Broward County news should not be reported in great detail.

23. Serialized mini-documentaries should not be used.

24. Minority group stories should be used only when really news; should be presented by a member of the minority group.

25. There should be news *analysis* on a regular basis.

26. Neither editorials nor analysis should last more then 60 seconds.

27. No repetition of editorial. No use of editorial and analysis in same newscast.

28. Both analyst and editorialist must be someone other than the newscaster.

29. Initiate Action Reporter feature.

30. Initiate consumer protection feature—once/week, one minute.

31. Initiate environmental feature—once/week, one minute.

32. Utilize brief, rapid-fire newsworthy items on *well-known* people.

33. Utilize stories on new and unusual products.

34. Weather should concentrate on *Miami* area with brief summary of rest of the country.

35. Weathercast should end with understandable forecast for next 24 hours.

36. Long-range forecast is desirable if viewers can be persuaded of accuracy.

37. Weather radar should be promoted heavily.

38. Sports action film should be used frequently, but restricted primarily to major events.

39. Coverage of participation activites (hunting, fishing, boat shows, camping equipment) should be included.

40. Promotion should emphasize the advantages of WTVJ news—what is special about it.

41. Promotion should concentrate on "Channel 4" rather than "WTVJ."

42. A slogan emphasizing friendliness and warmth of WTVJ news should be employed.

In that list are contained some of the most pernicious elements of cybernetic news.

A few of the suggestions are simple, common sense (10, 34, 38). Some are in the interests of good journalism—in terms of the topic suggested, if not the time limit suggested (18, 19, 30, 31, 33, 35, 39). Some are innocuous (5, 7, 9, 11, 13, 15, 28, 37, 40, 41).

The rest are either superfluous to good journalism or else explicitly anti-journalistic. They are included for their supposed audience-building value. And a heavy number of the suggestions, including some of the good ones, quite clearly transgress the realm of cosmetics and enter into the realm of content.

Magid's exhortation of brevity (an admirable enough virtue in itself, but not as a pretimed absolute) comes through in suggestions 17, 26, 30, 31, 32. Suggestion 22—"Broward County news should not be reported in great detail"—is part of this ethic, but its sheer anti-journalistic brazenness entitles it to a separate mention.

Suggestion 24, dealing with minority-group stories, would have been fashionable shortly before the fall of Richmond.

Suggestion 29—the Action Reporter—is a Magid trademark, and lends credence to those who argue that his firm propagates "franchised news."

Suggestion 36 provides an instructive insight into Magid's behavioristic instincts. Note that the sentence reads, "if viewers can be *persuaded* (italics added) of accuracy," rather than, "if accurate."

A list such as this might be expected to curl the lip of a professional newsman. And indeed, some lips were curled. CBS News president Richard Salant told the New York *Times* in early 1975: "Market researchers are an abomination. Perhaps I'm square, but I think our function is to determine what we *ought* to be doing. A journalist doesn't make a survey to find out what people want. You can do that in entertainment but not in news."

All too few of Salant's counterparts at local TV stations agreed. One year later, in April 1976, Marvin Barrett was obliged to report in the *Columbia Journalism Review:* ". . . The balance of opinion among station execs has shifted from a substantial majority against to three to five in favor of news consultants in the latest survey."

Barrett's finding was in an "Interim Report" on American journalism in the period from summer 1974 to fall 1975—the sensitive period immediately following President Nixon's resignation. Concerning news consultants, Barrett added:

> Further evidence of the impact of the consultants on the nation's news operations was indicated . . . particularly in the increase in number of news items per broadcast . . . and the increased use of film and tape on TV newscasts . . . four out of five stations increased their total news budget, and nearly two-thirds reported an increase in the size of their news staffs and the amount of time allotted to local news.

In too many instances, however, these increases were tied to implementing a news consultant's ideas for popularizing the news rather than improving coverage.

Almost as if in divine confirmation of Barrett's demonic apprehensions, a memo began making the rounds of ABC News at about the same time the *Columbia Journalism Review* article appeared. (ABC, both at its network and owned-station levels, has been the most unabashed booster of cybernetic news.) The memo was signed by William Sheehan, the network's news president.

After paying lip service to the verities of journalism ("Our basic task is communication . . . our NUMBER ONE mission is to cover the day's news . . ."), the memo arrived at the main item of business:

> After the major news stories of the day we must go after the stories that grab people where they're involved. And people are involved in a lot of things these days *that they are close to only vicariously.* [italics added] A recent poll in England showed that only 14 percent of the people knew who U Thant is while 80 percent correctly identified Mick Jagger. (He's the leader of the Rolling Stones.) I'm not suggesting that we slight U Thant, but I am suggesting that the Mick Jaggers of the world shouldn't be ignored. *I want more stories dealing with the 'pop people.' The fashionable people. The new fads. Bright ideas. Changing mores and moralities.* We should be quicker to jump on the muck-rakers' bandwagon and even do some ourselves.
>
> I'm suggesting that Truman Capote is news. So is William Styron . . .
>
> The back of our show must be different than the competition's. Provocative. Funny. Interesting because we're getting to the subjects that people are interested in, and people are interested *in many things that are not intrinsically important.*

Laughing beer drinkers. Life going on.

It is instructive here that ABC—the parent network of five Magid-consulted stations, including WLS in Chicago and WABC in New York—is the only network with a news consultant on its payroll. That news consultant is Frank N. Magid Associates of Marion, Iowa.

Sheehan's call for more stories about "the pop people. The fashionable people. The new fads . . ." had an ennobling patina of anti-elitism about it (although one may quibble that Truman Ca-

pote and William Styron are not big objects of gossip and speculation down at Joe & Mabel's Twelfth Street Bar and Grill). But his
motive becomes evident when one considers that "the pop people.
The fashionable people. The new fads," are not exactly overlooked by the rest of television. They are in fact the *stuff* of television, created by television, defined and examined by television,
elevated into global notoriety by television, then digested and spat
out by television to make room for the next pop idol, the next
fashion, the next fad. Many of ABC's own regular network programs, including "Good Morning, America," the game shows, and
the evening "Wide World of Entertainment," are among the most
consistent and enthusiastic showcases of the pop people, the fashionable people, the new fads. Why then, are they redundantly
courted by the network news — unless the network news is striving
to look more and more like the rest of television, for the sake of
building pop-fashionable-faddish audiences?

"People are involved in a lot of things these days that they are
close to only vicariously," notes newsman Sheehan, and evinces a
deadpan lack of skepticism about the value of this peculiar sort of
involvement, or about the reasons for its existence. (One good
reason, for the sake of argument, is television.) Sheehan's response to the phenomenon? Give them more vicarious involvement; they seem to like it; and if pop people and new fads
intrude on a network newscast's limited time to report and explain
complex issues — well, that's life.

Even before the celebrated $5-million hiring of Barbara Wal-
ters away from NBC, Sheehan's infatuation with show-business
values in the news was becoming evident to the nation's critics.

TV columnist Gary Deeb, in the February 4, 1976, editions of
the Chicago *Tribune*, articulated the trend in blunt language:

> Don't look now, but ABC seems well on its way toward becom-
> ing the first TV network to institute a lightweight "Happy Talk"
> format on its nightly news program.
>
> The ABC News With Harry Reasoner already has slipped
> into a sort of "Top 40" news concept in which stories are presented
> more for their "marquee value" than for their actual journalistic
> worth . . .
>
> Av Westin, executive producer of the Reasoner telecast and a
> dedicated professional journalist, was fired by ABC News president

Bill Sheehan. Named to replace him was Steve Skinner, the man who brought "blood-'n'-guts news" to San Francisco TV in 1974–75 before becoming senior producer of the Reasoner newcast last summer.

ABC insiders told this column that Westin was canned after a series of clashes with bossman Sheehan over ABC's increasing emphasis on "tabloid news" instead of serious, quality reporting . . .

Since shifting into its shallow approach last summer, the ABC nightly newscast has imposed some major on-camera changes aimed at improving the "visual attractiveness" of the program. For instance:

— Howard K. Smith, nearing retirement age and a fierce opponent of "Happy-Talk," was switched from co-anchor to commentator, à la Eric Sevareid. Reasoner remained . . .

— A new studio set was created in order to give the newscast a "comfy-cozy" aura. Resembling a basement rec room, the set soon became known in the trade as "The Plywood Minnesota News."

— A pair of "news windows" were built into the background set, in which reporters would pop up to gab with Reasoner. This "peeping tom" effect also triggered loads of belly laughs in the industry.

Those cosmetic changes — combined with the trend toward "soft" news, the dismissal of Westin and the promotion of Skinner — have convinced ABC News insiders that the onslaught of "Happy-Talk" at their network is just around the corner.

The emphasis on pop, fashion, fad — all with the idea of attracting a younger and more affluent audience for the news — the heavy emphasis on style, the reliance on softer news, the "cozy-comfy" set, the artificial attempt to convey interaction among newsmen through the "news windows" — all this bore the imprint of Frank Magid. At last, a news consultant had broken through the sacrosanct barrier of network news.

IN THE PALACE OF
THE ICE KING

Marion, Iowa, is the diamond pinkie ring on the outstretched hand that is Cedar Rapids. It lies south and east of its host city; one of those curiously seamless American bedroom suburbs, the bedrooms comfortable enough, encased in crisp white two-story frame houses that genuflect toward Iowa's heritage of agrarian plenty. But the genuflection ceases with the traditional architecture, the weather vanes, the cedars on the lawn, the occasional American flag drowsing from a rooftop like a war horse put to pasture. Like its host city, Marion is ambitiously addressing itself to the future: it is expanding, busy with subdivisions, billboards rampant, scraped earth where corn once grew. Here sleep the go-getters.

At the tip of one of these uncompleted subdivisions, at the end of a newly-poured street with no visible name, its back to a sloping ("unimproved") meadow that soon will be improved with ranch-style houses, rests a flat, featureless, single-story building. Look at it, then turn away; you will have trouble remembering what you have just seen. There is a suspicion of brick, of windows that yield no information. No cornerstones of chiseled granite here, no emblems of company pride. The building is seamless, as Marion is seamless. It suggests anonymous modularity; it will open its flank to a new wing as easily as Marion will surrender a corn field for one futher subdivision (as easily as Cedar Rapids will scrape the earth of homesteads for one more Marion).

The building could be a hopeful savings-and-loan branch or

a medical-association office. It is in fact One Research Center, the home of Frank N. Magid Associates, and thus the philosophical fountainhead for much of American telecommunications.

One Research Center manufactures the blueprints for cybernetic news.

At first it seems wildly improbable that America's largest and most influential broadcast consulting firm should operate, not in the Mies van der Rhoe chrome and glass of New York's Sixth Avenue, but in the loam of Iowa. It is not improbable at all. In a sense, One Research Center is one with Rockefeller Center. It is among the first edifices to appear on the skyline of the Global Village. As Marion reaches to Cedar Rapids, Cedar Rapids reaches to New York. The standardization of style, the uniformity of vision, the managed idea — all the benchmarks of the Magid blueprint for television, the great leveler — are inseparable from the motivating mentality of Cedar Rapids itself. One Research Center and Cedar Rapids each represents a different manifestation of an America trying to shake off its past, to jettison its regionalism, to amalgamate, in the name of cost-efficiency, of profit.

Disembark from a jetliner at the Cedar Rapids airport, and you will likely encounter a cab driver who will quote you a price of $5.60 to the Hotel Royale and bring you in right on the dime while delivering a Chamber of Commerce lecture about the city. For a few miles, charmed as the compact, finite skyline rises at you out of the plains, lulled as the cab driver banters in his hometown pride, you find yourself willing to reinvent the hope of Main Street — the hope that America's strength still lies in its diversity, and that its diversity is expressed in the idiosyncrasies of its towns and cities, each its own shading of the national mosaic.

The fantasy soon breaks down. Cedar Rapids is urbanizing the loam. The city of 105,000 is drawing its earth-mover claws across the adjoining earth. Fast-food chains have captured the land once held by homesteaders. Downtown, from a window of the Hotel Royale, you can see that the clean, sensible line of the central business district is still intact — Woolworth's, J. C. Penney, the railroad tracks all in fine right angles — but there are alien forces.

A MOVIE ARCADE/ADULT BOOKS establishment flourishes right next door to Postal Finance. The Cedar Rapids *Gazette* informs you that construction of a new community center is assured — with purchase of $7 million worth of obligation bonds from a Chicago financial firm. Cocaine valued at $85,000 was seized in town. The Hotel Royale bar, a triumph of nonindigenous design, with its wrought-iron grille and Spanish menu-ese, was even sophisticated enough to have its own floozy (a very *nice* floozy, it must be added; she turned aside every proposition I witnessed over a two-hour dinner).

Given this ambitious, eastward-looking context, this stripping away of the old verities of the Republic, the hum of Frank Magid's IBM 1130 computer out there in the Marion meadow is not exactly an anomaly. It is not the voice of the turtle, but then the voice of the turtle has not been heard in this land for some time.

Frank Magid, at age 45, is neither typical of his chosen environment nor atypical of it. He was born and reared in Chicago, the son of a chemical engineer and a member of an intellectually ambitious family (Magid's brother, Gail, is a neurosurgeon practicing in Santa Cruz, California).

Magid came to his meadow in the mildest and most domestic of circumstances — a fact that is characteristic of the man. He is the Pillar of the Community incarnate: Patron of the symphony; Rotarian (until his travels east and west forced these simple pleasures into neglect — he logs 250,000 business miles annually); indulgent father of "Chip," 15, and Brent, 12; accommodating husband who settled in Iowa so his wife could find a teaching job. Magid tells the story with a disarming, almost American Gothic modesty.

"I had been on the faculty at the University of Iowa," he recollects, "and my wife had gotten her degree—she had wanted to be a doctor—and was looking for a job, and we wrote to all the school systems because we were in Iowa City, and of course every instructor has a wife who can teach, so the school system has more teachers than they know what to do with, or can hire. So we wrote all the places that we could find within a 30-mile radius, and the Cedar Rapids school system was one of those who answered. She applied for the position. They accepted her, but on the condition that we live in Cedar Rapids. And then when I decided to go into commercial research, I thought, well, we might as well try here, so we began to do work here and began to expand and after a while, we began to do work nationally, and we found that we were situated in, I think, a geographically advantageous portion of the country and there are other things that I think are important to me and our people, and that is in many cities the commute is so long that it takes a toll on not only the number of hours you can spend working but on your attitude toward work—and here, research, being unlike a manufacturing operation where you can count on the machine producing *x* number of widgets within a number of hours, here there are many considerations to be taken into account. We're only five or ten minutes away from anyone's home. Somebody can always be here on a Saturday or Sunday. We have here the opportunity to give a great deal of thought without being hassled, bothered, you know, by the effects of big-city problems."

It is a remarkable performance, this bucolic reverie—evocative more of an old country doctor looking back on the rewards of honest, simple labor and a virtuous family life than it is of a ferociously contemporary sociologist-businessman at the peak of his power in shaping the informational style of a nation's electronic journalism.

What's more remarkable is that the performance does not seem contrived. There is an ingenuous side to Frank Magid, an unqualified belief in the self-evident worth of motivational research that balances his shrewd grasp of station managers' needs and mentalities, and his slick ability to persuade. It is not enough to dismiss Frank Magid as one-dimensional agent of cybernetics, the caricature of the futuristic man-as-automaton. Part of his soul is rooted in Main Street, in the very vestigial values of Iowa life that Cedar Rapids is busily scraping off the soil. He *cares* about the symphony. He *believes* in the Rotary. He has a Babbitt-like faith in the limitless efficacy of Yankee know-how; and if that know-how produced statistical research, why, then, statistical research is a good enough field for Frank Magid. It is not, paradoxically, the sophisticated and intellectually skeptical side of Frank Magid that supplies his power and his potential menace. It is his evangelical side: the side that elevates the very individualistic, exhortative values that his research-consultancy empire is leveling.

I visited One Research Center in March of 1976. A late-winter freezing rain had coated the city with ice. As the taxicab headed cautiously out of Cedar Rapids on East Post, past the Christian Science Church and the Country Kitchen (open 24 hours) and the Ample Lady Dress Shop (featuring a Red Tag sale) and the Hy-Vee Food Store, the approaching wooded avenues of Marion took on a surrealist aspect. Everything was encased in ice: branches, telephone wires, cars. We were in an Ice Universe, beautiful and spiked. One Research Center — when the cab driver finally located it, the landmarks being spare — was in the midst of an ice meadow; and I could not shake the half-joking fantasy that I was on my way to visit the Ice King.

Frank Magid received me in an office that did nothing to dispel the fantasy. It was a cool, correct, seasonless office, brightly lighted (the iced branches outside the windows served as mirrors to the sun) and noncommittal. There was an arching fern in one corner of the room; in the other, chrome-and-velvet chairs. Magid was seated behind his desk — a large, simple antique wooden desk. The surface of the desk was nearly bare, save for a telephone and a crystal decanter half-filled with Vitamin C tablets.

I sat at a far end of the office, away from Magid. We were to have begun the interview on the previous day, but when I telephoned to warn him of a touch of flu, he tactfully suggested that I stay in my hotel room and rest. Influenza germs were an unwelcome variable on Frank Magid's orderly agenda. Now he had unobtrusively placed me as far away from himself as possible; his desk, if not an "authority barrier," was at least a hygienic barrier. The crystal decanter of Vitamin C tablets sat gleaming between us like a sentinel.

Magid wore a white button-down oxford shirt, buttoned at the cuffs, a tie of muted burgundy and blue stripes, and the trousers of a glen-plaid suit. He looked somewhat like a junior Republican senator, with his iron-gray brush-cut hair and his clean, open features. The voice was a trifle high-pitched, and there was irritation in it. Magid has not been treated with unalloyed kindness by the press. The *Columbia Journalism Review* has displeased him particularly, and there have been less-than-flattering interviews in the *National Observer* and the New York *Times*. Part of the difficulty may lie in Magid's peculiar discursive style. When he is not talking about his family or his personal feelings — and he resists talking about these — he speaks in an almost Kafkaesque tumble of convoluted, purposefully oblique sentences, as though he were composing a prepared statement on the spot. He does not supply direct answers. He is a difficult man to interview.

I began the session by asking Magid why he thought he had been dealt with so critically by the press.

"My feeling," he said, "is that, because reporters are essentially a part of the journalism fraternity, there is a preconceived notion on behalf of those who are reporting that we are guilty of the sins that have supposedly been ours and have been laid at our feet by some of the individuals in the news business, the news directors. I'm amazed and in many cases appalled to see the lack of objectivity that supposedly those people who are supposed to be the most objective are exercising.

"This is our nineteenth year in the business." Magid went on, "and I'm curious as to why, all of a sudden, some of the critics . . . and, incidentally, I find that there are not as many critics as I think the public is led to believe, and that among news directors, as an example, throughout the United States, the number of critics could be counted on one hand."

It was a sentence that wandered off into nowhere, Magid beginning by stating a curiosity about "some of the critics," but losing the point somewhere along the way. Fine points get buried in his associative process: for instance, although Magid would refer repeatedly to his "19 years" in "the business," the fact is that he did not become a consultant for broadcast news departments until 1970. Previous to that, his firm had limited itself to providing market research for such clients as Coors, Schlitz, Harley-Davidson, and several universities and publishing houses.

But Magid was still groping to make a point about his unfavorable press. "Actually, our work began," he was saying, "if you want to go back and look at the record, at least two, perhaps three years prior to the time the first, quote, notice, unquote, of it appeared in the *Columbia Journalism Review*. Now, if these people are so sensitive to what's going on around the country and are so appalled by what is taking place, it seems very strange to me that for two or three years not a word was said, and that only until something surfaced in print and there was supposedly a rallying point, did individuals begin to talk about it. The same accusations, the same misinformation, and I just wonder, I really wonder who is writing these things, and who is believing these things?"

"What sort of misinformation?" I asked.

"Why, I think that there are a number of things. I did not bother to answer the *Columbia Journalism Review* article because I frankly did not feel the article was worthy of gaining an answer, but it was fraught, I thought, with inaccuracies.

"My memory may be a bit fuzzy and you might check it, but the article said you can always tell a Magid newscast by virtue of the fact that it is called 'The World Tonight' or some such title. And at the time, in serving close to 100 stations or what have you, we checked, and I think two stations used that title, so it meant that the vast majority, better than 90 per cent, you know, were not. Now, that's a gross inaccuracy."

(I later did check the article Magid had in mind. It was written in the November/December issue of *CJR* by Edward Barrett, former dean of the Columbia University graduate school of journalism. It did not, as a matter of fact, say that "you can always tell" a Magid newscast by vitrue of the title. It stated that "a fairly common title" for a Magid newscast was "The World Tonight." Does that statement amount to a "gross inaccuracy"? It is a fine point — but then, one finds oneself enmeshed in pursuing fine points after a conversation with Magid.)

Magid continued: "I think probably one of the more prevalent allegations has centered around the fact that we suggest that news stories be no more than ten seconds in length and there be, if possible, 100 of them in any half-hour newscast, and of course, the longer this goes on, the more absurd, you know, those figures become."

(Of course. The figures had become absurd enough by the time Magid enunciated them. No critic of Magid had ever seriously suggested his stations carried ten-second news stories, 100 at a time. But the short-length, high-story count has been an issue indeed. By exaggerating his own critics' claims, Magid defused them.)

But by this time, Magid was moving along to yet another example of his critics' "unfair" and "grossly inaccurate" charges against him. "It was just like the other night," he was saying, "in the question-and-answer period following my speech at a Sigma Delta Chi chapter. There was a student who rose and said, 'What about your suggesting to stations that they include blood and gore and things of that sort in order to gain audiences?' And I became quite angry and said, 'Now, look, I will pay your expenses to Cedar Rapids, Iowa, and if I can gain permission from each and every one of our clients to have you read through every set of recommendations we've produced in 19 years that we've been in business, and if you can find in there one statement to that effect, I will personally come back here and present to you a check for $1,000 or whatever sum you choose. . . .'"

Again, Magid was defusing the substance of a legitimate concern by exaggerating the charge—or, in this case, allowing a simplistic student to do it for him. There is little likelihood that a Magid list of recommendations would ever naively propose that a station go out and film "blood and gore." The process is more complex than that, and at its core is the crucial question of how a station manager *interprets* a given summary. If the summary suggests a higher emphasis on "actualities," or "visuals," it is likely that vivid film footage will be stressed. "Blood and gore" happens to fit the description of vivid footage.

I suggested to Magid that the student had oversimplified the question, and was in fact guilty of hyperbole, but that he had the nugget of a point.

Magid's response was vintage. "But wait a minute. The hyperbole seems to be going a bit far, and the fact of the matter is as you probably saw . . . and I was a bit disappointed, I think, in the article that appeared in the *National Observer.* . . ."

He went on to bemoan, in great detail, the *National Observer* article—leaving the Sigma Delta Chi student holding his bag of blood and gore—and then circled back for a counterattack on the critics themselves: "Now, I just believe, as an example, that a great deal of what these people are talking about is so much rubbish and I believe that it stems from the fact, as I have said time and time again, that these people's toes have been stepped on, and that they feel that they can take on this mantle of journalistic expertise and somehow try to shoot it out at the O.K. Corral, looking as if they were carrying on in the form of a white knight for those things that are pure and good in journalism, and I think that it is most unfortunate that so many people have fallen for this."

So—the bottom line at last. Magid's detractors are covetous, jealous souls who have suffered some obscure slight at Magid's hands, and are determined to wreak their revenge by holding up the red herring of "those things that are pure and good in journalism." The train of thought was taking a Nixonian turn.

I raised the question of content — whether Magid's surveys influenced the substance of nightly newscasts. I reminded him of the New York *Times* interview of October 12, 1975, in which he was quoted as saying, "We do not in any shape or form recommend the content of what the news should be." Magid replied with his "practical-point-of-view" remark: that it was "absolutely impossible" for him or his staff to be present in the newsroom of every client every night — therefore, the question of content interference was absurd.

I drew Magid's attention to the fifth DuPont *Survey of Broadcast Journalism,* which had reprinted his 1971 list of recommendations for station WTVJ in Miami. The recommendations had included, "Broward County news should not be reported in great detail."

"An interesting piece," was Magid's reply, "because I think it is inaccurate, false, and misleading."

The list was a false list?

Magid: "Well, now, wait. I think that if you were present at the discussion . . . and again, it depends upon the way you interpret that. If Broward County news is going to, in effect, preclude the reporting of other kinds of news that may be as interesting or important or what have you, and I don't recall the meeting and I cannot say and I would not, you know, certainly go to court about it, but I don't think that what we are saying is that you should not report Broward County news. Even what you have read to me was not that. There is a limited, a finite period of time on the air that you have to use in the best possible way and so that may have been reported there so we are able to get in other things and make the newscast more complete."

The point, I reminded Magid, was not that Broward County news *deserved* or *did not deserve* a given amount of coverage at WTVJ. The point was that the judgment on the question arose explicitly from the Magid staff's survey — not from the WTVJ news management. (It should be noted here that, in any case, WTVJ did not capitulate to the suggestion. Ralph Renick, the station's vice president for news, eventually succeeded in terminating the Magid group's services, and later characterized the service as "franchised news — like McDonald's.")

Magid's reply: "Well, no, but you see, what they do is, they hop on something like that, and say, you see . . . It's just like I read in the broadcasting article when I was quoted as saying don't do something about political news in Boston. It was kind of an interesting piece of reporting there, too. In the first place, the fellow who claims that I said that to him, the general manager up there, Mr. Coopersmith, is a man whom I've never met. So I couldn't have said that to him, number one, and it came perhaps second-hand from a disgruntled news director . . ."—and on and on in that vein for several minutes.

I was beginning to see that an interview with Frank Magid was about as productive—although, admittedly, certainly as interesting—an exercise as a conversation with the Cheshire Cat. Dutifully, I plunged ahead at the "content" question one more time: "Granted, what you say about Mr. Coopersmith [whatever he said about Mr. Coopersmith] may be true. But to return to the original question: Even if your intentions vis-à-vis Broward County news were the most benign in the world, and produced the best possible journalistic results, is it not at least a *semantic contradiction* to say, on the one hand, 'We don't involve ourselves in content,' and on the other to recommend a value judgment on a given category of news?"

It was at this point that Magid abruptly shifted ground, conceded the content question and, in doing so, revealed himself to be Frank Magid, Friend of Journalism.

"I think," he said, "that if we can be accused of dealing with content, the accusation might be more accurate if it, in effect, said, 'What they're trying to do is make news extremely broad in its concept or context.' And I think," Magid continued, magnanimously agreeing with his own interpretation, "that that's quite correct: that what we are trying to do is say, 'Look. The people are entitled to know all we can give them.' And that it is not our judgment or our concern that they have not been given that sort of thing, but our research shows that they are interested in more than you are providing them, and so therefore, if a television station exists, if a news department exists for disseminating information, then *please consider your audience* and disseminate more information than you are doing at the present time."

(A point well taken, on the face of it. Judged against UFO series, reports on bridges that wouldn't go up, sex fantasies, and porpoise-splashings, even the barest mention of the *existence* of Broward County should be deemed worthy of a George Foster

Peabody Award. But it does not come to one's attention that television stations are exactly erring in the direction of overcovering local-government news. Be that as it may, I wearied of the subject and yearned to change it. Magid, however, had a last, ennobling interpretation to apply.

"We say to people," he said, " 'Look. You have a show of 30 minutes' length time. *Let's not waste those precious minutes.* Let's make sure that it contains all we can possibly produce and we have a *responsibility to the viewers* to make sure that we provide them with every bit of out ability instead of taking a passive, you know, approach.'

"So, I suppose if we are accused of formulizing, then our formula would be that we want to see every one of our stations produce news of the very highest quality and to have people who are the very best people doing it. So I will accept that sort of thing."

Now Magid seemed preoccupied with this theme. He talked on, and as he talked, I realized how stunningly accurate were the broadcasters who had described him as "a super salesman." With no discernible leap of logic, Magid was suddenly the passionate defender of pure journalism against those who would deny the public its deeper, nobler interests.

"I'm troubled," he was saying. "I'm troubled by value judgments and who makes them and why. I'm troubled by what values or concerns the television journalists have. Those who seem to be against us appear to have, in many cases, *complete lack of regard* for the public they seek, or so they say, to *serve*. Now, you know, when they talk about the 'lowest common denominator'—I find that to be a little elitist. They are saying that 80 per cent of the people respond well and want certain kinds of things, and they are referring to the 80 per cent as the lowest common denominator. I find that very difficult to understand and I find it, frankly, a bit repulsive. Because *they are looking down* and are dictating and are saying that this is what they feel the public should have.

"You see, the critics are always saying that what we are doing is appealing to the lowest common denominator. How big *is* that lowest common denominator? It so happens that in many cases it is 80 per cent of the general population."

The populistic note was—as are so many notes that Magid strikes—a convincing and dramatic one. It takes a supreme effort at concentration to digest the above passage, and then consider that this is the same man whose organization told station WMAQ in Chicago that "... In terms of news, this means ratings are improved not when listeners are told what they *should* know, but what they want to hear." It's surprising to recall that this is the same man whose organization suggested that "Some very effective actualities can be delivered in ten seconds," and that an "enraged parent, a scared child, a marching picketer" are to be favored as on-the-scene news sources over a "disinterested" reporter.

"And why," I asked Magid, bringing the conversation back to TV news stories of murder, riots, fires, "why *is* there a preponderance of the easy, high-action film story?"

And this is what Magid replied: "Look. *I think you'd better turn to your journalism schools for an answer,* because that's what they consider to be hard, late-breaking news. As a matter of fact, you cannot find it, find one word that we have written about having, you know, fires, that sort of thing, and look at *19 years of recommendations,* and I don't think you'll find one reference to that sort of thing. But that seems to be standard in terms of what people coming out of the journalism schools think is news."

As it happened, I had come to Cedar Rapids directly from New York, where I had done exactly what Magid suggested — turned to a journalism school for an answer. Columbia University has perhaps the best-known graduate school of journalism in the United States, and Fred Friendly, the former CBS News president, is the Murrow professor of communications there. I had asked Friendly about his reaction to TV's emphasis on fires, crimes, and sex as news. His answer did not indicate that journalism schools were setting, up these categories as standards of news.

Said Friendly: "Television is becoming the tabloid, the instrument of the yellow journalist. It is doing the very thing that Hearst used to do, that the New York *Graphic* used to do. *The Front Page* is coming back, in television form.

"What's happened is that the newspapers have gotten pretty good. The newspapers that have survived are really quite good today. Television has taken over the crappy role.

"You get fire after fire after fire. One obvious reason besides audience-building is that those stories come right into a news department off the police wire. They're easy to cover. And, of course, it creates in this city, among older people especially, the feeling that this is a terribly unsafe city and you have to stay locked up in your room. And it isn't that way at all.

"News has traditionally been an anticipator of events, not just a voyeur of the sensational. If you can't anticipate, you can't report at all. What a journalist has to be able to do, is to see slightly beyond the curvature of the earth. To know what tomorrow's story is going to be. Not to go answering that fire alarm. Television is terrible about that.

"But among the local TV stations here in New York, you almost have—in a figurative sense—Nero fiddling while Rome burns. You should see how they were doing 'happy' news and fires while the biggest story since New York got sold for $24 was developing—the financial breakdown of the city!"

Magid was glancing at his wristwatch; he was scheduled to deliver a speech that afternoon, and wanted to bring the interview to a close. I decided to skip ahead to a topic I was very much interested in hearing from Magid's point of view: his role in developing "AM America."

"What were the differences," I asked Magid, "between your recommendations and ABC's execution of them?"

"Well," he said, "you see, there are a number of people in the creative end of any program development, and oftentimes these people have an innate distrust of research because they feel you cannot research certain things. *We* feel that you cannot research everything, but that research is a very, very valid instrument for doing certain things.

"I know that when we talked about Stephanie Edwards, as an example, the research which had tested her indicated that she would not be appropriate. And these people [at ABC] said to us, 'Look, give her time. She has to grow on you.' Things of that sort. We said, 'Look. Research says that *this* is the case,' . . . and that's where some of the differences seem to exist.

"I mean, we're all products of our environment, and we're all products of things we've learned, and that sort of thing, and what we do in research is try to take a view of what the public will re-

spond to. And these people are not privy to that information unless research provides it for them. But, you see, there is this distrust of research."

So far, Magid's account—boiled down to its coherent essen-
tials—provided a substantially different view from Stephanie Edwards'. According to Ms. Edwards, ABC blindly embraced the
recommendations Magid had provided. According to Magid, the
network was a reluctant dragon.

"Did your differences," I asked him, "turn on the Edwards
issue?"

"No, I think that there were a lot of other things. As an example, the set was inappropriate. It looked very small and people
looked uncomfortable on the set. I don't know whether you remember those first few days, but there were legs and shoes and
things dangling beside it, and when the people look uncomfortable, those who watch the people are going to be uncomfortable."

"There were stories," I reminded Magid, "to the effect that
your organization had called desks 'authority barriers'; hence, podiums instead of desks."

"Aww, you know, I wish that people would really come to
grips with some of these facts."

"Did you recommend podiums as opposed to desks?"

"I don't recall that we did, no."

"That the notebook paper should be orange?"

"Oh, yeah. That one. Some of these things are absolutely ridiculous. The fact of the matter is that, frankly, I thought the
show was, right from its beginnings, too much of a carbon copy of
what the 'Today' show was doing very well. We were not providing, as the research indicated we should provide, a viable alternative to the 'Today' show."

"How should it have been different?"

"Well, first of all, there are other things that people wanted to
know about. The 'Today' show rests very heavily on political news,
on interviews with political personages and other individuals,
newsmakers. The show on ABC was designed to provide a different kind of news . . . different *kinds* of information with different
kinds of people, whether it be experts on plants or animals or
weather or things that you do in terms of coping with problems on
a day-to-day basis. Lifestyles. Divorce and marriage. The sex situation. All of those things that people, you know, read about and

are interested in. So it was designed to be, again, a different show, concentrating on different things."

Plants. Animals. Weather. Lifestyles. Divorce and marriage. The sex situation. Different things. Different from the "Today" show's emphasis on "political news, on interviews with political personages and other individuals, newsmakers." (*"Broward County news should not be reported in great detail."*)

Frank Magid is very close to an absolutist in his acceptance of statistical research as a determinant of human impulses, tendencies, preferences, behavior. He is a true believer. And he is both dramatically right and dead wrong.

Magid's research for "AM America" produced the unsurprising information that television watchers prefer plant information over politics; lifestyles over newsmakers; day-to-day basics over foreign affairs. Perhaps a television show arranged around such categories can be a commercial and artistic success—as the improved performance of "AM"'s successor, "Good Morning, America," would indicate.

But Magid is not a consultant primarily for morning "magazine"-type formats. His principal area in television is the newscast. And the principal flaw, of both Magid and his rising army of consultant-imitators, is the assumption that light news, cute features, gossip, and folksy "how-to" information are all that people want, that such categories plumb the depths of the American public's curiosity, social concern, and attention span. (The principal flaw of Magid's clients, the station managers and one network news president, has been to turn such an assumption into news judgment. Recall William Sheehan's memo to the ABC news staff.)

No matter how stridently Frank Magid denies it—and he can, when he is in full rhetorical cry about "responsibility to viewers" and "disseminating more information," sound like a combination of Horace Greeley and Daniel Ellsberg—his thrust is basically anti-journalistic.

The best American journalism has traditionally proceeded from the assumption that it is mining areas that the public *did not even know existed*. How could any motivational survey, no matter how perfectly worded, yield the information—in advance—that Americans wanted to read the Pentagon Papers? Or that Americans wanted to know about the secret Constitutional assaults of the Nixon Administration? Or about illegal massacres in Vietnam, or faulty automobile-safety standards, or the rise of multinational corporations, or CIA involvement in Chile, or the Black Sox scandal, or Boss Tweed, or Teapot Dome? In none of these cases did the public (that is, a small sector of it) have the opportunity to "vote" on such coverage in advance—because the coverage *created* the category; made it visible; created and legitimized its own audience interest.

The reason why investigative reporting is anathema in the cybernetic newscast is self-evident: it is a revolutionary element (in that it commends radical change) and thus is counterproductive to audience-building. Yesterday's radicalism, to quote Garry Wills, "becomes today's common sense." But while a muckraking news story is in its "radical" stage, it upsets and annoys people; it activates hidden fears, biases, guilts; it creates in the TV viewer the strong preference to think about something else. The viewer is likely to switch to "Least Objectionable Programming."

This is why television has had to be dragged screaming by the hair to nearly every important "investigative" story of the past ten years: the developing awareness of official deceit in Vietnam policy and strategy (David Halberstam in Harper's); My Lai (Seymour Hersh in the New York *Times*); the inadequacy of automobile safety standards (Ralph Nader wherever he could find a forum); the Pentagon Papers (Daniel Ellsberg and the New York *Times*); Watergate (the Washington *Post* and Judge John J. Sirica); the various current resource shortages and fiscal crises (a noble exception being the three-hour energy-crisis documentary produced for NBC by the late Fred Freed in 1973).

There are strong parallels between investigative reporting's maverick role in the conventional news process (especially in television) and radicalism's role in the conventional political process, as articulated by Wills:[1] "All the initially unpopular political causes—labor, universal suffrage, Prohibition, civil rights, the antiwar movement—had their origins in the streets, or in back alleys, not in electoral contests. They were of questionable legality at the outset, or of open illegality. The first organizers did not end up in electoral office, but in jail [Note—for TV reporters, instead of "jail", read: "oblivion"]. Every strenuous moral effort begins with a handful of oddballs—the crazies, freaks, and street people; the prophets, the martyrs, the saints . . .

[1] "Feminists and Other Useful Fanatics" *Harper's*, June 1976.

"Prophets are a scandal in democracies. They are not representative. They cannot be controlled or called off by their 'constituents,' because *no constituency sent them. They create their audience, and compel it. They do not follow or submit to it.* They make a claim because it is right, not because it is wanted, even by its putative beneficiaries—normally it is not wanted."

As it is with the prophet in a democracy, so it is with the persistent, digging reporter of unpleasant truths in the electronic news media. No "constituency," in the form of an audience survey, sent him snooping in the county assessor's office or through the alderman's payroll. He creates his audience by presenting it with unexpected facts; and if he compels it, he often repels it as well. The investigative reporter does not "follow or submit to" the viewing audience—and, as a consequence, he is frequently reassigned, or else replaced by someone who is willing to follow and submit. (More typically, he is not hired by a TV station in the first place.) The dollar stakes are simply too enormous for TV news departments to play Russian roulette with their viewers by consistently taunting them with new threats to their comfortable suppositions about public ethics, official sanity, the degree of illness and starvation among fellow men, the proximity of catastrophe.

The use of audience research in TV journalism—any journalism—has the effect of turning the newsman's head backward, into the past. What "worked" before? What got results? Plant news? They like plant news? Good, we will devote time each week to plant news (come hell or high crimes and misdemeanors). Weather? Ah, we will give them a plethora of weather, more weather than they can possibly remember or repeat five minutes after having heard it. The "action" reporter? Get him on the air, every night. Sports; we have to have sports. Perhaps a "baby doctor" once a week. Celebrity notes—they always work. Faces and Places. The ombudsman, the "problem solver." The viewer-surrogate reporter. A little commentary by the co-anchorman.

And, if there is any time left, we will cover some news. That is, after all, our noble calling, our knightly mandate. We must remember our "responsibility to the viewers," and "disseminate more information." It says so right here, on Mr. Magid's survey.

Of course, we have to place news in its proper perspective. For example, Gloria Rojas, now a feature reporter at WABC, fled to the New York station from Chicago's WLS after a series of indignities, the most notable of which occurred when a report she had prepared on rape victims was pre-empted on the ten-thirty newscast so that Coleman and Company could have a few extra minutes to celebrate its eighth anniversary on the air. The same station lost Larry Buchman, a talented investigative reporter, to NBC radio, after the station's management told him they were not too interested in investigative work.

Dr. Lendon Smith is a good example of how this sort of soft, feature-oriented compartmentalization is replacing hard news on local stations. Dr. Smith is a 55-year-old pediatrician, popularly known as "The Baby Doctor" on the radio call-in and TV talk-show circuit. Dr. Smith is regularly seen and heard on "Good Morning, America," and on local stations in such cities as Cleveland, Washington, San Francisco, Los Angeles, and Seattle.

In early 1976, "The Baby Doctor" added another step on his rounds: he began appearing every Thursday on Channel 7 "Eyewitness News" in Chicago.

Before his series of "visits" on Channel 7 began, Dr. Smith candidly told a Chicago TV columnist: "I try to be reassuring, cheerful, intelligent and informative. The people want information, but they want it cheerfully presented."

How, the columnist politely asked Dr. Smith, would he manage a "cheerful" report on, say, leukemia or cerebral palsy?

"Well, of course, you don't," was the doctor's frank reply. "You just give it straight and get it over with. But I'd say my stuff runs 5 to 1 light to heavy."

Dr. Smith's penchant for the "light" was gloriously conspicuous in one of his first appearances. The subject was "hyperactivity in children"; it was, in the event, hyperactivity in Dr. Lendon Smith, and devil take the viewer seeking to squeeze a drop of information from the raffish doctor's verbal mulch.

Here, word for word, is how the segment proceeded:

NEWSMAN JOHN DRURY: Lendon Smith, author and pediatrician, is back with us again today. A subject that is on the minds of many parents is the subject of hyperactivity in children.

Uh — address yourself to *that*, okay?

SMITH: Uh — my mother wondered about this, but they had some other name for it. Like, uh "My, he's a touchy little thing." Or, "Isn't he sensitive?" is what was often said then, because I'm sure I was hyperactive. I think the only thing that saved me was that I was raisin-ably—uh, *reasonably* bright in school, and the teacher knew that my father was a, you know, a nice doctor; they said, well, let's not bug little Lendon, because he's got this nice father.

And I would smile. And I was *cheerful*. And I think that makes a difference. But as far as I'm concerned, hyperactivity is only a diagnosis, or is only meaningful if it interferes with a child's getting along in school. If he's, uh, if he's active but he gets his work done and he doesn't disrupt the rest of the class, why, you know, *leave him be*. Now, uh, I found, however, that, um, some children are hyperactive only in school. This is sort of really the best definition. If they're hyperactive at home and not hyperactive in school, there's something wrong with the home situation. And not at school. 'Cause hyperactivity is defined as a child who is unable to disregard unimportant stimuli. [*At last—the doctor defines what he is talking about.*]

If he's sitting in a class and a car goes by and he's WHHHHHHHISSSSSSSSSHHHT—off to the window, and telling everybody there's a car out there. Somebody drops a pencil three rows over, and he's the first one over there to pick up the pencil. That's called—uh, an *approacher*. He notices everything and he has to respond to it in a motor way. Now, if it's that sort of a child, then something, uh, could be done. Uh, if the teacher's upset with his behavior, then he may need medication, we're finding that other things, uh, red food-dye, uh, has something to do with this; we've all heard of studies . . .

DRURY: Izzat important?

SMITH: You bet it is. Yeah. But it's not the whole answer. Sometimes fluorescent lights, uh, are enough to freak out these kids. There's a whole bunch of things that can—that have to do with it. A tough teacher, too many kids in the classroom . . . we'll talk about it again some other time.

DRURY: Children grow out of this, don't they Doctor?

SMITH: You bet, and become, uh, uh, uh, news, uh, hosts and, and pediatricians.

That is, apparently, a working example of "different *kinds* of information with different *kinds* of people": a slickly commercial, self-consciously fey pediatrician-personality, advertised as an authority but in fact a monologist babbling on about his father, his teacher, red food-dye, fluorescent lights, a whole bunch of things.

An approacher. May need medication. We've all heard of studies. We'll talk about it again some other time.

Frank Magid is "troubled," he says, by journalists who "look down" and "dictate" what they feel the public should have. He finds such behavior, such talk of "the lowest common denominator," to be "a little elitist."

And yet, at up to 100 of the most influential television stations in the country, Frank Magid and his associates are doing most of the "looking down," the "dictating." And to proclaim that among the 80 per cent, Magid considers to be the lowest common denominator, "there aren't too many 'concerned' listeners out there"—as the Magid survey specifically informed WMAQ Radio—itself smacks of elitism.

The interview was drawing to a close. "I'm going to give a speech this afternoon," said Magid, "to the Iowa Sociological Association, and many of my former colleagues will be present and I'm looking forward to giving the speech because what I'm going to say is something they probably won't like, and that is that when I left the university both as a student and as a teacher and went into the commercial, that I felt that much of what I had been taught was not applicable to the real world.

"Now, I am going to lay the blame at the foot of the real world, so to speak, because I came in only partially prepared, you know, to deal with the things I found out, in terms of research methodology and what have you. Of course, I'm going to urge them this afternoon to, in effect, poke their head out of the cocoon and to see, you know, what's really there.

"But the fact of the matter really is, I must take it upon myself, as I hope I have over these past 19 years, to build a better situation; to learn more myself and not, you know, lay it at the foot of something as these people are laying it at the foot of commercial television. I will say that, to a large extent, the individuals who are employed today lack a great deal of imagination. They lack the ability to go beyond the supposed parameters that exist at the present time."

"Do they," I asked Magid, "lack the ability to understand what you are telling them?"

"Yes. And, as a matter of fact, they confuse and misconstrue, and as I think I've mentioned in a number of articles that have been written or at least I've been quoted, I speak of a sign I saw once in the office of a college president. It said: 'New ideas are always in danger of being beaten to death by those of insufficient knowledge, or by those whose apple cart they would upset.' And it's so true. Because we are a purveyor of new ideas. We come in and we, in effect, as we walk in the door, come in with a large sign that, in effect, says, 'Change.' We represent change. The only thing is, we don't know what it's going to mean until the study is through. And people are resistant to change because it can be a very unsettling thing. The news director worries whether, you know, this or that or the next thing. I think that's wrong. Because we should be regarded as someone who is going to give us some information about what people are responding to, and if we work together we can make this a more effective newscast."

"Why are you in the business?" I asked Magid.

"I am, I guess, inquisitive. And I'm curious as to why people do the things they do. And I suppose I am a student of human behavior. I'm intrigued. I'm interested. And there is, to my way of thinking, a great deal of satisfaction that one gains, aside from any monetary remuneration there may be.

"And I do honestly believe that seeing a station grow in its news ratings . . . and I know this comes back again to, 'All we're interested in is ratings.' *Well, that's what we're retained to do.* A station is interested in gaining ratings, but I really don't know of any station that is dominant in the ratings that doesn't do a good job. Now, you and I may travel all over and we have a broader view of news than the person in any given market that sits home or watches television news in his market. Everything is relative."

I asked Magid what his own news sources were.

"Personally? I enjoy reading newspapers. As a matter of fact, and because I travel so much, I read daily such things as the *Wall Street Journal;* I'll read the newspapers that are available in the given market. I try to read the national news magazines. We take quite a number of magazines. I enjoy such things as *Atlantic* and *Harper's* and *The New Yorker* and *New York.* I listen to radio only when I'm in the car because that is the only time I have available outside of when I'm in hotels or things of that sort. I try to watch a bit of the morning news in terms of comparing how they look so you get a full spectrum of everything. And then, wherever I am, because I'm interested in television news, I watch television news."

It was an interesting set of informational priorities for the anti-elitist, the booster of television as the best disseminator of American journalism: newspapers first, and particularly the quintessentially Establishment *Wall Street Journal.* Magazines second, with a nod to the eastern, low-circulation, high-prestige periodicals such as *Atlantic,* and *The New Yorker.* Radio *third*—only when he is in the car. Television news *last,* and then with a pointed qualifier: *"Because I'm interested in television news"* (as its architect).

Magid was warming to the subject.

"You know, I enjoy reading a great deal. For instance, I was intrigued with Tom Wolfe's book *The Painted Word* because I am interested in art as well, and I was interested in what he had to say about the art establishment, so to speak. But I'm also interested in the philosophy of ideas. I was intrigued with Saul Bellow's book *Humboldt's Gift.* Such things as *Night Work,* by Irwin Shaw, or whatsisname's very enjoyable book—Doctor . . . *Ragtime. Ragtime* I especially enjoyed because I enjoyed the style. *And there was a very interesting amalgamation between fact and fiction. . . ."* [emphasis added]

Magid was speaking with real animation now. The formality was gone. For the first time in the interview he seemed at ease, friendly; the defenses down. The carefully oblique businessman-academic in the starched oxford shirt was giving way to a more *spontaneous* man; and, for the first time, it occurred to me that there was a clear correlation between Frank Magid's distinct lack of personal spontaneity and the same lack that comes through so painfully on Magid-counseled newscasts.

But now Magid was reminiscing; the memory that followed offers perhaps the most revealing, and poignant, insight into Frank Magid's identity. "If I may recall the days that I went to school," he began almost shyly, ". . . I recall one thing that impressed me very much. I had just gone into graduate school and I had to take a course in statistics, and I really had a very poor background in algebra and things of that sort.

"And the first day, the professor gave a math test, and I got about 20 out of a possible 100. And I went up to him and said,

'Look. Will you tell me the name of a tutor; I have to have this course to get a master's degree, and I know my limitations in math and I want to do well, and please.'

"And he said, 'Why don't you sit down.' 'No, you don't understand. I have to; if I don't do it now, I'm going to fail.' He said, 'Why don't you sit down.' I did — and that professor *made statistics so meaningful, so important, so wonderful.* He was so facile, so able, and that sort of thing, that I was intrigued, and I did extremely well in that particular course. I went on to take every statistics course that they offered, and ended up taking my Ph.D. qualifying exams in statistics, and ended up teaching statistics at Coe College here in Cedar Rapids."

That Frank Magid, the reserved, bookish don, the diligent acolyte of charts and graphs and abstract data — that this austere Ice King received his motivating inspiration from the *personal style of a charismatic mentor,* is one of the master paradoxes of the Magid empire. But Magid was absorbed in still another reminiscence. "I have a minor in anthropology. And the professor at the time was David Stout, a fellow of the Royal Society, probably the world's foremost authority on the Kuna Indians of Panama, that sort of thing. And I never took a note in that class — and worried — and yet, on the other hand, didn't, *because he brought everything so much to life every time he spoke,* whether it be of one culture or another, that I could visualize everything. If we were talking about South American Indians, or whatever it is, I could visualize them in front of me. *I could see tribal rites. I knew precisely what the homes were like.* I knew everything he was describing, and it was there in living color, right before my eyes. It was wonderful, and most of those things, believe it or not, I can still recall today."

"Now," continued Magid, and his voice was softer, "there were others in that university who were teaching statistics. I tried it when I taught at Coe College . . . but I know I failed, I mean, in my own mind, I'm sure that no student was . . . uh, enlightened and enthused and concerned and wanted to do something with it as David Gold made me. The same with Dave Stout and a few others." He paused, and looked up; spread his hands, a trifle embarassed by what he had revealed. When he finally spoke, it was with a shrug and a sense of anticlimax: "But there is a difference in terms of what I received by virtue of their enthusiasm, their manner of presentation. All of the things that they did."

The interview was over. Magid had to make his speech before the Iowa Sociological Association. He gave me a brief tour of the research center; we inspected the IBM 1130 computer, met some of the young Ph.D's on Magid's staff. And then we shook hands.

As I left Cedar Rapids ($5.60 from the Hotel Royale to the airport) I found myself trying to place Frank Magid in the repertory of American archetypes. It was an elusive game. Magid has few distinctive edges. The effect of his startling authority within electronic journalism is clear, but it wants a personal stamp. The most influential televison theoretician since Marshall McLuhan (save, perhaps, Paul Klein), Magid is, like McLuhan, an academic; but he lacks McLuhan's fantastic idiosyncrasy and playful synthesizing. More important, McLuhan — though his historical premises could be faulted for accuracy and his historical analogies be endlessly debated on grounds of logic — *has* a historical sense. It is Frank Magid's peculiar fascination that he seems cut off from history. Just as his strange modular research center has nothing in common with Iowa's agrarian history, no organic continuity with the historical *fact* of Iowa any more than with the Kuna Indians of Panama, so Magid's vision for television news has nothing in common with the inquisitive, disinterested history of American journalism. (Yes, Magid builds on "what has worked" in past TV newscasts; what has worked within the relatively few minutes of television's tenure in the American life. And, yes, One Research Center builds on the recent ambition of Cedar Rapids go-getters. History, for Magid, extends back approximately 19 years.)

If not a McLuhan, who then? A salesman? Yes, but no Willy Loman, way out there in the blue riding on a smile and a shoeshine, whining about getting some seeds in the ground. Magid is a breed of salesman Willy never dreamed of.

George F. Babbitt? Magid has something in him of the small-town booster, the Rotarian, friend of the symphony, but he is far more patrician than Babbitt in his innocent coarseness. Professor Harold Hill? Some hope there: Magid knows the territory, all right — but he isn't in Iowa just to organize a boy's band, he's there to orchestrate a national cacophony into the ultimate negotiable hum, the one perfect note that will have the 18-to 49 age group marching in perfect consumer-cadence behind him, past the advertisers' reviewing stand. More Paid Piper than Music Man.

If Frank Magid conforms to any national type, it is likely the Self-Made Man—the Emersonian self-improver, the Horatio Alger out to fill up the empty spaces in the world, and, in the process, the empty spaces in himself. Such men and women tend to regard life as a series of arenas in which one tests and improves one's soul by meeting and defeating obstacles, or "opponents," or "competitors." Incentive is all; expansion an unquestioned virtue; rating points are the merit badges of moral worth.

As a medium conceived for the purpose of moving goods, television is a natural breeding-ground for this marketplace definition of an ethical system. It is no contradiction that Frank Magid and his rival news consultants are consummate masters of audience-building subtleties, and yet stumble into incoherence and contradiction when led into the subject of news "content." "Content" is, after all, incidental to the game. It is someone else's worry. Let the moral weight of "content" fall back on those millions who choose one newscast over another. If they choose the entertaining newscast over the serious-minded one, is that not evidence enough of the rightness of the course? (Never mind that the millions have not been let in on the rules of the game: have not been told that they are not the *objects* of television programming but *commodities in it*, to be turned over to advertisers en masse like cattle; and that the entertaining newscast does not *signify*—although it manifestly *implies*—that the world is free that night from more significant stories, deeper crises, more and various impending agonies.)

Magid's sharp, sophisticated, fatuous "researchers," out there in the communities, gathering their foreordained "attitude and opinion summaries" for their clients to use toward rating-point merit badges, are on a fixed and sterile course. They are as surely enmeshed in meaningless charade (for all the good they do for public enlightenment) as are the eigth-graders described by Jonathan Kozol:[2]

> It is conceivable that eighth grade children in an innovative
> and experimental junior high *might*, in the course of "field work,"

[2] *The Night Is Dark and I Am Far From Home*, Houghton Mifflin Co.

hear at least a couple of divergent views on urban problems, welfare, trade, taxation, voting age. They will hear, perhaps, from
those who favor low-cost housing, those who feel that water-fluori-
dation is a good idea, and those who think that smog is a bad problem. They will hear from Democrats. They will hear from Republi-
cans. They will hear from liberals, from moderates and from
conservatives. They will hear from those who favor health insur-
ance as a national priority, and those who think the whole thing can
be handled better by Blue Cross and by Blue Shield. They will hear
of "know-how," "in-put," "out-put," "programs," "structures," "systems."

What we must ask, however, is what they will learn about starvation? Needless hunger? Conscious exploitation? Purposeful in-
justice? What will they learn, not of the friendly Mayor and City
Council, but of real power? What will they learn of the accountability of public officers to those in corporation offices and private-
interest lobbies, "funds" and "fronts," whose cash donations make
their re-election possible? What will they learn about the power and
control of schools *themselves* [read: "TV stations"] and of the ways in
which the schools, the publishers and the educational consulting-
firms labor together to expropriate the candor and the courage of
the pupils who are locked within these schools? How much of *this*
will get to children, unassisted, undirected, unprovoked, by "random" accident of "open" access and untutored inquiry? I think we
know when we are in the presence of overt deceit.

Kozol is close to the point of Frank Magid here, with one important distinction: Magid, whatever else he may be, is not a prac-
titioner of "overt deceit." He is not a dishonest man. In a peculiar
way, he is as much marionette as he is puppeteer.

And, in the field he has perfected, he is surrounded by a vast
and growing community of competitors — many of whom would
be only too happy to cut his strings.

COLORS IN A
DIAMOND

As far as Phil McHugh is concerned, Frank Magid is an upstart, a Johnny-come-lately, and a lot of baloney.

The fact that Frank Magid has soared past Phil McHugh as the nation's most influential news consultant has not done much to temper McHugh's judgment.

"Magid never was a consultant," growled McHugh in the high-rise executive offices of McHugh & Hoffman, Inc., Communications Consultant. The offices are at 7900 Westpark Drive, McLean, Virginia, a rapidly-expanding little oasis of urban glass and steel rising out of the lush forests about 20 miles south of Washington. Ten years ago, the land on which McHugh's high-rise offices rest—an area with the quaint name of Tyson's Corner—was a farm. In another ten, given the present rate of expansion, it will be inner city.

"Magid was always a research man," continued Phil McHugh, a squarely-built, feisty, balding fiftyish bulldog of a man whose voice can fill a room to bursting. "I know he likes to use that '19 years' figure, but for most of that time he was a research man. When Magid *became* a consultant, he hired Les Atlas' son [Atlas was a Chicago broadcast baron] and it didn't work out worth a damn. He then turned around and hired Lee Stowell from us, about four or five years ago, and Lee Stowell set up the consulting division for Magid in broadcasting. Now, that's a fact. Magid has been doing research in broadcasting for a long time, but he had never been doing consulting."

Perhaps Phil McHugh can be forgiven his animosity toward Magid—an animosity that has tinges of a modern-day Hatfield-McCoy feud, fought out with computers and questionnaires instead of Kentucky long rifles.

For if Frank Magid perfected the business of news consultancy, it was Phil McHugh who invented the damn thing—way back in 1962, along with his partner, Peter S. Hoffman.

At that time, McHugh had already been in what he calls "the radio, television, agency field" for 26 years, starting out with a radio directing job at the University of Notre Dame in 1936. Two years later he joined the CBS Radio Network in New York in *its* research department, but quickly moved into the broadcasting side as an associate network producer.

After World War II, McHugh held a variety of radio jobs, some of them news-related, and in 1950 he began a long and profitable career in the "agency" arm of his chosen field. He joined the Campbell-Ewald advertising agency in Detroit; under his management, the company's radio-television billings rose from $4 million to $40 million a year. In those days, companies and corporations still sponsored individual TV shows in their entirety—as distinct from the "spot buying" of air time in practice today—and McHugh proved to be a cagey operator indeed when it came to purchasing "commercial vehicles." He bought and supervised, for clients such as Chevrolet and Delco, such "commercial vehicles" as the Dinah Shore and Bob Hope shows, "Eyewitness to History," "High Adventure," "My Three Sons," "Route 66," and "Bonanza."

All the while, McHugh, a hardheaded businessman from first to last, was getting more and more curious as to why people developed loyalties to certain TV shows—curious as to why the ratings turned out the way they did.

He had, in the meantime, met Peter Hoffman, who had joined Campbell-Ewald's research department in 1954, upon being discharged from the army at the close of the Korean War. (Hoffman, the smooth and persuasive Dartmouth gentleman-salesman, was also tough enough to have been an infantry platoon leader and a Ranger.) Hoffman's main fascination was research; at Campbell-Ewald, he organized the TV-radio research section, which became a pioneer in the pre- and post-testing of radio and TV commercials.

The careers of McHugh and Hoffman became intertwined in 1957, when Hoffman became McHugh's assistant as an account executive for Chevrolet, General Motors, Firestone, Kroger, and other large clients. Hoffman also coordinated TV and radio research for these clients.

In 1962, the two men resigned from Campbell-Ewald to form their own research firm. McHugh & Hoffman, Inc.—its offices then in Birmingham, Michigan—became the first consulting company to employ the techniques of social research to make specific recommendations for improvement in radio and television.

And, from the first as now, "improvement" was defined as upward movement in the ratings. At the time I visited with McHugh, his firm was working for 31 television stations around the country.

"The concept that we're consultants for news, and news only, is one of the misapprehensions that's sprung up about this business," said McHugh. "Certainly, we *evolved* into a greater concentration in news. But that was a result of several things.

"We started out consulting for stations in all the areas that were outside network control. Now, back in those days, you have to recall, there was Bozo the Clown, there were the morning shows, the cooking shows—a lot more programming under local-station control. All kinds of things in the early sixties. We would study all of these things. Over the years, we became very much aware that the primary relationship between a station and its audience was established, really, through its news. That was where the dependency began to develop."

I asked McHugh if he would explain what he meant by "dependency."

"We began to develop," he said, "what I call a 'home-station' relationship. We were interested in finding the reasons why viewers kept coming back to a particular station to find out what happened today—to find out the news. We were looking for the elements that made a given station more attractive than its competitors. We studied all the stations in a market at the same time. And, as we studied, the news itself became a more and more important factor. It went from a 15-minute format to a 30-minute format to an hour, and now, in some cases, to a two-hour format.

"The late 1960's—the time when local TV news made its big move—was a major period of transition. It was probably most notable for the fact that the visual content of a newscast began to improve significantly. Editing began to improve. The coverage of stories began to improve. And the audience began to feel that it was much more at the scene of what was happening, rather than being told what was happening with a silent picture."

"Was this," I asked McHugh, "a result of the unrest going on throughout America in the late sixties—the riots, the demonstrations, the Vietnam War protests?"

"Yes," he said. "I think the news became more important in the daily routines of viewers. We had never had a war going on in our living room before. We had never been as close to events. And, too, color television was then beginning to make its big impact."

I asked McHugh to explain the principal differences between his company and Magid's.

"I've always said this," replied McHugh. "If colleges and universities are similar—if Antioch, Harvard, and Johns Hopkins are alike—then Magid and we are alike. But you know the kind of education and the approach to education at Antioch. So we don't have to go into it. But we are different from Magid.

"Frank Magid runs a tremendously big company. I have no idea what percentage of his income comes out of his consulting part of the company, but he's got a whole lot of bodies to work on.

"We, by contrast, are a very small company. There are four men and five girls, and the men are the only ones who consult and travel. Our whole concept is not to spend our lives looking at tapes and visiting a station only once. I think Magid's plan is to visit only once a quarter. Ours is entirely different. We go every six weeks, sometimes every three weeks, sometimes every other week, depending on the problem.

"And the principal executives of our company are always involved with the client. The principals of Magid's company—with the exception of one station—sell. They sell beautifully; they're master salesmen. But they are not around afterward."

"What do you mean," I asked McHugh, "by 'sell'?"

"They go out and make sales presentations and persuade stations to come with them. Then they are hardly ever seen again. Frank has been able to accomplish it; it's no discredit to him, but I don't know that I would. I don't know if I'd want to. He has set himself up in such a way that, really, other than selling—and the servicing of ABC—he's really not that much involved."

Selling and servicing—it all sounded vaguely like a feud between two competing automobile dealers. " 'Involved' in what?" I asked McHugh.

"In service. I suspect that Frank Magid reads a very small percentage of the studies. I read every study. He doesn't. He claims to handle 100 stations on a consulting basis. We know that he handles a maximum of 50. That's a fact; I know it because we are in negotiations with a man from his company who was going to join us just two weeks ago.

"Their system of consulting is very different from ours. We're all-involved. They assign an individual from the company, and he becomes responsibile for, let's say, 13 stations. Now, those stations tend to assume a look and a feel, a certain common denominator of things that is very much the point of view of that one guy.

"Magid has a tendency to be—which he hotly denies—much more formulized than we are. You can, if you spend enough time at it, go into almost any city and pick out the Magid station."

McHugh & Hoffman, to compensate for the smallness of its staff, does not perform its own audience research—the distribution and collection of surveys that supposedly provide the basic insights into the public consciousness. Rather, the firm farms out this task to one of several research companies on a contract basis.

"We tend to have far less computer information than does a Magid study," said McHugh. "We started out that way. We think you can get more of a subtle understanding of why people feel the way they do, and why they're reacting the way they do, then you can ever get by compounding statistics.

"Magid is very big on statistics. In fact, his concepts go way beyond our concepts. He's in a lot of areas we don't necessarily feel that we should be in."

For instance?

"We don't coach talent. He coaches talent. I think it's a highly specialized thing, the coaching of talent. There's nothing in the world wrong with it, but we don't see that as our job. Another thing Magid does is a tremendous amount of bicycling tapes around, from station to station among his clients. This leads to a movement of talent from station to station. We don't do that. We don't run around brokering talent. We're not a clearinghouse."

McHugh paused, clasped his hands behind his head. He leaned back in his chair and sighed. Then he went on.

"There is an inherent susceptibility among broadcast people," he said slowly, "to rely on the quick answer. Some people in the research field tend to promise more than they can actually deliver in terms of panaceas.

"Changing somebody's mind about something they like is the most complex and difficult thing to do. What you have to do is come up with something so much better that they become uncomfortable about a habit that they were very comfortable with." McHugh paused again, and when he resumed, he chose his words carefully.

"I think," he said, "that if there is a selling distinction between Magid's organization and our own—and, God knows, it has cost us clients—it is that some of Magid's clients were promised, literally, that within a year they would be Number One. This is based on conversations with some of their former clients that we now have.

"Almost all station managers are former sales managers. And what they want to hear is that it's going to be a great next year. What *we* say is, if you really want to know the truth, if you do everything right, it'll take about three years, because that's about what it takes to change somebody's mind.

"It's not like prime-time situation comedies. It's a whole different thing. A prime-time relationship is only good for that one show, only good for a year or two or three at the most. But the news relationship is much more dependent on the relationship between the community and the station. News viewers are not as fickle or easily swayed to change, and since a tremendous amount of the station's total image is dependent on news, you can't expect overnight miracles. It's a hard job."

If blunt, plain-talking Phil McHugh wastes little love on enigmatic Frank Magid, he wastes less on anyone who questions the propriety of news consultancy. I found this out when our conversation turned to the reasons why the business has been criticized so severely. "Could it not be," I suggested to McHugh, "that there is an unreasonable pressure on TV news to assemble large audiences not only for itself, but for the parent network's prime-time schedule? Is not TV news being asked to perform a business function that no other news organization. . . ."

"That's outrageous!" snapped McHugh.

How so?

McHugh leaned forward at his desk, folding his arms and drawing his bullet head down between his shoulders.

"What do you think the Washington *Post* is? Don't you think it's a business organization? It's in business to make money. That kind of thing is pure bull. They are out to fight the bloodiest fights for circulation the world has ever known! They redesign their formats for circulation.

"If there isn't show business and claptrap in Ann Landers, which is your highest traffic page, and the comic page and all this stuff. . . .

"You know, this is the biggest illusion that print journalists have ever heaped upon themselves—that they're so pure and the other guy is so bad. They are in show business *up to their very tails!* When that poor girl in Boston and her baby dove off the fire escape, the Washington *Post* ran the picture boom-boom-boom down the front page, as did lots of other editors. Is that show business or not? Or is it the truth? Is it a dramatic way of presenting the truth? You decide. I just say it's a lot of baloney. Secondly, newspapers, from the beginning of time, have used consultants. All of them."

Discounting the hyperbole—I doubted that Tom Paine ran the mockups for "Common Sense" through a battery of smart cookies from Ye Colonie Consultants, Ltd., or that Nast looked at a "Summary of Community Attitudes" before drawing his Boss Tweed cartoons—discounting that, I told McHugh, I agreed with him. Nevertheless, I suggested, the point is that television—which is primarily an advertising medium, a mover of goods, and a federally-regulated entity as well—perhaps has been saddled with an unfair burden. Perhaps television, unlike the print press with all its faults, is simply not a news medium. Why, if this is true, even keep up the pretense of television news?

McHugh got up from his desk and crossed the room. From behind a file cabinet, he pulled forth a large cardboard square. On the face of the square was drawn a diamond. The interior of the diamond was segmented by several horizontal layers, each a different color.

"I will tell you something about the television viewing patterns of people in this country," said McHugh, as he propped the cardboard square on top of his desk. It was clear that he was about to launch into a favorite lecture. He turned to the board and pointed toward the top.

"This," he said, "is a visualization of the social-class structure of the U.S. population. This diamond is in proportion to the numbers of people in each of several classes—so where it's fat, there are the biggest numbers of people. Where it's pointed, there are the smallest numbers of people.

"Up at the top here, you have the 3 per cent. Now, this three per cent—which, oddly enough, has diminished to about 2 per cent since I drew this chart—this is the social elite. This is the control segment, socially and business-wise. This is where the money is and where the real power is.

"When we come to their attitudes toward television, we don't talk about them at all, because the only influence they have on television is financial. Television is not something they watch or care about. Nothing in their life is planned around television. They may be upset if the symphony isn't on at four o'clock on Sunday afternoon, if they haven't anything else to do, but that's about all. They have a lot of power relative to television, as they do to newspapers. This is where the advertiser power, the manufacturer power, the owner power is.

"Now," McHugh went on, dropping his hand to another color area, "when we get to this 12 per cent, which is the upper-middle, we are getting to the managers, the middle- and lower-level executives and professional people. In *their* attitudes toward television, they watch less than the rest of the people on the diamond. They are the most selective and the most critical. The three per cent don't use it; these use it, but they tend to use it for the things they want to. Their wives are involved with the upper end of the PTA, and complain about television as no good. This class, however, performs one very valuable role: they are the communicators to these people"—he lifted his hand to the 3 per cent—"of what the rest of the people are doing.

"The pieces of paper pass through their hands on the way up—whether they are profit-and-loss statements, or audience and circulation figures, or whatever. They are the bridge between this and the lower classes. The 12 per cent *carry up* to the 3 per cent."

McHugh dropped his hand another notch. "Then you come to the lower-middle and the upper-lowers—and for the most part, you can treat them interchangeably, because you have the white-collar, the small businessman, some semiskilled professional people and the top skilled workers.

"And in their attitudes toward television, it's a primary source of information and entertainment. They are somewhat selective and becoming more selective, but their selectivity comes from picking up the newspaper supplement or *TV Guide* and looking at the plot lines and deciding what they're going to watch tonight. This is particularly true in the case of movies, specials, and so forth. Very often, they measure the plot line of a favorite show of theirs against the movie plot line and make a decision that way.

"But television is a very heavy element in their lives—the upper-lowers, particularly."

The hand dropped again. "At the bottom is the unskilled 20 per cent. In this category are the unskilled, the unemployed, the unemployables—some people who are incapable of working for a whole lot of reasons: schooling, recent immigrants, or the poverty-stricken. *Tremendously* heavy users of television. And they watch, for the most part, entertainment rather than information, and they are the least critical.

McHugh turned away from the cardboard chart and folded his hands in front of him. "Now," he said, "for a TV station to be successful, it has to succeed in the lower-middle class, which is 30 per cent, and the upper-lower, which is 35, so there is almost 70 per cent of the population in the middle that a station must be able to communicate with in order to really perform the function of mass communication.

"When you're doing this, communicating at levels which these people can understand, and relate Vietnam or Angola or whatever to their lives, it needs a special kind of communicator to put it in focus for them."

McHugh returned to his chair behind his desk.

"Edward R. Murrow," I remarked, "did not seem to have any special trouble reaching those same people 20 and 25 years ago, without the benefit of consultants. Why, now, a generation after the age of Murrow, do newscasters have to be coached by outside agencies on how to communicate?

"They are using far more complex tools than Murrow was using. Murrow was just talking, and for the most part, Murrow's biggest success was during World War II, standing on the roof of a building in England and saying, 'look at the damn bombs falling while people are spending another night.'"

"Yes," I said, "but he went on from there to distinguish himself in complex television stories. The McCarthy broadcast. 'Harvest of Shame'. . . ."

McHugh waved a hand. "Yes, but the things he was known for later were 'Person to Person'; his one-on-one kind of interviewing of *relatively famous people, celebrities.* Lowell Thomas and I were talking one time, and Lowell said, 'One of the things the public understands but the broadcast executive has never understood is that *I never give them the news, I tell them the human-interest stories in the news.*' You must be able to communicate in ways that people can understand. . . ."

There it was again: the notion, so frequently encountered in Magid's maxims, that there is this big, amorphous bulge of people in the United States, squeezed between the very rich (who don't count because they know better) and the very poor (who don't count because they can't buy), and that this big bulge cares only about celebrities and "human-interest stories." If American schools are not teaching us to read, to the tune of 2 per cent functional illiteracy, American television is compounding that shabby omission by adding an active element: it is encouraging us not to think.

To trivialize Edward R. Murrow, a founding father of television journalism, as nothing more than a celebrity interviewer, a sort of intellectual antecedent to Rona Barrett, is to badly misunderstand the history of the genre. More to the point, it reveals more about the meretricious elitism behind McHugh's endeavors than perhaps he would like to reveal.

Phil McHugh, with his neatly-colored diamond-shaped chart showing a United States firmly partitioned among castes labeled "upper" and "upper-middle" and "lower-middle" and "upper-lower" and "lower"; McHugh dismissing, with a drop of the hand, the "lowers" as being the "least critical" (though they are, by his admission, the most faithful users of television); McHugh deign-

ing to treat the "lower-middle" and the "upper-lowers" interchangeably—all this suggests news consultancy as an agent of
American broadcasting's most imperialistic instincts.

The Communications Act of 1934, under which radio and
television stations are to this day licensed, recognizes no social or
class priorities among the American citizenry which collectively
owns the airwaves.

It does not stipulate that the "lower-middle" or the "upper-
lower" classes become the primary target of broadcasting, any
more than it legitimizes the will of the "3 per cent" above that of
the rest.

The Federal Communications Commission grants and re-
news licenses on the condition that broadcast stations serve "the
public interest, convenience and necessity." This philosophy, as
Fred Friendly points out, derives from a 1929 decision of the Federal Radio Commission, which stated: "Broadcasting stations are
licensed to serve the public, and not for the purpose of furthering
the private or selfish interests of individuals or groups of individuals. The standard of public interest, convenience or necessity
means nothing if it does not mean this. . . ."

To isolate a lucrative buying group from the total pool of
American television viewers, and then to create programming
that supposedly meets the specific tastes and interests (needs be
damned!) of that group, is to discriminate against groups both
"above" and "beneath" the target audience.

In entertainment programming, this practice is merely unfair and counter to the intent of FCC licensing policy. In news
programming, it is pernicious. Television managers and owners
have a right to make a profit—yes. But as has been pointed out
before, profit-making has never been seriously threatened as a
way of managerial life in American TV. At what point does this
right to profit interfere with the public interest, convenience, and
necessity? At what point is the process reversed, with the public
serving the interest, convenience, and necessity of television?

But the really ludicrous aspect of a Phil McHugh, with his
diamond-patterned chart, fat with its "lower-middles" and "upper-lowers"—the really ludicrous aspect of a Frank Magid prat-
tling on about "the 80 per cent"; or of John Coleman celebrating

the laughing beer drinkers; or of a Joel Daly pretending to frater-
nize with truck drivers—the really ludicrous aspect of all this is its
transparent element of slumming.

Phil McHugh doesn't hobnob with truck drivers and steel-
workers. He lives in burgeoning, expensive McLean. His peer
group is the 12 per cent on that little diamond chart. How does *he*
presume to know the precise manner of speaking down to those
social underlings? Magid, with his interest in art and the Kuna Indians of Panama and the symphony, is hardly a proletarian.
Whence comes his special insight into "the 80 per cent"? Coleman's only brushes with the laughing beer drinkers have occurred
on the Chicago elevated trains to and from work; he, like Daly,
lives in the exclusive suburbs, and when his fans from the common herd have approached him on the train to "do" his weatherman persona, Coleman, by his own admission, has recoiled.

Robert Wussler, the president of CBS, maintains a family
home in Winnetka, Illinois, and commutes to New York weekly.
Why? Because he wants to "keep the common touch; to know
what people outside New York are saying and thinking." Ho.
Have you ever been in Winnetka? Placed there blindfolded, you
would not be able to tell for sure, from the clinking of ice cubes,
that you were not in Scarsdale.

It is a beautiful picture: our great defenders of middle-class
needs, tastes, and interests, perched up there on the comfort of
their 12-per-cent bar, gauging the motivational pattern of the rest
of us by baiting a hook with a questionnaire and dropping it in the
waters of "lower-middle" and "upper-lower."

Phil McHugh and Frank Magid would argue that, through
their surveys, they *are* in fact discovering the true interests of the
public, and in doing so, are acting in the service of the Communications Act.

Such sophistry begs the question of the various levels of "interest" within a human being, the range of complementary and
contradictory needs any person may experience at one time.

It is human nature to turn toward pleasure and away from
pain; to prefer the sweet to the bitter; to respond to the cheerful
and shun the severe; to lament "all the bad news" in the media
and demand more "good news."

This is the level of human behavior on which the news consultant makes his entrance—and his exit.

The questionnaires cannot express the duality of human nature — not that the survey-takers would be inclined to deal with it if they did know how. The questionnaires cannot reconcile the respondent's willingness to be entertained *and* his active, legitimate, and proprietary curiosity as to the safety, the financial security, and the political state of the world around him, his demand for accountability among his leaders.

"What is it about the news on Channel 8 that you don't particularly care for?" asks a survey question, and in asking, it stacks the deck: for it implies that the news, like any other consumer commodity in America, can be restructured, improved, smoothed out, bolstered with miracle ingredients, and topped off with a hearty, rich flavor that the whole family will enjoy. Finger-lickin' good.

And that's the way it isn't.

RESEARCHTHINK:
THE RISE AND FALL
OF "AM AMERICA"

In early 1973, Frank N. Magid Associates embarked on television's version of the Manhattan Project.

Magid's client was the ever-covetous ABC Television Network. The mandate: produce the blueprints for a television program that would draw rating points away from the reigning lyceum of the TV network airwaves, NBC's "Today" show, with its $10 million yearly profits.

The methodology: cybernetic research.

It was an undertaking unrivaled in the history of television. Certainly, the idea of audience testing was nothing new. For years, prospective prime-time entertainment series, before hitting the airwaves, were routinely subjected to the tender mercies of "sample audiences" at test centers on the West Coast. Groups of men and women, selected at random from shopping centers and on the street, sat in darkened auditoriums and viewed "pilot" episodes of the fledgling shows. As they watched, they pulled or pushes levers attached to electronic graphs that recorded their "responses" to what they saw—whether they felt the impulse to laugh or frown, how much they liked each character, whether they generally approved of the total "package." This raw data was collated and delivered to network vice presidents, who could be found each spring worrying at their desks over strips and reams of what appeared to be readouts from seismographs—which, in a manner of speaking, they were.

Through the wonders of audience testing, such creations of manifest destiny as "Me and the Chimp," "Needles and Pins," "The Cop and the Kid," and "Planet of the Apes" found their way forever into the hearts and minds of America.

But this project was going to be different. This project was going to be to previous prime-time testing apparatus as the Apollo II mission was to the flight of Wrong Way Corrigan.

In the past, the testing came into play only after a given piece of work was completed. But in the case of "AM America," there would be no such variables in the completed piece of work. For the first time, the research would be an *integral part of the work in progress*. Nothing would be left to chance. Magid's minions, with their sophisticated questionnaires backed by that humming IBM 1130 computer out there in the Iowa meadow, would probe into the psyche of consumer America and uncover the mysterious chain of conditioned responses that would lead to the collective switching to the ABC channel at seven o'clock in the morning.

It was a brave, new, worldly undertaking indeed. . . .

Seldom in the annals of broadcasting have two more differing forces been arrayed against one another than in the case of "AM America" *vs.* the "Today" show.

It was the steam drill against John Henry; Astro Turf against infield grass; the urban planners against Piccadilly Circus.

The "Today" show is a comfortable vestige of the early days of television. A perfect tomato, ripe and lovingly cultivated, it has roots going deep into the soil of human intuition, enterprise, trial and error, tradition and continuity.

NBC is not innocent of audience research, to be sure; the network has perhaps the largest in-house research department in broadcasting. And the "Today" show staff is as fiercely competitive as any in television.

The point, however, is that "Today" had been allowed to develop, sharpen, and modify its personality over a period of years that stretched back to 1952, to the serendipitous era of Dave Garroway and his chimp, J. Fred Muggs. (Question: Would J. Fred Muggs have passed a modern personality-preference test? If so, would he have been history's first anchor-chimp?)

"AM America," by contrast, was coming in as the complete

cybernetic challenger. In comparison with the "Today" tomato, it was to be a hothouse hybrid, more perfectly round and of a hue scientifically predetermined to catch the consumer's eye. Magid's technicians were allotted two years to produce a blueprint that would have the same effect as (correction: a more efficient effect than) a quarter-century of natural growth.

Dennis Doty, then the brash and youthful (at 33) vice president of ABC's morning programming, and a man wholeheartedly at ease with the wisdom of cybernetic research, had no doubts that "AM America" would succeed where another assault on the "Today Show" had failed.

Doty had in mind the infamous experiment by the CBS Morning News, in August of 1973, with the unlikely anchor team of veteran newsmen Hughes Rudd and Sally Quinn, the glamorous Washington Post feature reporter. Following a graceless publicity buildup that suggested a personal rivalry between Ms. Quinn and the Today Show's Barbara Walters, Ms. Quinn endured six disastrous months of critical scorn and her own compulsion for malapropisms before retiring from the field.

Nevertheless, it was not the bungled show-business approach of "The CBS Morning News" that inspired Doty's disdain. The program, he told a reporter early in 1975, had erred in trying to counter-program "The Today Show" with an emphasis on journalism!

"AM America" would not be so naive. "AM America" would offer the sweet-toothed American public what it really wanted: more entertainment.

First, there was the small matter of determining the audience itself. Magid's expeditionary forces ventured forth—and came back with good news. ABC was in luck. There was a whole untapped morning-show population out there, a Lost Tribe of potential viewers not being reached by the "Today" show. Better yet, they were the very people that advertisers wanted; they were bona fide, card-carrying members of that most desirable group around, the 18-to-49 age group.

The "Today" show, the reasoning went, appealed mainly to an audience of women aged 50 and over—a group outside the mainstream of American spending. Therefore, the "AM America" counterpunch would not be more of what "Today" did best—news and news-related interviews and features—but kicky-trendy material of which the 18-to-49'ers are so fond. Pop people, fashionable people, new fads, as it was later to be expressed in another context.

A young audience naturally called for kicky-trendy hosts to match, and ABC plunged into a highly-publicized nationwide talent search for the genetically perfect blend of personalities, the ideal "chemistry," as it is charmingly called in the trade.

ABC executives studied hundreds of candidates. Out of the mix came three: Bill Beutel, then 43, the co-anchorman of the Channel 7 "Eyewitness News" team in New York; Peter Jennings, then 36, a lean and dashing newsman who had proved his mettle as Beirut bureau chief for ABC News; and Stephanie Edwards.

Ms. Edwards, who would eventually take the fall for the failure of "AM America," was in many ways the show's brightest promise. At 31, she had the requisite bright good looks—she is a tall, slim, red-haired woman with high cheekbones and flashing eyes—and she also had a proven record in a morning-show capacity similar to her "AM America" assignment: she had been co-host for three and one-half years of "AM Los Angeles" for KABC, along with Ralph Story. Crisply intelligent and humorous, Ms. Edwards had been trained as an actress and musician. By her own admission, she had limited experience as a journalist. But then, journalism was not to be emphasized. Stephanie Edwards was an inspired choice. A computer couldn't have done better.

As these personnel selections were being made, Magid's team was hammering and chiseling away at the show's concept. No nuance was overlooked for possible subliminal content. For instance, the research somehow determined that the colors orange and yellow were good "morning" colors—so various and sundry articles of the "AM America" set were done up in yellow and orange. These included the notebook paper for Stephanie and Bill. (Stephanie's hair, by one of those fortuitous strokes of nature, nearly matched her notepaper.)

Jennings would anchor the show's newscasts from Washington and would speak to Bill and Stephanie through a "news window" (sound familiar?). Bill and Stephanie would operate out of the ABC studios in New York. Would Bill and Stephanie sit behind desks, as TV hosts have done since Jack Paar descended from the trees? No, they would not. Desks, the Magid researchers declared triumphantly, were "authority barriers." Bill and Stephanie would perch on stools behind podiums.

It did not occur to Dennis Doty, or to anyone else on the ABC

staff, to ask for a definition of "authority barrier," or how such a
barrier would be overcome by a podium.

The blueprint expanded. Magid's surveys discovered, as they
had so often in the past, that Americans go gaga over celebrities.
A regular feature entitled "People" was decreed. Another maxim
held that viewers fall hard for practical information, such as home
economics and beauty tips. Another regular feature: "Coping."

An original musical score was commissioned and wrought in
the Standard Consumer-American Uplift genre of a hamburger
ditty or an airline fight song. Sam Ervin, the grandfather in the
successful daytime drama "Watergate," and John Lindsay, the
movie star, were hired to do political commentary.

The advertisers found it all too wonderful. The first three
months of "AM America" were sold, in advance of the premiere,
at $3,000 a commercial minute. ("Today" commanded rates of
over $12,000, but one must not be unseemly impatient. Wait a few
weeks.)

On Monday, January 6, 1975, this failure-proof epitome of
cybernetic technology, this electronic Big Mac, made its debut to a
waiting world.

On Tuesday, January 7, 1975, the following remarks appeared under my by-line in the Chicago *Sun-Times:*

> "AM America" is not a new television series; it is a new stage
> of human evolution. As I watched its premiere Monday morning
> on ABC, I had the strange sense that my television set was watching
> me as well: It knew, or thought it knew, exactly what sounds and
> colors and faces and personality mixes and thematic rhythms
> would please me the most, would make me the most disposed to
> march trancelike to the marketplace and buy Era detergent and
> Mazola corn oil.
>
>   . . . The two hours of its telecast Monday were an Orwellian
> tour de force. There was not one second of spontaneity; not one
> remark, one ad-lib, one gesture, on twitch was left to chance. From
> the careful timing of co-host Stephanie Edwards' opening giggle
> (my TV set wanted me to believe that she and Bill Beutel had en-
> joyed a casual, lighthearted joke a split second before air time) to
> the color of Stephanie's and Bill's note paper (orange, to match the
> orange sunburst behind them) to the researched and rehearsed
> wisecracks (Stephanie said that weathermen keep their money in
> cloud banks) to the stopwatch-segmented interviews ("Forty-five

seconds," Beutel muttered to guest Tom Corcoran), the program was marked by fake reality; by synthetic enthusiasm.

What other process could hit on trendy-kicky-handsome John Lindsay, the former New York mayor, as a "guest contributor"? Lindsay, presumably in the role of newsman, began an interview with British Home Secretary Roy Jenkins by introducing Jenkins as a man "who happens to be a very old friend of mine." And his first question was a capital specimen of investigative incisiveness: "What is your outlook on the state of the world?"

. . . Normal courtesy might require that a few days pass before any final judgments are handed down on a show such as "AM America," to allow "bugs" to be "shaken out." "AM America" is beyond such folksy considerations. It is a new and unsettling element in morning television. In a strange, Researchthink sort of way, it is beyond criticism.

But it was not beyond failure. Four months later Stephanie Edwards, the finest flower of a sophisticated nationwide search, was off the program. The ABC publicity department let it be known that she had left "to get married." Ten months later, the program that had been given a grace period of two years by ABC was—ah—neutralized, replaced by an entirely new format called "Good Morning, America."

The Manhattan Project had run true to its nickname. It had produced the biggest bomb in the history of television.

VICTIM: STEPHANIE EDWARDS

In the early spring of 1976, a year after she had departed "AM America," I met Stephanie Edwards for breakfast in the sidewalk cafe of the Century Plaza Hotel in Los Angeles. The giggling readhead who had seemed so giddy and frivolous as Bill Beutel's co-host was, I discovered, an intense and articulate woman, a serious professional who was an unlikely source of jokes about "cloud banks."

I asked Stephanie Edwards—who was both a creation and a victim of cybernetic research—to recall her experience with "AM America."

It wasn't all bad. There were interviews that worked wonderfully well, and there were moments on "AM America" that I'm proud of. But there were not very many. What I eventually came to realize was that they did not have any new ideas. If they'd had a new idea, I think they'd have done it . . . but the people who were responsible for putting "AM America" on the air literally did not have anything new to say. But let me back up a little bit and start at the beginning.

First, I should make clear that my very career in broadcasting had started out as a fluke. I came to California from Kenyon, Minnesota, aspiring to be an actress. And I learned that 99 per cent of the women out here were aspiring to be actresses. So I'd gone from being a secretary for an advertising firm to working for a Lutheran church to teaching modeling when I spotted Ralph

Story on KABC. I thought to myself: If there's a man who can help me find something, that's the man. I wrote to him — and he hired me as his secretary.

While I was working as his secretary, Ralph learned to know me well enough to feel that I had a performer's spark. So when KABC offered him this morning slot, which at that moment was sort of 90 minutes of bare air time for Ralph to fill whatever way he wished, he said to me, "If you like, let's do this thing together."

I was co-host of "AM Los Angeles" for three and a half years. It was the show that came to be, as I understand, the prototype for "AM America." When the ABC people in New York began discussing "AM America" — I guess they'd been chewing on the concept for a couple of years — they came out here to talk to Ralph and intimated that his show was the prototype they'd like to base it on. I was an observer at that point. Nothing was said to me about whether or not they would wish to use me — but eventually, by a kind of osmosis, I began to recognize that they were considering me.

This, I was to discover, was pretty much the way people communicated at "AM America."

Nothing was explicit. Nothing specific was mentioned at all. At first, I decided I was not available, because I had never felt particularly comfortable in a journalistic endeavor. But later I realized I might be looking a gift horse in the mouth — it might be the easiest route to finding where I did belong. So I contacted ABC and said, "If the job is still open, I would be very happy to talk to you about it."

Within a week they had hired me.

But the vagueness, the mystery never stopped. Even after I was hired as a co-host, I had trouble discerning what it was that ABC wanted me to do. They told me they wanted me basically to carry myself to New York and do what I'd already grown comfortable doing in Los Angeles. *We did not ever speak of particulars.* There was never any definition of whether or not I would do interviews or features, or whether I would review films or not. Whether I would write my own material or read whatever someone else wrote.

I was told as the weeks progressed toward air time that "it would all come together," and, "We do know what we want of you,

Stephanie, but at the time when we can begin to talk particulars we'll let you in on it. Right now we're involved in technical problems. We're dealing with how the set should be designed."

At that point, I began asking a question that I was to ask many, many times before we went on the air: "Wouldn't you like those of us who will be on camera to be involved in these meetings as well? Maybe we can help you figure out what would be a comfortable chair for the on-camera talent to sit on."

There was a resistance. And I think that part of it had to do with the research they had already done. Research that they kind of wanted to lock into. As I look back on it now, I believe—in fact, I know, because I've heard it several times—that there had already been a very tight summary and analysis made of me by Mr. Magid and his associates, telling ABC what my character was and how best it might be used. That research was never discussed with me.

To this day, I don't resent them for asking Mr. Magid to make that analysis. I do think they made an error in not bouncing it off me before we went on camera, so I would know either what they did expect of me or did not expect.

So I went on the air that first day, in January, having been through many hours of production meetings, *still not knowing what I was expected to do.*

There were hints of what was to come beforehand. Once, in all innocence, I ran across some files—I was trying to find some space for my own papers and books—in which there was a letter that was addressed to me, but that I'd never received. It was from a group of women ABC employees. It said, basically, "Stephanie, we've seen your closed-circuit introduction to our ABC affiliate stations. And we are concerned that, during the interview, you talked only about what kind of clothes you'd be wearing and how your hair would look and the lighter issues, while Peter and Bill were asked the heavier questions. We hope you won't let us down and that you will push for the discussion of issues as weighty as those discussed by the fellows."

Well. Pinned to the top of that letter *addressed* to me was a note from one of our executives to another saying: "I'll let you decide whether or not Stephanie should see this. I wouldn't want her to overreact. . . ."

Had I not stumbled on that letter, I never would have seen it.

So I think there was a secretiveness to a degree that was not necessary, and was indeed harmful, from the beginning.

That first day on the air — the one you reviewed so negatively — was a nightmare. I was told, I can't tell you how many times, to "have fun and relax." No one around me was relaxed. Indeed, I think everyone was as close to urinating on the stage the moment we went on the air as ever they were again. The production people. The minds behind the show. And I don't mean necessarily the floor producers, I mean the big minds in the sky — they were obviously petrified. And that fear showed itself.

I don't think they would have had to have been that frightened if they had sat down weeks before and admitted, "We have to have the 1-2-3's, *and we don't know how to do it.*"

I remember there was an amazing amount of concern over the most incidental questions. I had a pants suit on that first day and it came up gray instead of brown on the monitor screen. *Thirty seconds before I was on camera that stage was an absolute uproar* over Stephanie not being allowed to go on camera in a gray suit.

And there were other things that were of much more import. It was that kind of problem that continued, and I realized by March that my inquiries, suggestions, demands, and supplications were simply never going to be heard. I was horrified, and later infuriated, at the lack of ability to make a decision among those people who were hired to do so.

By this time, also, I had begun to get a lot of mail. I found that people all over America were not different from people in southern California; they wrote the same kind of letters. And they were very sharp, contrary to what you hear in the halls. They are not Neanderthals. They know the difference between a person who is being dumb because she is dumb, and a person who is a fish out of water because she's doing what she is not good at doing.

That was the one flaw. I think that was the basic problem. ABC decided to do things the way they did because they did not trust the audience to *identify*. They kept saying, "They'll not understand. The audience has to get to *know* you, Stephanie, before they'll *understand* that kind of remark, or that kind of an interview."

I can give you one example of this: I can remember specifically a feature that was written *for* me by one of the staff writers, having to do with calling women "persons." They used, as an example of how ludicrous the feminists' requests were, the fact that a song like "I want a person just like the person that married dear old Dad" just really wouldn't sound right.

And my angry response, after I read that feature, was that, one, it had nothing to do with the logic behind the request of the women's liberation movement or anything else. Women were simply tired of being called "chicks." Two, it was ill-written. Three, it was grammatically incorrect. It was a feature that, if I were to do it, would have been better written by me, from my point of view, rather than by a writer whose words I was supposed to mouth.

When push came to shove, I was told to either go on the air with that feature or not do the feature at all.

I could have easily written the piece myself, but for some reason they did not want it—even though one of the criteria for having hired me was that *they were impressed with my ability to write!*

I did it—to my undying distress. And I got letters. From people who said that the feature didn't make sense.

The people were writing, "Why are you doing that? Why do you look like this? Why are you sitting like you are stuck on the top of a flagpole?" I said to the ABC people: "You know, they are giving us suggestions. Why don't you listen to them, to the response from the people?" And the executive staff said, "Well, how many letters have you got there? Fifty? A hundred? Three hundred? *We've got surveys that were taken all over the country.*"

And there's no way you're going to fight that.

And here we were, on the air with a set that looked like a Buck Rogers reject, and it cost many thousands of dollars. It looked like it had been culled from some alleyway from behind a hardware shop, and I said, "Can't we at least put a plant on that set to warm it up?" They said, "No, Stephanie, this is not a local show any longer, this is a network show. *Plants look local!*"

Now, of course, David Hartman on "Good Morning, America" has to fight his way through what looks like a tropical rain forest.

But it was this preoccupation with that kind of minuscule piece of junk that prevented all of us from doing what that show really could have done: bring issues of substance to the public.

And if our mandate was to do something different from the "Today" show, surely, in wading into the same bailiwick, we'd better do something *better* or not be on the air. They were describing

"AM America" as vastly different from the "Today" show. Those of us on camera knew full well that we were not only pretty much like the "Today" show, but much less good at what they already did well.

And for someone like myself, who is not a producer, to see the realities of those simple facts—and then have highly-paid executives say, "That's not true"—was such a puzzlement, that finally, after the end of March, I just left. I knew there was nothing I could do.

"The news stories at the time," I pointed out to Ms. Edwards, "announced that you were leaving the show in order to get married."

Unfortunately, that was one of the pieces of publicity that was very early released. I'll go to my grave only having a guess at how it was released, and it's just too bad, because all that junk was not necessary.

When I finally was given permission to leave, I was asked not to discuss in particular why I was leaving. And I, on the other hand, made very strong requests that ABC would not release inaccurate publicity. Inaccurate publicity was very definitely released. I *did* get married—to Murray McCloud, who's an actor and musician. But that wasn't the reason I left "AM America." If a man had left a show like that, and at the same time married, there would have been no attempt to link the two events. Both my husband and I love this business, and we would really love to be a part of the best of it.

"Are you bitter?"

I'm fighting it, because I realize bitterness is really useless and, in fact, detrimental. But I do resent what happened, not only for my sake but for the sake of the public who tuned in, thinking they might see something innovative after 15 years—and I resent that one of the best opportunities to broaden television in the last 15 or 20 years was badly botched. I resent that on the part of all of us who invested so much in it, and on the part of the public, who, I think, was given a piece of drivel when there was really no good reason for it.

* * * * * * *

On November 3, 1975, ABC's great morning experiment returned to the airwaves in a more subdued, altered format. "Good Morning, America" seems to be making almost a conscious effort to disassociate itself from the taint of "newsiness." It features two former actors as hosts: David Hartman, a pleasant, low-keyed journeyman of several TV series, and Nancy Dussault, an amiable singer-comedienne in Broadway theater. (It fell to Ms. Dussault to report each moring's "People Poll," which dispenses such vital information as the fact that more Americans prefer chocolate ice cream than prefer vanilla. Or possibly vice versa. Perhaps it was that level of reportage which inspired Ms. Dussault to resign the show April twenty-ninth 1977 to resume legitimate acting.)

Regular contributors to "Good Morning, America" include Rona Barrett on gossip, columnist Jack Anderson on Washington inside-stuff, Geraldo Rivera as a roving "national correspondent," John Coleman as the visiting weather clown, and Erma Bombeck, whose repertoire of self-deprecating gags about middle-aged women is apparently inexhaustible. Except for a few flashes of conviction, mainly from Rivera and Anderson, "Good Morning, America" gives little evidence of having any purpose whatsoever for being on the air—which, apparently, was exactly the idea. It is militantly innocuous. True, certain "controversial" issues are "treated" from time to time on the show. They are in a manner of speaking, treated and released. "Good Morning, America" is the mucus that held commercials together. It is Paul Klein's L.O.P. brought to its ultimate. ABC is very pleased.

"Good Morning, America" might seem totally unrelated to any discussion of television news. (The show has no connection, for example, to the ABC News division, save for the half-hourly news feeds.) But in fact, the program's assumptions and techniques can be traced back along a line of continuity that has, as its source, the very origin of the team newscast itself. That origin— which in fact held high promise for the broadening of television that Stephanie Edwards desired—was, not surprisingly, within the ABC empire.

PRIME MOVER: AL PRIMO AND THE "BEAT SYSTEM"

The progenitor of "Eyewitness News"—the Prime Mover in the process of the local television newscast as it looks today—was a young news director with the prophetic name of Al Primo.

"Eyewitness News" hit the big time in November 1968 at WABC in New York (although, in keeping with its show-business heritage, it had had a successful tryout in Philadelphia).

In that month, in that year, as the laughing beer drinkers were setting about to elect a President who had campaigned by shrewdly manipulating their legitimate civic concerns, the newscast that would form the prototype for the cybernetic era was in its genesis.

Interestingly (in view of what soon happened to it), "Eyewitness News" in its original concept held high promise as a tool for useful television journalism. Primo, then 32 and a fast-rising innovator out of Pittsburgh, had a genius for making changes that boosted a news team's ratings *and* significantly improved the news product. It was Primo who broke local TV news out of its in-studio paralysis by pioneering the use of "beat" reporters, à la print journalism, to augment the Neanderthal anchorman-weatherman-sports format. It was Primo who insisted on specialists to cover specialized beats; Primo who hit on the idea of ethnically identifiable news personalities (he hired Geraldo Rivera, the Jackie Rob-

147

inson of TV news superstars) to cover news of interest to minority audiences; Primo who insisted on a neat, uniform appearance by the news team; Primo who first perceived that sloppy writing was a hidden detriment to many TV newscasts.

Innovative though he was, Primo could not claim the "news team" concept as his own for very long. He arrived in New York in 1968 to find stations there working on concepts parallel to his Philadelphia system. Lee Hanna, now an NBC executive but a CBS man in the sixties, was organizing the WCBS news department into a cadre of specialists: Earl Ubell as science editor; Jeanne Parr as consumer reporter; Jerome Wilson, a former New York state senator, as political reporter; Ed Wakin, a professor of education at Fordham University, as education editor; Chris Borgen, a former New York City detective, as police reporter; Leonard Harris as arts editor; Frank Gifford as sports editor; and so on.

"I created that staff," says Hanna. "We built the single largest local news staff in the country. It was my conviction that we had to get away from 'daybook' journalism—just keeping up with the agenda of events. Local news broke open in that year, and we helped make the break."

WNBC, in those days, was still several years from its golden age of "News Center 4." It had long enjoyed the status of New York's Number One news station—mostly through default—and had grown complacent in its success. "Before 1968," recalls Hanna, "NBC was Number One and CBS was Number Two. There wasn't a Number Three."

NBC's flagship station, therefore, was totally unprepared for the revolution in local news that soon took New York. WNBC reacted to the bewildering changes with the classic gesture of futility: it began shuffling anchormen. In the space of several months, each of the following personalities occupied the WNBC anchor desk: Gabe Pressman, Bill Ryan, Robin (now Robert) MacNeil, Frank McGee, Lou Wood, John Palmer, Sander Vanocur, Carl Stokes, Paul Udell, Jim Hartz.

In two years, CBS had unseated NBC as the top-rated news station in New York. In three years, ABC had moved from total obscurity to surpass everyone.

It was no discredit to Primo that his journalistic innovations were also highly marketable; that within two years of "Eyewitness

News'" startling success at WABC in New York, most of his ideas would be cross-pollinated with the new Happy Talk concept being pioneered at WLS in Chicago, thereupon to breed a generation of cliché: endless news teams, each with its uniform blazers, each with its own mustachioed local Rivera-derivative, each with its handsome, concerned "action" reporters out in the field, relaying snappily-worded capsules of inane information to the wryly-smiling anchor team, all tossing good-natured japes at the weatherman-card, all full of sound and fury, signifying . . . ratings.

I met with Al Primo in the spring of 1976, during his last days at ABC. Just eight years after he had scaled the heights with WABC's news team, turning it into the pre-"News Center 4" New York ratings leader, Primo was a forgotten man at the network. He had lost a couple of internal power struggles; he had developed major philosophical differences with Sheehan, the network's news president. He was disillusioned, but had the saving grace of a sense of humor. He was cleaning out his desk at 1330 Avenue of the Americas to embark on a new career: News consultant.

At 40, Primo looks and talks like a younger, thinner Hal Holbrook. The hair is prematurely white, the eyes dark and knowing. Seated behind his desk in a half-cleared office, Primo was still dressed in the uniform of the television executive: a charcoal pin-striped suit over a white shirt and noncommittal tie.

I was interested in the notion that most TV news executives developed their broadcast experience in the sales departments, and I started the interview by asking Primo whether that was true in his case.

I started out at a station called WDTV in Pittsburgh in 1953. WDTV was owned by the DuMont Television Network—shows you how far back *that* was. I started out there as a switchboard operator, newsroom assistant, copyboy, whatever. Within the year, I was working in the newsroom, doing everything that one did. There were only three people in the newsroom: me, the anchorman, and the cameraman.

I started out learning the trade from the people there—total television. I never had any print experience at all. I went out on stories, I did telephone checks, I did the police beat, the whole routine. In those days you filmed the stories, you edited the film, you put the film together, you worked with the director, you had exposure to every aspect and element of the televison broadcasting experience. I was a cameraman, I was an anchorman, I was a reporter, I was a producer, I was a director, I was a writer, assistant news director, news director, All of these things over a period of 12 years in Pittsburgh.

So to answer your question: no, I did not start out as a salesman.

In 1965 I went to Philadelphia, to KYW, and was news director there until 1968. That station, basically and really and truly, was where the "Eyewitness News" format came into being. And it came into being in a very interesting way. Through a quirk.

When you come to a television station as news director, the very first thing you do is pull out all the labor agreements, all the past history, and try to familiarize yourself with what the rules are, the ground rules, what you're committed to, what you're not committed to.

I found in the KYW contract that everybody in the news department belonged to the American Federation of Television and Radio Artists—AFTRA. Writers, reporters, producers, anchormen, sports men—*everybody*. And there was a master contract which said, among other things, that *any member of this union* could, in pursuit of news coverage, write, report, and present over the air news material without extra compensation over their base pay—which was, I don't know, $200, $300 a week.

Prior to this point in time in the history of broadcasting, anytime anyone went on the air, he had to be paid an extra amount of money—a small amount, $5 or $10 or $20, but when you add that up times five or six or ten times, it amounts to a lot of money.

In my experience, and I think in the experience of most television stations at that point, the only people who were ever on the air were the news person, the weather person, and the sports person. So the fees were kept to a minimum.

So I see this contract, and I say to myself: "*Wait a minute. Does this mean what it says?*" I called my lawyer in New York, the station's lawyer, and sent him the contract . . . and he said, "Yes, it does. What do you have in mind?"

"Well," I said, "I think that I'm going to be able now to use any person I want on the air." He said, "That's right."

That day, the day I got the permission to do that, there were

16 people in the news department. We had a meeting, and I said, "One person is going to produce the early news, one person is going to produce the late news, and one person is going to be the assignment editor — *and everybody else is going to be a reporter.* So, on that day, KYW got 13 reporters.

So here I was, in 1965, with 13 reporters, four film crews — an army! What to do with them? I decided to create a "beat" system, organized along print journalism lines.

I tried to find the guy who had the most contacts at City Hall, and he became the City Hall reporter. Another guy had medical/space interest; he became the science reporter. There was a labor reporter, a transportation reporter. . . .

I had a very long session with each and every reporter there. I said, "This is what we're doing. You're going to be given a reasonable amount of money to go out and take people to lunch, and I'm expecting you to work more than eight hours a day, to call people at home, and do the whole routine" — *and they did this!* They did this with an eagerness and an incentive, because when they got these stories on the air, they'd be on the air themselves. And lo and behold, we found that within a very short period of time — less than a month — we were breaking stories well ahead of the Philadelphia newspaper. We were filling a tremendous void in the Philadelphia community, because they had two fairly docile newspapers.

I tried to generate a certain amount of excitement in the community. I got into a little controversy with the city editor of the Philadelphia *Bulletin.* We used to call each other names. He'd say, "They're not really serious," and I'd say, "They haven't broken a story in years and we're going to show them how to do it." That sort of thing.

So that's how "Eyewitness News" began — largely as the result of this quirk in the contract. It led to a basic approach to journalism which I believed in and still do believe in.

We went on this way at KYW for three years. And then one day I got a call from someone at WABC in New York. He had heard about what I had done, and could I come up and talk to him. I did. Like any good newsman, I came a day ahead of time, looked the place over, watched the news — just got scared to death. Because I never saw anything so bad in my life.

ABC had a horrible reputation, even then, of not having a

commitment to news. So the general manager and I had a meeting, and I said, "What the hell would I want to come here for, with this kind of product? There's no commitment here; I can see that on the air." He said, "You don't understand. We *have* a commitment; we must win." This man, in effect, telegraphed to me that his job was on the line unless WABC improved. So I asked for a certain salary, and they said okay, and I came here. That was in 1968.

Now, let me tell you what it was like in those days. Roger Grimsby was already working here, as anchorman. It was Grimsby, Tex Antoine doing weather, Howard Cosell on sports, Rona Barrett doing what she does, and one other person from time to time who would do theater reviews.

It was jokingly called, "Roger Grimsby and the *Noise Makers*," and it was the most horrible, humiliating . . . I mean, I've never seen anything like it in my life. All these strange-looking people. Roger's a little strange-looking; Howard is certainly not the matinee idol; Rona, back in those days, was a little raggedy; Tex, with his red hair and his *smock,* and he used to have this artist's brush and that whole thing. Remember that?

So this is what I had. A zoo. It was a real zoo. I set about to decide how to approach this . . . problem. I told myself, "What a marvelous opportunity. I have no one here, but I do have the budget to go out and hire whom I want — so I can not only *have* 13 reporters, I can *hire* all 13 of them."

I set a couple of rules for myself: the only people I will hire at this station as reporters are people who have had at least ten years' experience in broadcast journalism, and who'd had anchor experience.

There were a lot of problems in that original group — Cosell, Grimsby, Antoine. First of all, Howard Cosell would only work the early news. And he would only be on the early news when he *could* be here, because he had baseball, football . . . so many days of our sports consisted of Howard Cosell on this very raggedy, tacky film that they used to film right in the newsroom: "A story From Howard Cosell." No scores, no nothing. That was our sports report.

We made a number of changes. One of the things, as I mentioned, was that everybody was so seedy-looking; this was a raggedy station. *And here's Tex Antoine with that smock;* that's part of his "image" and all the rest of it. So I said, "All right. We will buy dark blue jackets for everyone to wear so that there will be a certain uniformity." They could all wear their green pants or whatever; the audience couldn't see *that,* but they'd all have a nice look for what the audience *was* able to see. So we did that. Tex Antoine gave us a tremendous amount of trouble about this.

I always laugh about the Antoine business. I really, in fact, did say this, and I don't know how I had the smarts to say it at the time: Tex Antoine had said, "I can't do this. I can't spoil my image"; I said, "Tex . . . we're either all going to wear *jackets,* or we're all going to wear *smocks.*" Which is the funniest thing I've ever said. I still laugh at it.

So, at any rate, we began. And, as I say, there were lots of problems. Howard Cosell wasn't going to wear the jacket. Howard Cosell wasn't going to be there live. And finally I said, "Look, there's going to be one rule here: that no one is going to be on the air on film. We're going to approach this from a real point of journalism." And, of course, Howard liked to come around even then and say that he was the first *journalist* in sports reporting. And I just used to say, "Well, fine. Be that on the *air.* We'd love to have that. We *don't* want, 'I can't be here tonight because I have to speak' or 'I have to do a network thing.' *There's nothing more important to this company and to this station than this local news program.*" And that's the spirit that we built.

There was one other revolutionary thing we did on that station. For the first time on a local station, we had two men sharing the anchor role. It was done for very realistic reasons.

One reason was basically that Roger Grimsby projected such an I-don't-give-a-damn, seedy, nonchalant attitude, and had such a cold, austere look that I felt it was a major problem. The first thing I thought was, what the hell, let's get rid of him. No one was married to the fact that he was here. But I thought I saw in him something that was good. He was in fact a journalist. He was a good newsman and did have a certain dedication to what he was doing; he just had been shell-shocked and brain-damaged to the point where he just didn't give a damn.

So I thought, let's get someone who is exactly the opposite of Roger, and we'll put the two of them together and they'll read the news in tandem. Obviously, the Huntley-Brinkley thing was in my mind; I knew it had worked at NBC. So we hired Tom Dunn, who had been let go by WCBS. The two of them worked together fine, and we were on our way.

(I asked Primo at what point McHugh & Hoffman—the news consultants hired by WABC—became involved in the planning.)

I came to the station in September 1968. November 17 was when we had the set built, the reporters hired, and went on the air. Up to this point, *I did not even know we had a McHugh & Hoffman*. I guess the first inkling I had that there was a research organization came at a meeting in January. The manager called me in and said, "Hey, we've got these people, name of McHugh & Hoffman." And I said, "What are they and what do they do?" "Oh, they're researchers." "Well, call the research department." I didn't know what this was all about. They said, "No, they work with the news program. They're going to do a study of our program to see and measure its impact." And I thought, gee, maybe that would be good. So we had a meeting. They introduced themselves. Phil, Pete. Nice guys. They were very complimentary. The thing really looks good, first-class, nicely done, and so on.

Phil McHugh then began this attack on using reporters in the studio. He said, "There's one thing you have to understand and that is, you don't know anything at all about show business or this business, television. But I do. One basic premise is that you never supplant the star performer, and what you have done by putting all these people on the air is that you are draining the strength and impact of your anchorman."

And I said, "*You* don't understand. It's exactly the opposite. All these people in the studio are going to build the anchorman because the anchorman alone can't do it all by himself. We've already had the experience; we know he can't do it all by himself."

McHugh said, "Well, look, I'm just telling you. . . ." I said, "Fine."

I got through that meeting. I had to really go into a very strong attack mode to get through. After McHugh and Hoffman left, we agreed that they would do a study of the program. They did a study. Two or three weeks later, they came back with a big folder. "This is the impact of 'Eyewitness News,' and this is what's happening." A number of things came out of that.

One was that the audience was sensing that there was change in the air of WABC, and a positive one. We were being sampled.

Two—according to McHugh and Hoffman—was that Roger Grimsby cannot, based upon his "popularity charts," make it. They recommended that he be fired. Three: reporters in the studio aren't useful; in fact, they're screwing things up, and so forth.

When you looked at McHugh and Hoffman's report, and cut away all the jargon, *they were saying that this newscast was a failure.*

Okay, fine. They carried me out of the room quietly or whatever it was, and McHugh & Hoffman let us alone, and we did *not* follow their recommendation, which, in fact, was to tear down the "Eyewitness News" format as conceived and operated and developed at this station. That's how close this thing came to never existing, to being aborted.

It was incredible—and what happened next was even more incredible. Strangely enough, WABC allowed them to do an unprecedented third study, and on the third study, it came back that everything was terrific. McHugh & Hoffman said, "Yeah, well, you changed and that's great, and you have listened to our suggestions"—when, in fact, *we didn't do anything different.*

"Based on this experience," I asked Primo, "do you feel that news consultants are good or bad for television news?"

It may surprise you to hear this, but I think that consultants generally have been good for many television stations, because they have done a number of things. They have created an awareness of the importance of the news effort of a station to the news department and, as a result, have provided the incentive for stations to do better in their news.

So in that regard, I think they're just terrific.

It's a shame that this industry has had to have outside forces bring its attention to this vital area. It should have been for all of us in television to meet this public trust on our own, meet the responsibility head-on. But we didn't.

"Why not?" I asked.

Because—I don't know. I've never been in top station-management; I've always been in the news, a newsman. The general feeling is, it's been a big pain in the ass; it costs money, made problems with the sponsors, and all the rest of it. I think that is what the real reason is.

But back to the consultants. As far as the negatives are concerned, I think that in the desire to make news programs have a larger circulation, more watchability, the consultants have tended to concentrate not on the basics of journalism, but rather on the other elements connected with the programs. So it's entirely conceivable that consulting companies oftentimes would recommend as the anchorman some guy named Joe—an actor, a pretty face, not a journalist. I think there are enough dedicated journalists around to avoid that kind of approach.

I quoted to Primo Fred Friendly's characterization of the "complicated-dull" story, and asked whether consultants tended to steer stations away from that kind of journalism.

This is where I disagree with Fred Friendly tremendously. The type of story you have just described is what has *always* been the prime motivation for someone like me, and anyone who has ever worked as a news director. That's why we put people in City Hall; that's why we have investigative reporters.

There is no such thing as a complicated-dull story in television. There is no such animal as being dull about covering the way government operates. The trick is to find people with the expertise to illustrate, to visualize, to conceptualize, to tell the story. We've had a lot of bad writers in a very good medium.

There is nothing better than a man sitting there, live on camera, telling the viewer a very interesting, compelling story. You don't need "visuals" with it. You don't need pictures if it's right.

I don't think there's any question that a number of the things that we see today on local television news are a direct result of the input of television consultants, and the input is of little or no journalistic value.

I believe that the next thing in television news is going to be news. And, as a consultant myself, this is what I intend to suggest to my clients.

* * * * * *

There is some support for Primo's concluding optimism. Certain of the country's larger stations have, in the past two years, shown evidence of a renewed commitment to substantive journalism.

But the men who make the decisions in TV news are still hardheaded pragmatists, not crusading idealists. And within the arcane fraternity of broadcasters, only a broadcaster can appreciate fully just how coolly and ruthlessly these decisions get made.

"SALESMEN SELLING SALESMEN": AN INSIDER SPEAKS

We will call him Ishmael.

In 1976, he was one of the most dramatically successful broadcast executives in the United States. He had assumed control as station manager of a network-owned operation that had for years been a punching-bag for its competitors. Within a year, Ishmael had turned the station into a highly profitable winner.

He achieved his success by an outrageous combination of talent-raiding, ferociously aggressive promotional campaigns, and a highly sophisticated system of audience research that he had devised with the help of his youthful, brilliant staff.

Ishmael is far from an altar boy in the back-alley brawls of broadcast competition. He is a quick, tough, arrogant, intelligent, and supremely confident veteran of the ratings wars; a nomad, a soldier of fortune who has taken on challenges at several stations and won more than he has lost. A large man, still young after 20 years in the business, he has shrewd, owlish eyes, a booming broadcaster's voice, and a habit of slapping his desk to emphasize his frequent pitches of anger and humor.

He has no illusions about the realities of airwave competition. He accepts cybernetic research with the fatalism of the born pragmatist — but the hustler in him sees beyond even the slick pretensions of the major research firms themselves. He will deal with them — and has — but he knows when to draw the line.

On the stipulation that his real name not be used — his parent network employs some of the big firms at various points in its corporate structure — Ishmael agreed to provide an insider's appraisal of cybernetic news.

You asked me why stations need to hire news consultants in the first place, when presumably the men running TV news departments know something about journalism. Let me answer you this way: without a shadow of a doubt, broadcasting is the worst-managed major industry in the country. Stop and think about it. You are given a limited monopoly. The product is in high demand. Television stations in major markets make a 30 to 40 per cent profit. Radio stations make 50 to 60 — 100 per cent profit in some cases. In terms of return on captial investment, it's unbelievable: 50 to 60 per cent net profit on sales!

Does it sound like I've just made a contradiction — broadcasting is mismanaged and yet highly profitable? Listen, you've got to be an idiot — *a raving idiot* — to lose money in television. I mean, some of the biggest idiots in the world run television stations.

I'm not kidding you. Because what happened was, in 1948, all the big newspapers applied for TV-station licenses, and when they got them, they said, "Oh my God, we've got this new toy over here and what are we going to do? Look, George is a drunk and he's not doing too well in the classified department. Have him go over and sell some television time." And then ten years later, George was the general manager of the television station supporting the newspaper. That's exactly what happened.

It was like any tremendous growth business. The people in it, all of a sudden, were getting these fantastic ratings and were unbelievably successful, and they said, "Oh, look how smart I am." Not "How lucky I am to be here," but "How smart I am." The people at the Harvard Business School will tell you that, generally speaking, the top management people in television and radio are *just now* getting into professional management sciences and that sort of thing. That's one of the major points of the whole story you're after: they are incredibly poor managers, and their instinct is to turn to outside research.

Now, the best audience research is research that reflects people's behavior. *Not* what they *say* they want; not what they *say*

their attitudes are, because people lie to you. The first part of au
dience research, the quantitative part, the demographics of it, is
easy. Nielsen and the American Research Bureau do a good job
on that. When you get into qualitative matters is where you get
into terrible problems. It is the most difficult kind of research to
do.

So here's where the problem comes in: many of the executives in this business come out of sales. Most of them. And salesmen have learned to manipulate research to suit their own needs.
That's their job. I mean, I would not hire salesmen who could not
manipulate research to sell time because that's all research is for,
really. That is the kind of stuff the ad agencies want. They are the
ones who say, "We want to know how many people 18-to-49 are
watching. Or listening." So we pay for the research, and we give it
to the agencies. *But I wouldn't hire salesmen who didn't have enough
sense to manipulate the research in order to go out and sell time.*

I asked Ishmael exactly what he meant by "manipulate."

It's just exactly what the newspapers are doing with "Markets
in Focus." You write for the Chicago *Sun-Times.* Okay. Well, the
Chicago *Tribune* will run a double-page ad in *Advertising Age* that
will say, "We're Number One in Chicago." Well, pretty soon the
Sun-Times will come out: "Number One in Chicago." What they're
doing is playing with figures and facts, to make themselves look as
positive as possible. Maybe the *Tribune* is Number One in the total
market area, and the *Sun-Times* is Number One in the city itself.
So they both have a claim to "Number One."

In broadcasting, a salesman can take a rating book and say,
"See? We're Number One in audiences 18-to-49." His competitor
can say, "See? We're Number One in audiences 18-to-34, and
that's a more powerful buying group." Manipulating.

My point is that salesmen are trained to use research to reinforce their position. Okay? That's the point I'm making.

Now, a salesman becomes a station manager. What is he
trained to do? He is trained to use research to reinforce his own
position. So if he has a gut feeling that he needs a new anchorman

for his eleven o'clock newscast, and the research comes up and says, "You need a new anchorman for the eleven o'clock newscast," why, that manager says, "Of course!" He's just seen some research that corresponds to his own built-in bias.

Take it a step farther: outside consultants, primarily, are *also excellent sales people*. Frank Magid is one of the slickest salesmen who ever lived. That *ever* came down the pike. Willis Duff of Entertainment Response Analysts is one of the slickest salesmen you would ever want to talk to. I mean, he will sit down and tell you about ERA and the galvanic skin response and how it works and what it means and the whole thing and you're *mesmerized*. You feel like you are *crazy* not to take it. He has given you the greatest opportunity of your life to make millions of dollars for your business. The same thing is true of the McHugh & Hoffman people. Peter Hoffman went to Dartmouth, and he's a very well-educated, a very slick guy.

But they're *salesmen* first. So you've got a *salesman selling a salesman!* And one thing that salesmen are trained to do is find out what the guy they're selling to wants. There is this subtle little gyroscope inside that tells a salesman just what his client wants. A good salesman can sit down across from a guy and read him like a book inside of 15 minutes.

So the research people will interview the station manager. Then they'll interview his staff. The department heads. *Then* they put their researchers in the field, and it is fascinating to see just how reinforcing the data is that comes back. Fascinating.

What do I think of Magid and McHugh & Hoffman? In my opinion, ABC is crazy to pay for them. Research companies have systems, just like anyone else. Once you get the system down, you know that 90 per cent of the surveying is going to show consistent truths. So you just organize. It's the McDonald's principle. Once you get something that works, you organize it beautifully. Standardize the parts. It's mass production.

I will say this in defense of the big research firms, and it is an extremely important point: the ultimate responsibility for the quality of a newscast, or a total station, lies *not* in the research, but *in the interpretation of it and the way management uses it*. That, plus execution. That's more critical than anything else. I think the most common misuse of research is in the fact that a station manager will take it literally. A summary of recommendations might say something about, "Many stories can be done effectively in less than 90 seconds." And a memo will go around the newsroom: "NO STORY IS TO LAST MORE THAN 90 SECONDS."

The suggestions become ironclad, and that is crazy. You see, most of these station managers don't have the confidence of saying, "Well, this part of the Magid report is useful, and the rest of it is crap." They can't throw the crappy half away. And this gets us back to our point of salesman-selling-to-salesman: the consultant gives the general manager what he wants.

The consultant tends to be the reinforcement of the desires of management.

There is nothing immoral in using research. There is nothing immoral, there is nothing sinister, about putting something in a very attractive package. Where you can criticize a network or a station—where I do, in fact, criticize ABC—is when they go a step too far. When they start making decisions on news based primarily on its attractiveness.

"What," I asked Ishmael, "do you think the next big phase of market research in broadcasting is going to be?"
"Better," is all he answered.

"...SUCH ANGER!": BARBARA WALTERS

Early in 1976 the emerging national debate over television news as show business coalesced around one personality: Barbara Walters.

In April of that year, Ms. Walters—who for 12 years had been a principal member of NBC's "Today" show "family"—resigned to join ABC as co-host of the "Evening News" with Harry Reasoner. Her position (as the first regular anchorwoman in the history of network television), her salary ($1 million a year under a five-year contract), and her public image as celebrity-in-her-own-right (highest-rated substitute host of the "Tonight Show Starring Johnny Carson," sometime luncheon partner of Henry Kissinger) all blended into a single and powerful symbol of TV news's drift toward entertainment.

The brotherhood's most sagacious chieftains themselves beheld the symbol and were sore afraid. CBS's Walter Cronkite, for years a gallant defender of the integrity of television news, and normally the most courtly of men, set the tone for qualified Solomonic rebuke. "The Barbara Walters news did shake me up at first," he told a CBS affiliates conference in New York shortly after Ms. Walters' salary was announced. "There was a first wave of nausea, the sickening sensation that we were going under, that all of our efforts to hold network television news aloof from show business had failed."

Cronkite went on to acknowledge that "after sleeping on the matter, with more sober, less hysterical reflection, I came to a far less gloomy view of the matter." With what might be interpreted

163

as tending toward faint praise, he pronounced Ms. Walters' qualifications as "not all that lacking—it is not as if ABC had hired a
singer, dancer or ventriloquist to share the 'Evening News' duties
with Harry... She is an aggressive, hard-hitting interviewer. She
does her homework."

Nevertheless, the terrible label "show business" had been uttered and hung around Barbara Walters' neck. For Cronkite, the
reservations probably had less to do with Ms. Walters' sex or her
salary than with her credentials for admission to electronic journalism's Olympus.

Walter Cronkite and the men of his generation, who came to
television news after years of grassroots training in the honorable
field of "print," regard as interlopers those who ascend to the anchor without such apprenticeship. (In many celebrated cases, this
point of view is highly justified; as witness the almost militant vapidity of WABC's preening Tom Ellis or the high-school forensic
overkill of his former anchor-partner Bill Bonds, since banished
to the Detroit from whence he came.)

"Her background is not what I would call well-rounded," ex-
UPI ace Cronkite candidly submitted to the affiliates. "—newspapers, press services, the police, county courts, statehouse beats.
But," he conceded, "who is to say that there is only one route to a
career in journalism?"

Cronkite also allowed for a certain amount of "hypocrisy" in
linking Ms. Walters' salary to the threat of "show business." "My
friends," he said, "if salaries alone are the criterion, we in television news have been in show business a long time...."

But Walter Cronkite's carefully balanced demurs had little
counterpart in the rest of the journalism community—either electronic or print. Most people reacted as though a topless dancer
had just been appointed to the Supreme Court.

"Yecch," muttered Richard Salant, CBS News president. He
added: "I'm really depressed as hell. This isn't journalism—this is
a minstrel show. Is Barbara Walters a journalist or is she Cher? In
fact, maybe ABC will hire Cher next. If this kind of circus atmosphere continues, and I have to join in it, I'll quit first."

Even august Fred Friendly, hardly the stereotype of a male
chauvinist pig, could not resist a reproving cluck: "We make all
kinds of statements about the right of the public to be informed.
Those things can't get mixed up with million-dollar-a-year per-

sonalities. It's sort of a throwback to the days of Walter Winchell, when news was done by name people with a lot of money—but there wasn't much journalism in it."

Ms. Walters' colleague-to-be, Reasoner, was reported to have considered quitting. A salary raise, extending his own $400,000-plus compensation, quenched that desire, but it did not stop Reasoner from moaning about injured "personal pride." From John Chancellor, who might have found himself sharing anchor duties with Ms. Walters had she remained at NBC, there came equally vague intimations of threatened mutiny (Liz Smith, writing in the New York *Daily News*, reported as much in an "exclusive" column.) For the record, Chancellor said, "Happily, I didn't have to do any soul-searching on the question."

The flow of sarcasm poured in from unexpected sources. *The New Yorker* magazine, that soul of civilized compassion, that torch of considered reason, published a cartoon of Walters in a chorus line, holding a hand mike and telling viewers, in mid-kick, of the latest news from Beirut.

And Pulitzer Prize–winning cartoonist Paul Szep, in the Boston *Globe*, caricatured Ms. Walters (who was reared in Boston and attended Sarah Lawrence College) as a torchy tease in a low-cut evening gown, holding a script captioned "Barbie's Evening All Newsy Show, With Harry What's His Name." "Barbie" was saying, "But first, a word from *my* sponsor."

Most scabrous of all were the newspaper headlines. As Judith Hennessee put it in the July/August 1976 issue of *(COLUMBIA JOURNALISM REVIEW)* magazine, newspaper coverage generally "left the reader with the erroneous impression that Walters, not ABC, had set the fee."

"BARBARA LEAVES JIM FOR HARRY," giggled the San Francisco *Examiner. Newsweek* styled her as "THE $5 MILLION WOMAN" (which, as Hennessee pointed out, brought to mind two ABC potboilers, "The Six Million Dollar Man" and "The Bionic Woman"). *Newsday* called it "THE NEWS, STARRING BARBARA WALTERS." Even the staid *Christian Science Monitor* could not resist a deaconly simper at its subject's gender: "TWO NETWORKS WOO BARBARA WALTERS."

It was left to the New York Daily *News*, however, to summon up the ultimate condescending graffitous: "DOLL BARBIE TO LEARN HER ABC's."

✳Coldly true to form for network competition, NBC, the organization Ms. Walters had served so long, bothered little to discourage this accelerating public ridicule. To the contrary: after NBC News president Richard Wald had tried to retain his star with a series of hastily improvised counterproposals, and after she announced her final decision, NBC suddenly turned abstemious. The network let it be known that it had "pulled out" of negotiations before Ms. Walters made up her mind because it was offended by the "carnival atmosphere" being created. (Salant's circus is Wald's carnival.) NBC sniffed that its ex-employee's demands "were more fitting of a movie queen than a journalist." The demands in question, said the network, included a hairdresser, limousine, and press agent. (NBC never did explain how those "demands" could be reconciled with the fact that Ms. Walters already had one of each.)

Clearly, Barbara Walters was looking down a double barrel of public (or media) opinion. One barrel was labeled "Show Business." The other was labeled "Women." Symptomatic of the times and of the industry, the two barrels tended to fuse.

If Barbara Walters was the most publicized anchorwoman of 1976, she was not alone in her hazing. In the last two or three years, the important question of news-as-show-biz had repeatedly been reduced to a discussion of women's place in the news. CBS's 1974 experiment with Washington *Post* reporter Sally Quinn, as co-host of its "Morning News" (and the attendant hysteria of her imagined Armageddon with Ms. Walters) is aready a legend, an epic travesty. Stephanie Edwards' Ordeal by Silence at ABC was another chapter in the same epic.

Such nationwide farces overshadowed the fact that, in every major American television market, local anchor positions were suddenly being offered to women on an unprecedented scale. That market research helped clear the way for such hirings by discovering that women anchors were "acceptable" to viewers, there can be no doubt.

ABC officials insisted that Frank Magid had nothing to do with testing the market prior to the hiring of Ms. Walters. Be that as it may, the move was classic Magid: the bold, extravagant, highly visible, "personality"-oriented gesture, rather than any systematic, patient attempt to improve structural or organizational weaknesses in the news division. ABC had one "weakness," and one "weakness" only: it was third in the ratings. Irrespective of her legitimacy as a journalist, Barbara Walters was acquired to repair that weakness.

ABC News president Sheehan himself gave the lie to any question of higher purpose in the selection of Ms. Walters. Magid may not have dictated the move, but even so, Sheehan announced, ABC *had* commissioned "a series of surveys" that analyzed the reactions of sample audiences to the hiring of a female anchor. One sample, he said, showed 20 per cent of the audience in favor, 10 per cent against—and an imposing 65 per cent that did not care. With the leap of logic that is peculiar to the cybernetic mentality, Sheehan concluded: "We figured that added up to 85 per cent of a potential audience."

* * * *

Since about 1970, citizens' groups have been discovering a previously obscure tool for making TV stations receptive to public demands: the license challenge. Station licenses are renewable every three years (the specific renewal year differs according to regions of the U.S.) and the renewal is granted, at least in theory, only after a station has demonstrated to the FCC that its programming has met the public "interest, convenience and necessity."

Station licenses had been challenged on infrequent occasions down through the years, on a variety of complaints. Few challenges were successful, but the very specter of the license challenge and its long-shot potential for turning off a station owner's profit-spigot had a chilling effect (or, to be more accurate, a thawing effect) on stations' restrictive practices.

In 1970, citizen "watchdog groups" in a number of American cities began challenging broadcast licenses on the basis of inequality in hiring practices.

This trend—accompanied by "affirmative-action" programs throughout industry, the advent of the Equal Employment Opportunities Commission, and women's heightened self-awareness generally—sped the dissolution of the all-male enclave in broadcast journalism, and opened the ranks to women reporters and anchors: Melba Tolliver and Norma Quarels in New York; Jane Pauley, Terry Murphy and Susan Anderson in Chicago; Sandy Hill, Christine Lund/and Diana Lewis in Los Angeles, to name a few. (Pauley, of course, has since moved on to "The Today Show"; Quarels to Chicago, and Hill, away from Los Angeles's KNXT.)

The curious thing about women's ascendancy in TV journalism is the degree of hostility they have encountered among critics as well as their male colleagues. Granted that the sins of motivational research apply as much to women as to men — only the most beautiful are hired, and no one looks too closely at Cronkite's standard of "credentials" — still, many critics react as though women alone are the interlopers, as though the very *presence* of a woman on a newscast constitutes a sellout to show business. Thus Jane Pauley was scored by a Chicago critic, weeks before her debut on the air at WMAQ, as "having the IQ of a cantaloupe." ("I looked in the mirror and cried," the rather extraordinarily self-contained young woman admitted later.) On the air, anchorwomen are often presented with bouquets by weathermen-clowns seeking to make a baggy-pants comic's point about femininity.

Into this sunlit garden, in the summer of 1976, stepped Barbara Walters.

Her apartment, in an old but graceful building not far from the television plexus in midtown Manhattan, does not reflect the personality of a Barbie Doll or a chorus-line kicker. The living room is comfortably dark and substantial, anchored by a grand piano in one corner and a cluster of tall, potted plants diagonally opposite. The furniture — mostly small, black-and-white patterened sofas — is clustered in intimate, right-angle groups about the room.

The glass-topped coffee table adjoining the sofas nearest the window is heavy with jeweled cigarette cases, music boxes and, on this day, a vase of one dozen fresh yellow roses. Around the room, displayed with a sense of pleasure rather than ostentation, are some other mementos of Ms. Walters' travels with the "Today" show: a grouping of miniature earthenware jugs, one of which bears the inscription: "To Barbara Walters, All Best Wishes, Moshe Dayan — 4000 B.C."

On the wall, are a signed Andy Warhol dancing slipper and a signed Calder print.

Scattered on the various coffee tables are commemorative medallions from Russia and Greece, a crystal camel, a turquoise elephant, a few intricate antique clocks. Propped up on the surface of the grand paino are 20 or so black-and-white snapshots of Barbara Walters with her relatives — principally, her eight-year old adopted daughter, Jacqueline. Opposite the piano, on a round table, is an outsize apothecary jar filled with candy in twisted wrappers.

The bookshelf, which covers the wall at one end of the living room, is filled with titles that are respectable almost with a vengeance. There are volumes of Chaucer, Ibsen, Balzac, Thackeray, Swift. There is a life of Renoir. There are *The Second Sex* and *How to Raise a Human Being* and *Wines and Spirits* and Bishop Fulton J. Sheen's *Life of Christ*. There is — for mad reading, possibly — *Haji Baba*.

I visited Ms. Walters during the week of the Democratic National Convention in New York. She had completed her duties for NBC, and would not assume the ABC assignment until September. The subject of TV news-as-show-business was very much on her mind, as was the subject of women's treatment in electronic journalism. Just a few weeks previously, her long-time colleague on the "Today" show, Frank Blair, had added a sour-tempered denunciation of Ms. Walters to the already blazing bonfire. From his retirement home in South Carolina, Blair had grumped that Barbara Walters was cold, hostile, no fun to work with, and that NBC was glad to be rid of her.

Now, dressed informally in a lime-colored cotton pants suit, a bandanna wrapped about her head in lieu of a coiffure, Barbara Walters sat in her living room and nibbled at a celery stick coated with onion dip as she sorted out her feelings about the tumultuous past months.

"It staggered me when Frank said what he said," she began, speaking softly, "but it didn't amaze me.

"I know that Frank was bitter. I think he was bitter about the show — and, I think, particularly bitter about me and my success. After all — well, he knew me when I was a *writer*. You know: 'Why should she make it and not I?' We were friendly enough on the show, I thought, but we were never very close friends off camera.

"I called him after it happened. I said, 'Frank, *why* did you do this?' I said, 'You lived in South Carolina for a whole year. How do you know how NBC feels about me?' He said, 'That's what I heard.' I said, 'Frank, do you know they offered me the same kinds of things that ABC did?' He said, 'Well then, why did you leave?' And I told him. I said, 'There was *this* opportunity, there was *that* opportunity. . . .' And he said, 'Well, I'm not the only one. Have you seen the cartoons about you, you're fair game.' I said, 'Frank, the day I left the show you sent me flowers.' He said, 'Yeah, you know how much those flowers cost?' And I laughed and said, 'Look, never mind.'

"I think he was bitter about the show, and I think the fact that this *girl* should make it. . . ."

Barbara Walters hesitated, as though she were reluctant to continue the thought toward its obvious, political conclusion. Through her years at NBC, Ms. Walters had kept silent about her ideas on the condition of women in broadcasting. But Frank Blair's gratuitous broadside had apparently crystalized a number of accumulated resentments. With a certain studied matter-of-factness in her voice, she went on.

"That episode hurt me. And it hurt me because if it had been something *nice* Frank had said, it wouldn't have been in all the papers. If it had been something about Jim Hartz or Gene Shalit, it wouldn't have made any of the papers. But because it was *me*. . . ."

She paused, head lowered, and scraped at the onion dip for several seconds. She was down near the nerve now, worrying at the edges of old wounds.

"I think," she said at last, "that there is this image, in part sustained by the press, of my being very cold and very difficult.

"I *am* aloof. I *don't* become very friendly. I don't drink; I'm not a drinking buddy. Frank loves to drink a little bit. But I can't offer that kind of camaraderie. As I said, I can appear cool, aloof . . . I am somewhat shy."

Barbara Walters glanced up, and for a moment there was a trace of defiance in her gaze—an oddly anomalous quality in the temperament of a woman paid $1 million a year for her ability to attract viewers to a network. A vulnerability.

"Look," she said. "When I left the 'Today' show we got 5,000 letters. 'Wherever you are, we'll watch you.' So supportive. And this business of, 'Gee, she's so cold,' and, 'Gee, she's so aggressive,' I think that's the kind of thing that's come up because I'm a woman; because I was the *first* woman to really go in there and ask some tough questions." She gave a shrug. "A lot of people don't believe I'm so tough. Tom Snyder said, "I don't think you're so tough. I think you're too *easy.*'

"I think it was because I was very *businesslike* on the 'Today' show. 'Aggressive,' perhaps, is the wrong word. 'Businesslike'—it's the first time I ever used it. I *wasn't* just a girl who was there to be cute and charming."

What came next was a startlingly blunt appraisal of someone soon to be her network colleague.

"Now," she was saying, "I look at 'Good Morning, America' on ABC, and they have Nancy Dussault, who is lovable and sweet and warm. But there's no *businesslike*, there's no *crispness*, nobody takes her too seriously. *Most* of the women on television shows are like that—somewhat in the pattern of Dinah Shore.

"And *here*"—fingers flying back to tap her shoulders—"was a woman who was crisp and cool and businesslike, and they thought, 'Aha! Therefore she has to be ice cold' . . . and I think that is why the Frank Blair thing hurt me so much. Because I thought, *this is what* people are going to think."

I reminded her of Walter Cronkite's speech to the CBS affiliates.

Barbara Walters nodded. "I felt bad about that," she said, "because . . . first of all, Walter Cronkite gets three months a year vacation. Does anybody complain about that, or say he's not entitled?

"Look, there is one thing about my salary contract that has not been made clear. Let's say Cronkite makes $400,000 a year; I believe that's about right. Every time he does anything else—space shots, election-night coverage, conventions, radio, special interviews—*for every single one of those things he gets paid extra.* I don't know what Cronkite's total salary is, but I dare say that it is not too far below mine. Plus three months' vacation. Great! He deserves it! And Walter Cronkite, of all the correspondents, of all the anchormen, is a kind and lovely man.

"But *nobody* is going to talk about my working hard. My base pay for anchoring the ABC news will not change, no matter how much extra I do. Who else does 12 'Issues and Answers,' one every month? Who else is doing four prime-time specials? And whatever I do, I won't get any more money. That's it. That's the blanket fee. I'm not *complaining* about it. But, I mean, this *anger,*

this . . . 'Who does she think she is?' . . . You would not have had
that with a man. And this business of, 'Oh, she's going to be show
biz.' " Barbara Walters raised her eyes again, and again there was
in them the trace of defiance, at least a wariness. Her visitor, after
all, was a man. And Barbara Walters—undoubtedly like countless
other, less famous women in broadcasting—has kept to herself
her reactions to male jealousy, to male condescension. Now the
feelings were beginning to spill over, and the voice was taking on
an edge.

"Why?" She demanded. "*Why* show biz? If you make
$500,000 a year as an anchorman, that's *not* show biz? I mean, you
know, the *hypocrisy* of it all." She jabbed another celery stick into
the onion dip.

"It is *still,*" she went on, "in this day and age, such . . . *anger.* I
have, in many ways, bent over backwards not to wave the feminist
banner. I thought of it this week at the convention: I didn't go to
any of the women's caucuses; I don't want to be categorized just in
that orbit.

"But there still is this picture of the strident female: 'Who
does that bitch think she is?'—and that's what comes out."

I recalled an interview with some "Washington wives" during
the time of the Representative Wayne Hays—Elizabeth Ray scandal. In it, the wife of Supreme Court Justice William O. Douglas
observed that although women have learned to regard men in a
professional sense, men cannot yet deal with women in any way
other than a personal sense.

"Well, I think so much of the reaction to me when I made the
switch to ABC was personal. Suddenly all my credentials were examined. Is she a journalist? All the years of the Kissinger inter-
veiws, the Nixon interviews, the Haldeman interviews—everything I'd done: Cuba, China—that was all down the drain.
Suddenly I was a female showgirl. They immediately believed the
makeup and the hairdresser and the limousine, even though, logically, they knew it had to be untrue. . . ."

I was considering Barbara Walters' remark about not waving
"the feminist banner." For much of her career, I pointed out to
her, there was no feminist banner to wave. Without having had
the benefit of foresight in the early years—without knowing such
a cause as "feminism" would be institutionalized—did it rankle
her that she was placed in a special category, that of the "girl interviewer"?

"It didn't rankle me then. It rankled me later on, when I was excluded from the serious interviews on the 'Today' show. Frank McGee, when he was host of the show, had an agreement with the producer: he had the right to say *what interviews he wanted to do*. I didn't; I was *assigned* interviews. He could pick any interviews he wanted to do; let's say, four interviews a week—which meant that he could take the four major political interviews.

"Furthermore, in an interview in Washington, where we would be talking to somebody in our Washington studio and where they are almost always political interviews, *Frank could decide whether or not I would participate*. And if he decided I would, I couldn't *unless or until he had asked the first question*. And if he did not ask the first question, or if he chose not to ask a question [allowing the NBC News correspondent to do so instead], I could ask one.

"This never showed on the air.

"And that is why I used to go out on my own and get my own interviews. I got Haldeman, Nixon, Dean Rusk, Kissinger that way. I got them when nobody else could get them. I would take the film crew, I would edit the film, and bring it in.

"If the guest came into the studio, I would be excluded. If I *arranged* it, and the guest came into the studio, the interview would be done by Frank McGee or Hugh Downs, and I would *join*.

"It was only if I went outside the studio and got the interview myself that I ever had the opportunity to *do* it myself. And that's why I tried so hard to get them, and that's where I gained the impression of 'She's so aggressive, she's so pushy.' "

"The question of your salary aside," I asked her, "do you think there is any merit to the charge that television news is entering the realm of show business?"

She gave a curt nod. "We saw some of that this year during coverage of the presidential primaries: NBC spending what they said was $50,000 just to make a *set*— a mobile set to take from New Hampshire all the way through to California. Now, they didn't *have* to, they could have gone in and used whatever set there was. But there was this wonderful, red-white-and-blue set that must have cost them several hundreds of thousands of dollars to move every time they did it. By the end of the primary, it must have cost them a million dollars just to have this glorious *set*. What is that? Is that show business or is that news?

"Look. As soon as you *talk* about television, and people who put on makeup and go on the air, you are talking about people who are to some degree performers. When David Brinkley tells a littel anecdote and laughs at the end of it, he's obviously heard the anecdote before; that laughter is the laughter of someone who is to a degree doing a performance.

"Tom Snyder considers it all show business. He asked me, 'What if you find out that the role, as called for on ABC, is a role that should be played by a man?' That was one of the things that troubled me; it was on my mind when I asked the very first question that I asked of Bill Sheehan: 'How do you know that a woman will be accepted?' He mentioned a poll that amounted to the fact that 85 per cent of the audience either liked a woman or didn't feel that it made any difference. And it was not until that poll was taken that they felt comfortable about hiring me."

Has she herself ever seen the results of an audience research survey?

"In a peripheral way. NBC, this past year, did a long study on the 'Today' show to find out how people were accepting it. And it was at that point that they found Jim Hartz was not as well accepted as he should have been. His days were numbered from that point."

"What form did that research take?" I asked.

"They just asked thousands of people two things: one, which feature do they remember most on the 'Today' show, from one half-hour to another (and they had to be careful, because many people watch one half-hour but not another); and two, what was the impact of the person they were watching? How much did they like him, and how much did they remember him?

"What was coming out of that was that Jim was not being as recognized as he should be; he was not as strong as he should be. So then there was this great effort to give him more of the kinds of things he did well. They sent him to Alaska to do the clubbing of the seals, to do more outdoor things. But his career was altered because of this so-called 'recognition factor.'"

I asked Ms. Walters how NBC had tested the waters before embarking on its Great Experiment with her 12 years ago — an experiment that eventually led her to an Emmy, the 1975 Broadcaster of the Year award, inclusion in *Time* Magazine's "100 most influential leaders" list, honorary doctorates at two universities, her own syndicated program ("Not for Women Only"), the memorable interviews with Richard Nixon and Henry Kissinger and Fidel Castro and Spiro Agnew.

"There was no advance testing of the waters except that the audience knew me. Before I joined the permanent cast, I had been the 'Today' show's reporter at large. I had traveled all over the country doing all kinds of stories; I was a very serious, hard-working girl. I'd *write* them, I'd come back and *edit* them, I'd put them on the air, and once in a while I'd go on with them. So the audience was just beginning to know me.

"I certainly wasn't a performer." she said, and again, there was a trace of defiance in the voice. "I was not beautiful. I was not even very pretty. I was not as attractive as I am now; I am better looking now, at 44, than I was then, 12 years ago. I didn't really know how to project myself, I was in no sense an actor. I didn't smile enough, I—you know—I still don't talk as well as I should; my enunciation is not that perfect. I had the little lisp or whatever anyone wants to call it.

"But people *believed* me," she said, leaning forward in emphasis. "I talked to them absolutely straight. I went off and did my own reports, and I came back on the air with something tangible."

Barbara Walters' leap from reporter at large to "Today" show regular was facilitated by a blunder that seemingly has become chronic in television: the misuse of a woman personality—specifically, the mistaken assumption that a beautiful woman from show business could handle news-related features and interviews.

On this day of our interview, as the Democrats were selecting their presidential nominee not 30 blocks from her apartment, Barbara Walters recalled the occasion with more than a touch of irony. It was the Democratic National Convention of 1964, in Atlantic City, in the time of Lyndon Johnson, the grand champion machismo pol of all time.

"The last woman the 'Today' show had hired with enormous fanfare was Maureen O'Sullivan. Al Morgan, our producer then, had seen her being interviewed and thought she was terrific. Well, as we never seem to learn, there is a difference between being terrific when you are being interviewed and when you are interviewing yourself.

"That assignment was terribly hard for her, as it is for many actresses. She couldn't take the time cues, she had no idea of the rigidity of the 'Today' show—you know, it's a very tightly segmented program. And it was the time of the conventions, and Maureen simply couldn't cope. I remember that she said at one point: 'There's simply no place for women on this show; a woman is only a book end.'

"I knew Maureen and liked her. She was a very bright, fey woman. I wrote for her — I wrote for everyone. But it just didn't work. In Atlantic City, when Lyndon Johnson was nominated, they had this problem. They had now had Maureen O'Sullivan for six months. It had been a disaster. They had to pay her off, because she had a contract. They had also had such a big publicity campaign when they hired her, and I remember there was this wonderful picture of the convention with her in the front row, and I'm back in Row 14 or something, as one of the writers of the 'Today' show.

"So Al Morgan wanted to put me on the air for 13 weeks. *Over the sales department's dead body.* 'Who knows her? She'll never sell.' And Al Morgan said to me, 'If at the end of 13 weeks it doesn't work out, we'll keep your other job for you.'

"They put me on the air — *for scale.* And that was, uh — 12 years ago."

"Do you now find that you are considered a prototype by young women coming into television?" I asked her.

"I think that there is the feeling now, by many women, that they have to be stronger and tougher. There are women who ask *much* tougher questions than I, and do things that I would not do. Connie Chung of CBS is a very tough interviewer. It's funny that when Connie Chung was interviewed about me, she said, "Oh, *I'm* a journalist; I go out and cover stories. She doesn't." And I thought, 'What have I been doing all these years?'

"But that's rare. It's very rarely the women who say this kind of thing. The women, and especially the young women, I find enormously supportive. I go out and they say, 'Right on,' and 'Congratulations.'

"It's as if, in doing this ABC thing, I've opened new vistas and . . . conquered something for women."

Just as enterprising local anchormen have taken to aping Tom Brokaw and Tom Snyder, many young anchorwomen around the country are now being said to imitate Barbara Walters' style. One of the accused is Ms. Walters' successor on the Today Show, Jane Pauley. (Asked directly about this, Ms. Pauley blithely denied it, saying that her model was in fact Nancy Dickerson.)

"Yes, I've heard that," said Ms. Walters. "What I do think

some women might be trying to do is imitate my style of questioning. I have seen some women on NBC—I won't mention any
names—but one time Senator Eugene McCarthy was on, and one
of our correspondents was doing an interview with him from
Washington, and she said, 'Well, aren't you aware that you're
making a fool of yourself?'

"And I thought, 'No, that's not the way you do it. You don't
ask that. You ask him a question in such a way that he either does
or does not make a fool of himself.' "

The question of Barbara Walters as a prototype points up another dilemma of network news-as-showbusiness, one that is
shared by men and women alike: network reporters and anchorpeople inevitably become celebrities in the same league as the
newsmakers they cover. Walter Cronkite was mentioned on
George McCovern's list of possible vice presidential candidates in
1972. Geraldo Rivera considers running for mayor of New York.
Barbara Walters socializes with Kissinger. Doesn't this fusion of
identities interfere with covering the news, or at least covering it
objectively?

"The celebrity thing is a factor," said Ms. Walters. "It is happening to me now. I find that, during this convention, when I'm
not working, that I am still recognized by delegates and by politicians. Today, I went to a convention party that *Newsweek* gave.
Last night, I went to a party that *Time* gave. I've met all the Carter
people; they recognize me. And it's killing me that I've met them
all and I can't put them on the air.

"But up until very recently, the fact that I was a celebrity
hasn't hurt me in terms of getting stories. It has *helped*, occasionally, in terms of meeting the Washington hierarchy. That's because Washington is very impressed by celebrities. You know,
Elizabeth Taylor goes there, the *world* falls apart. She comes to
New York and, you know, so what else is new? It *may* have made it
a little easier for me to get an interview now because people know
my name. But that's relatively recent."

"What about the popular image that you move in the same
circles socially as the people you cover?"

"That's a small amount. First of all, if you live in New York,
that factor is very small. It is far less here than it is for most of the
newsmen in Washington. It's far less than for a Rowland Evans or

a Joe Kraft or any of the Washington columnists, who are at these parties—you know, the Ben Bradlees and Sally Quinns. This is their life.

"I live in New York, so I'm very rarely in Washington. When you go to Washington, and I go rarely, you tend to get your picture taken a lot, or it's a big deal when you walk into a party, so there's a feeling that I'm in Washington more than I actually am.

"My social life is very private. Most of the time, I don't see people in television, and most of the time, I don't see people in politics. Remember, I had those terrible hours at the 'Today' show. You would *hear* about me a lot. But I really didn't . . . yes, I did use to have lunch with Henry Kissinger—haven't, really, in years—but even *that* would be twice a year. I think he was always sophisticated enough to know that it would not affect my interviews. If anything, I bent over the other way.

"Let's take the H. R. Haldeman interview—the one in which he said that people who disagreed with Mr. Nixon's foreign policy were, in effect, traitors. That interview didn't happen because I was a woman. Or a celebrity. One of the ways you get an interview is to decide what will make somebody want to *give* you an interview. And in the case of Haldeman, nobody had appealed to him in this way, although everybody had put in their bid to get an interview.

"I used to write long letters to people, telling them what we would do, what we would offer. And I remember with Haldeman, it was at a time in which Richard Nixon's image was particularly bad. And there was a conception of Haldeman being—as it turned out, rightly—this kind of ice-cold, glacial figure who guarded the door. And therefore (my reasoning to Haldeman went), since *Haldeman* was not understood, and since *he* was considered so cold and forbidding, *Nixon* was considered forbidding.

"And I said to Haldeman: 'Let people see you. Let them see you in your office, with the fire; let them know what you're like. We'll talk about your job.'

"And I remember having lunch with Kissinger—one of those biannual lunches—on the day I was going to try and talk Haldeman into it. Kissinger said, 'You'll never get him.'

"But Haldeman, and I *knew* this when I went there, was going to try to give an image of himself that would help the Nixon image. I got the interview. But not because I was a woman or a celebrity or whatever. Because I *tried*."

Now that she has endured the hazing, the sarcasm, the questions about her "credentials," and now that she has secured an anchor position on a major network—how, I asked Barbara Walters, does she intend to use this new opportunity?

She nodded. She was well acquainted with the question.

"I hope that what I intend to do that is different will be apparent as soon as I begin," she said. "Because unless I come on the air with firecrackers coming out of my ears—if I just come on and do what David Brinkley does now, read the news, or write some of it, they're going to say, you know, 'Big deal. This is what they hired her for?'

"I think you are going to see a tremendous difference in network news in the coming years. The anchor people are going to have to do more than read; they'll have to create their own news. They'll have to create it by interviews; perhaps, by a different kind of analysis of the news. You're going to have anchor people being questioners. You're going to have much more interplay between the news anchorman and the reporters in the field.

"You're going to find more *creation* of news. When we had Watergate, when we had Vietnam, the news created itself. You turned on the dial and it all washed over you. That has changed now. You are seeing more—almost a magazine format on the network news. You see investigatory things; you see different kinds of features and personality profiles. And this will continue.

"There is a new phrase at the network—it's kind of pompous—it's called 'Reality Programming.' It parallels the growth, in the last five years, of popular interest in nonfiction over fiction.

"What this means in television news is that programs such as CBS's '60 Minutes' are attracting audiences and making money. Reality Programming is making it in prime time. So you're going to have more of this: more consumer features, more of an awareness of subjects that women are interested in *as well as* men.

"In terms of what I'd like to do—I'd like to develop what I call the 'So-What Factor.' I listen to the news and hear that the gross national product has gone up 5 per cent. *So what?* And we've all been afraid to say 'So what?' because Walter Cronkite and John Chancellor can't say 'So what?' They should know better. I would like to do some news features that ask, '*Why* do we bring you the gross national product? The Dow Jones averages? What do they mean to you?' I want to get us to the point where the anchor people are not demigods and can question and can give answers.

We have to get to that point because the news audiences are so much more sophisticated than they used to be."

Whatever Barbara Walters accomplishes on the "ABC Evening News," it will have been achieved despite one final, galling, self-contradictory pratfall on the part of the network and its affiliate stations around the country. It is perhaps the ultimate mockery of Barbara Walters' aspirations in the peculiar milieu of broadcast journalism. Taken as a scenario, it reads almost like a chapter from *Catch-22*.

In a nutshell, it is this: ABC hired Barbara Walters away from NBC in large part by promising her that the network would expand its half-hour nightly newscast to 45 minutes — and that the extra 15 minutes would be devoted to Ms. Walters doing her specialty, namely, interviews.

Then, once Ms. Walters had committed herself to the network, ABC found that its affiliate stations would not accept the extra 15 minutes of network air time. The project was scrapped — with the result that Ms. Walters, on the nightly news at least, is basically a newsreader.

But there is a further twist. "During the last week of my negotiations," said Ms. Walters, "all hell broke loose at NBC. I understand that for two days, everything stopped while they suddenly confronted the fact that I was about to leave. They said, 'Why do you want to go?' And I told them that one of the big reasons was that ABC was offering a 45-minute newscast.

"At that point they said, 'Look. Stay with us. Give us a week or so. Let us try to line up our affiliates and try to do the network news for an hour.'

"I'd already known — or thought — that I would have the 45 minutes at ABC. I thought, for a variety of reasons, that I should honor my negotiations with ABC. So I went ahead with my decision to switch networks.

"Two things happened. One, the ABC affiliates balked at the 45-minute plan, and the project was lost.

"Two, as a result of ABC's starting the idea, both NBC and CBS are committed to an hour-long network newscast in the near future. CBS is already doing dry runs. And instead of an hour newscast being three to five years away, as everyone thought last April, I will tell you that within two years, and probably within one year, you will have the network news shows going to an hour."

Barbara Walters smiled at the absurdity of it all. She scooped another celery stick into the onion dip.

"I enjoy it," she said in a quiet voice. "I am a child of television. When I was brought on the air, I knew about film, I knew how to cut and edit, I knew how to write for film. I am the oldest of that 'new' television generation who were trained entirely *in* television, not in print journalism.

"What has happened with me is this: even though I came along before the women's movement, I showed that a woman could *do* it. I took a lot of fire and abuse for being a woman who was navigating in a man's world, asking the tough questions, and, in some cases, tougher than the men's. The fact that I could—oh, it sounds so funny, so awful—the fact that I could *get this kind of respect* meant that other women could. Now that I've left the 'Today' show, they will *not* hire a model to replace me. They will hire another—to some degree at least—working journalist.

"And really, the one who took my place is Tom Brokaw. *He* is the new host. Whatever woman they hire won't be 'me.' *Tom Brokaw is me!*

"And, certainly, I can't tell you that I am not pleased to be the first network anchorwoman. Yes, part of it was the salary, part of it was the 45 minutes that we talked about, but beyond that, I am pleased to be the first.

"Of course I know I'm not going down in any history books— and if I fail, it isn't going to make me happy to know that I was the first anchorwoman. But the fact that I *am.* . . .

"If I make it, within two years—and especially if the news goes to an hour, but even if it doesn't—you will have anchor*women* on every news show."

"And if you don't make it?" I asked.

Barbara Walters sat very still, and looked at me for quite a long time. "I will," she said at last.

By March of 1977, it was far from certain that Barbara Walters had "made it." Her interviews with newsmakers were branded as "theatrical" by the critics. Reasoner's discomfiture with his co-star was apparent on the air; he was, on frequent occasions, openly snappish and scornful of Ms. Walters' remarks. The ratings languished: six months into the new format, the "ABC Evening News" continued to attract only 18 to 19 percent of the nightly news audience—approximately the same figure Reasoner had drawn before Ms. Walters joined him. ("The CBS Evening News" with Walter Cronkite, meanwhile, was at its ratings peak —29 percent of the audience—and the "NBC Nightly News" with John Chancellor and David Brinkley attracted a healthy 25 percent.)

Certain of Ms. Walters' interviewing ploys reinforced the suspicions of her male colleagues that she was, simply, not an issue-oriented broadcaster: on one of her prime-time specials, she asked President and Mrs. Carter whether they slept in the same bed. And her closing supplication in that interview—"Be good to us, be kind to us."—became an in-joke at television stations around the country.

In an uncharacteristically acerbic radio broadcast, CBS correspondent Morley Safer gave Ms. Walters a tongue-lashing, suggesting that she lacked the seriousness and the background to be a network anchorwoman. And in March, *TV Guide* magazine, the best-read television periodical in the country, published an editorial calling for Ms. Walters to resign.

Television columnists such as Frank Swertlow of the *Chicago Daily News* began to print speculations that Ms. Walters would be switched from New York to Washington, to ease the tension between her and Reasoner. Others guessed that she would be reassigned to a documentary unit. Although both Ms. Walters and news president Sheehan denied it, the feeling in the industry persisted that America's first network anchorwoman would be off the job by year's end.

As for Sheehan, he had career anxieties of his own to think of. The well-connected Swertlow published a column reporting that ABC was considering replacing him—with no less a news eminence than Roone Arledge, the head of ABC Sports.

And Arledge's rumored choice for an addition to the network newscast?

Howard Cosell.

THE BEAUTIFUL ETHNIC: GERALDO RIVERA

There are times when Geraldo Rivera allows himself to wonder whether, but for the grace of cybernetic news, he might still be a $210-a-week lawyer for some New York street gangs.

"One day Gloria Rojas [a WABC reporter] called me up and said that ABC was looking for a Puerto Rican," he said, recalling the circumstances of his transubstantiation. "Just like that. I mean, she didn't pull any punches. She wasn't kidding around. I mean, I had no experience, so obviously they didn't want me for that. They had an ethnic slot available."

It is true that TV news went looking for the Beautiful Ethnic in the early 1970's, and Rivera — half Puerto Rican, half Jewish — was there like some divine apparition from *Godspell*. What Sidney Poitier did for the white middle-class idealization of blacks in the movies (*Guess Who's Coming to Dinner?*), Rivera has done for the white middle-class acceptance of minorities on television newscasts (Guess who's staying for breakfast?).

Today there are countless clones of Rivera on TV news staffs around the country: soft-haired, mustachioed, handsome devils with *Latino* surnames, all smoldering with ill-contained outrage on behalf of the downtrodden common man (within acceptable limits, of course).

Meanwhile, the original item is one of broadcasting's superstars and a shining light among the nation's celebrity-journalists: a
master of that curious, schizoid style once known as "Radical
Chic," which depends on a careful fusion of faded jeans, just-plain
brogan shoes, a borderline-profane "street" dialect, a palpable air
of Involvement, lots of straight-ahead Brotherhood handshakes—
plus incredible good looks, sex appeal, power, and notoriety.

Rivera understands all this. He has a ready rationale for his
seemingly contradictory status as superstar spokesman for the
teeming masses.

"They *make* celebrities, man," he said, sitting in his small office at ABC—an ostentatiously casual cubicle festooned with
"Doonesbury" comic strips, glossy photographs, likable pieces of
carnival-souvenir trinkets and pop posters—the kind of office that
strives mightily to be "storefront," even though it is several stories
above West Sixty-sixth Street, near Lincoln Center.

"I mean," continued Rivera, "the television news bosses see to
it that their personalities become stars. *Stars*, in direct proportion
with their popularity. With power."

Rivera allowed himself an ironic shrug—feet up on the
desk—and there was a conspiratorial glitter in the soft brown eyes.

"So they created me," he said. Now there was the faintest ironic curl at the lips, a trace of amusement creeping into the voice:
Geraldo was sharing a secret; he had *put one over* on the Establishment. ". . . They *created* me, and here I became a star, and they
came to me, and they could no longer tell me what I could do, you
know, at the local level, because, then, suddenly, I could say, 'I
ain't doin' that.'

"You know, you see, what they did was, I mean, they created
a *monster;* they really created somebody they could not control.
And that," said the monster, smiling an irresistibly warm smile, "is
how it all happened."

There is obviously, a generous quotient of hype in the dashing *comanchero* that is Geraldo Rivera—a hype so distinct at times
that it has led the unseduced to speculate whether the name itself
is not an artful embellishment of "Jerry Rivers." (It is not; Rivera's
father, Allen, of West Babylon, bears the authentic surname.)

But if Rivera is partly a self-created media celebrity, he is un-
deniably an extraordinary person and a journalist of considerable

ability. He has a legitimate claim to the "street" style that he still affects, having run with a neighborhood gang, the Corner Boys, in his boyhood West Babylon community. (Typical of Geraldo's later upwardly-mobile shrewdness is the fact that he became president of the gang.)

Another experience that Rivera shares with many of the "fringe" people he covers is bewilderment about American public education. He struggled through West Babylon High School, and was accepted into New York Community College on a conditional basis: he could study only remedial courses in English and math. Rivera's crazy-quilt wanderings took him next to the Maritime College of the State University of New York, the merchant marines, a stint as a clothing salesman on the West Coast, a professional soccer interlude in Arizona (to help him finance his way through the university there), and then brought him back East, where he worked in the basement of Alexander's Department Store in the south Bronx.

Rivera's scholastic abilities began to stabilize in the mid-1960s, and he entered Brooklyn Law School. It was during his work for two storefront legal-aid operations—the Harlem Assertion of Rights and the Community Action for Legal Services—that he had his first brush with the TV cameras. Rivera was an occasional spokesman for his clients during news conferences. Among his questioners at those events was WABC's Gloria Rojas.

Rivera's work since he entered TV journalism gives strong testimony to the fact that he is far from a passive mannequin representing the Latino category of cybernetic news. His 1972 documentary on the archaic and inhumane conditions at the Willow-brook State School for the Mentally Retarded in Staten Island led to radical reforms there—and a Peabody Award for Rivera. He has also done noteworthy investigations into drug addiction among children, the plight of migrant laborers, prisoners, motorcycle gangs, and other fringe aspects of American life not normally covered on the "Evening News." His occasional late-night magazine show, "Good night America," has won some critical acclaim, if not massive ratings. In 1976, Rivera was the travelling correspondent for ABC's "Good Morning, America," compiling filmed essays from various corners of the United States.

On the local level in New York, he was director and reporter for the Channel 7 newscast's "Help Center," an ombudsman feature that purported to intervene on behalf of private citizens against corrupt merchants and indifferent bureaucracies.

Television news was not totally a caucasian-male preserve when Rivera was hired by WABC in June 1970, but then it was not exactly "Sesame Street," either. A few blacks and fewer Latinos held reportorial jobs around the country. There were no blacks or any other minority representatives at the anchor desk—except in one or two cases, during weekend newscasts. With a few exceptions in large cities such as New York and Los Angeles, there are still no minority anchormen or women.

This rather conspicuous lack may be attributed to racism, but it is an indirect, even an impersonal racism. Station managers are not notable for the bigotry as a group; only their slavishness to presumed mass-audience tastes stands in the way of inroads against the color and ethnic barrier. The surveys and ratings books make it clear that the most important *buying segment* of TV news watchers are middle-class whites. Best not to court their disapproval with an unpleasant symbol at the anchor desks, especially when an archetype of White America is just a flick of the dial away.

If, in the early seventies, minority viewers were not yet "ready" (in the sense of economic power) for representatives at anchor, their numbers were at least impressive enough for the station managers to throw them some sort of bone. Hence the emergence of the minority "specialist" reporter, brought to apotheosis by Geraldo Rivera.

"It was an incredible experience," recalled Rivera of the phone call from Gloria Rojas. "It was at the height of all the hysteria," he said, "and I was getting on TV a lot as a kind of spokesman, because they were going through the whole 'We-don't-deal-with-the-pig-media' trip, you know. So the lawyer gets pushed into the forefront in that kind of situation. So I was meeting a lot of reporters as a newsmaker, you know, in that sense."

Did the heady experience of TV cameras and attentive reporters prompt Rivera to begin thinking of himself as a TV newsman?

Rivera's face was deadpan. "To tell you the truth, I never noticed the equipment. I never noticed anything about it, and I hardly noticed the reporter. I just noticed whether the people were polite or impolite, whether the people were sympathetic or not. And then I met Gloria Rojas that way."

Did her phrasing of the invitation imply to Rivera that some sort of audience-measuring blueprint was at work?

He gave a contemptuous chuckle. "Oh yes. I mean, the implications of it are that someone sat down with a yellow pad and pencil and said, 'Okay, what do we have in New York? All right, we got a million of these, two million of those, three million of these, five hundred thousand of those. All right, we got to go after *this*, got to go after *this*, got to get these *Italians* . . . all right. What do we have left? We have no Puerto Ricans! Well, we have got to get one. Who we gonna get? They can't talk English, they got kinky hair. . . .' "

Rivera chuckled again, more humorously now. "So that is about what happened. Gloria called me up and that was the basis on which I was approached.

"So I came down to ABC and I met Al Primo. I talked with him. And he impressed me. I think he is a good man. He talked with me for about five minutes, and I think he was surprised to find that I spoke English—that it wasn't accented English. It was a *Brooklyn* accent, but he could deal with that. I didn't look funny, and I wasn't too short. I was not too swarthy. All those things.

"Then Kenneth MacQueen came down—vice president, general manager of Channel 7. He just looked me over like I was a piece of meat. Up and down. 'Okay, what we want you to do is go to Columbia University for the summer in this minority program that they have.' I decided to give it a try. It was as cut and dried as that."

Once ABC's cybernetic apparatus had proclaimed the need for a Puerto Rican symbol, and once an appropriate specimen had been found, a ludicrous—but oddly commonplace—development ensued: the specimen was left to learn the complicated skills of television news reporting by himself.

"The first reporter I saw working, after I was hired, was myself," said Rivera. "The first TV reporter I saw reporting a story was me. I remember very clearly what it was. I was still at Columbia, but ABC wanted me to help cover the Democratic primaries. I

got the losing candidate in the primary for state attorney general.
ABC just wanted a little news clip, just to say they covered it all. So
I got this guy; his name was Robert Min. So I went up there and
recorded the concession speech, and then I did what is called a
'standup wrap-around' . . . you know, an opening and closing.

"I got in front of the camera, and I had the microphone, and
I had memorized what I was going to say . . . and it just came out."
There was real amusement in Rivera's voice now.

"I had this cameraman who works with me still—Edgar
Pressman, from Trinidad. The sound man was Kenny Smith,
from Jamaica. You know, just real West Indian people. Giants,
they were. So Edgar shuts off his camera, comes walking over to
me, puts his hand on my shoulder. I'm trembling. My palms are
sweating. I had just . . . *recited* this. It sounded like a limerick; you
know, a children's limerick. It was terrible.

"Edgar says, 'Hey, man . . . no good, man. You got to take it
easy, man.' I mean, that was the most advice I *had,* up until that
time." Rivera paused and shrugged. "Anyway," he said, "they
didn't use the piece."

Rivera's humiliating debut parallels the incomprehensible
treatment described by another TV news "specimen," another
creation of cybernetic research, who quickly fell victim to it: Sally
Quinn of the Washington *Post,* and late of the "CBS Morning
News."

When CBS decided to take a run at the "Today" show in
1973, the network's news executives hit upon Ms. Quinn as an
eminently marketable commodity: a Woman, a Blonde, a Washington Insider, a Confidante of the Famous—and a personality in
her own right, complete with a certain sexual mystique, never defined, but exploited to the point of nausea in CBS's publicity campaign. Hired as the co-anchor along with Hughes Rudd, Ms.
Quinn was thereupon virtually ignored in terms of broadcast
coaching. (A highlight of her book about the affair, *We're Going to
Make You a Star,* was the revelation that no one had bothered to tell
her that the red light above the TV camera meant that the camera
was on.) Predictably, Sally Quinn failed, quickly and decisively, on
the "Morning News." CBS officials expressed surprise and regret.

Rivera survived. But, like other "minority specialists" around
the country, he was struck with the nagging suspicion from time

to time that his employers, having hired him in a flush of humanitarianism, had no idea exactly what a "minority specialist" was supposed to do.

"Let me tell you what it was like when I first started," said Rivera. "Remember that I'm coming from a radical background. Plus, I'm in long hair. I was the youngest member of the news staff at that time, about 27.

"So I was politically far out, I was chronologically far out, and, certainly, I was far out in style. So I was covering things like fashion shows—no, really! Fashion shows, any demonstration of twelve people or less that had no political connotations—I mean, I really had the dregs to do. I mean, it was very frustrating. I was ready to quit a million times in the beginning.

"It was just by accident that I got into the other stuff. I was in the village one day with Edgar, and we were going to cover a Levis fashion show. You know, because I'm a young guy, and who else is going to cover the Levis denim fashion show, right?

"So we were walking down Bleecker Street, and I look up, and there's a crowd of people right on the corner of Bleecker and Sullivan. A bunch of people, and they are all looking up, and there's a guy poised to jump off the ledge of the goddamned Greenwich Hotel.

"So I start blabbering right away to Edgar to film this guy. Of course, Edgar had already been filming this guy for 45 seconds, you know, before I realized what's going on. The guy jumped. He jumped right there—right on camera!—right on TV, he *jumped*."

Rivera was growing excited now, with the memory. "But it gets better," he continued, and immediately sensed the gaffe; "I mean better, you know, in the news sense—better means awful. His twin brother's right there when the guy lands! Twin brother! We are running over there—*and the guy recognizes me!* And he starts blabbering about him and his brother being junkies. They are twin sons of a Marine colonel from southern California. They just made this odyssey across the country, looking for junk. And his brother just got to a hundred-and-fifty-dollar-a-day habit, and he says, forget it, I can't do that any more, you know—and jumped. And his brother sits, telling me all this shit *right here!*

"The brother did not die for some reason. He was taken to the hospital. But the other guy is crying hysterically and grabbing me—like *this!*—and the camera is on all the time. So it was on the eleven o'clock news that night. They let it run three minutes, which, at the time, was a really heady experience."

Thus it is one of the exquisite little ironies of cybernetic news that the country's premier "minority specialist"—the newscaster hired to go beyond the sensational headlines and probe for the neglected stories of abuse, unfairness, and corruption suffered by ethnic groups—got his big break covering what TV news covers best: the flashy, sensational tearjerker. At that horrific moment, on the corner of Sullivan and Bleecker Streets, much to his own surprise and quite beyond his volition, Geraldo Rivera joined the Club.

It is a tribute to Rivera's sense of values that he has remained a "serious" journalist at ABC almost in spite of himself, and certainly in spite of the network's own maneuvers to transform him totally into a pop-cultural idol, a figurehead. The Willowbrook documentary was in fact a distinguished work. Since that time, Rivera has brought to the screen a number of people and issues that, undoubtedly, would otherwise have been ignored by network television. Nevertheless, his status as a celebrity—as a personality who often is larger than the events he covers—is unavoidable. His marriage to, and subsequent divorce from, Edith Vonnegut, the daughter of Kurt Vonnegut, Jr.; his movements among the social elite of New York; his rumored impulse to run for *mayor* of that beleaguered city—all attest to the fact that the token Puerto Rican of 1970 had sampled television's most sumptuous advantages in 1977.

Rivera, a man of genuinely candid instincts, was characteristically blunt about the forces that influenced his identity at ABC. "I went on the air with 'Good Night, America' in 1973—did one show that year," he said. "I put it together myself—formed my own corporation to do it. And I'll tell you why.

"In 1973 I had the highest-rated documentary in the history of television, 'The Littlest Junkie.' It was a helluva show. So, I am saying to myself, when is ABC gonna say, 'This is your chance, this is the time to go out there and do it.' They never did. I told them, I told the president of ABC News, 'I'm ready now. You know, I've done a thousand stories on the local level.' He said, 'No, you're not ready yet, you are not ready yet.'

"So I created 'Good Night, America,' and the reason I

created it was to *circumvent* the network news. To give me a chance to be on a national program, doing what I do, because as far as the network was concerned, I was shut out of it, I was just really shut out.

"So I formed a corporation and went—not to the news division, but to the *entertainment* division of ABC. I went to them because they saw me as an audience-grabber; they didn't care what the commodity was as long as it sold. They didn't care if I was out there talking about *shoes,* as long as people were watching.

" 'Good Night, America' made its debut in the summer of 1973. I wanted it to be a magazine, a mix of news and entertainment. I mean, they were pressing for more and more show business, and I was pressing for more and more news things. So we compromised.

"The pilot did rather well—I mean, in terms of audience. And then the next year I had twelve shows, and the year after that I had twelve shows. This takes us up to 1975. In 1976, it was cut way back. I think it will be four 'Good Night, America's. Total."

Now a darkness had crept into Rivera's face. The breezy humor was gone from his voice. He scuffed at his desk top with a paper clip as he went on. "You know, if I'd tell you my theory as to why it was cut back. . . ." He stopped, and was silent for a moment or two. Then he went on, speaking faster. "Like, I have all the ratings for the 'Good Night, America' show. I have them all written down, and I always did better than the other 'Wide World of Entertainment' shows [the umbrella title for the 90-minute segment in which Rivera's show appeared]. I mean, it was obvious that people who did not watch 'Wide World of Entertainment' were tuning in to watch 'Good Night, America.' But now it's 1975 and you have a situation in the morning where ABC has a gigantic investment on a two-hour bloc that's going to be network. Okay, so first they start with the 'AM America' show. I have nothing to do with it. The show, for one reason or another, is a colossal failure, probably the worst in the history of the network.

"So ABC has a huge investment. They are losing money; it is going down the tubes. My theory is that ABC looked at 'Good Night, America' and said, 'Rivera can't do both. Let's put him where we need him, rather then where he wants to be.' They came to me when they were gearing up for 'Good Morning,' 'AM' 's replacement. I said, 'I'm not taking that morning show.' They said,

'You don't take the morning show, you don't have the night show.' Rivera sighed, raised his eyebrows, and spread his hands.

"So I do the morning show," he said. "And I've done some of my best work on it. Unfortunately, not many people see it. But from time to time, ABC says, 'Do more entertainment and more personality stuff.' And they've *always* said that about the night show. Always said, 'Come on, you've got to get more into personalities, you've got to get more into show business. So that's where I find myself right now."

If Geraldo Rivera, with his awards and his renown for tough reporting, is being pressured to do "entertainment and personality stuff," what of his less-famous colleagues who cover local news in New York?

Rivera made a grimace and shook his head. "Investigative stuff is not being covered," he said. "I mean, *no* one is doing investigative work. No one is doing the kind of stuff that you don't get on the air every day—the stuff you've got to hold off for three days because you are doing the backup work on it. Nobody's doing that. Absolutely nobody!

"Like, take Betty Furness over at Channel 4, who does the consumer stuff. She does 'success stories'—just like the 'Help Center' here. They told us: 'Success stories, success stories, success stories!' They don't want you getting sued—so do success stories. Yeah, it's happened here, right here in my own shop. I mean, instead of pointing your finger at the guys who are ripping people off and getting away with it, they want you to publicize the firms who do good. Or spotlight the lady who got a new color television set because we told her story. That's what they want—not systematic, investigative stuff."

Rivera paused and stared for a moment or two at his hands, which were folded in his lap. "It's not that the reporters here wouldn't love to dig into corruption and malfeasance stories," he said. "It's just that they have no time to look. And there is the money thing, also, you know—the way our reporters are getting paid.

"As long as the stations pay these guys for *piece*work, as long as they pay the guy who gets three stories in a day more than the guy who does one story in a day, there'll be no investigative work. See, the way it works is that a reporter gets a guarantee—a guaranteed minimum salary. And then he works against the guarantee. You do one story, you've recaptured a percentage of your guarantee. You do two stories, you've matched your guarantee. You do three stories, you go above—you get an increase; you get more than the guarantee.

"So," said Rivera, leaning forward and spreading his hands, "you are rewarded for *quantity!* For *mediocrity!* A guy goes to a location and covers a demonstration. Maybe it's not time to leave yet. Maybe he doesn't understand what's going on yet. But he *wants* to leave because there's now a fire in the Bronx. There's flames, and they can photograph flames, so he knows that he will definitely get on the air. And then maybe he can think of something else—maybe something at City Hall, maybe there's a crash on the four o'clock express . . . and you wonder why nobody spends time on investigative stories." Rivera gave a chuckle that was more of a snort.

Does Rivera sense that similar pressures will soon overtake him at the network level—that there will no longer be a place for the kind of reporting that made him a media celebrity?

"Well, if there isn't, then I'm not staying. I mean, *that is it . . .* as soon as they tell me no more of that, screw it. I don't need it. I'll be a lawyer. I'll practice law, or I'll write books or something. I'll just do something else."

There are times when Geraldo Rivera allows himself to wonder whether, but for the grace of cybernetic news, he might still be a $210-a-week lawyer for some New York street gangs.

And other times when he wonders whether he might not end up being a street-gang lawyer anyway.

THE CURATOR REACTS: WALTER CRONKITE

Walter Cronkite came to CBS long before there were such things as news consultants, although a rumor persists that William S. Paley hired God to do the necessary market research. In many obvious ways, Cronkite is the symbol of the classic network news anchorman, the ultimate "talking head," whose punctilious eight minutes, minimum, of on-camera time on the "CBS Evening News" each night is referred to as "the magic" by the producers. He is the inheritor of Murrow's truly mythic hold on the popular imagination; more than any other newsman of his time, Cronkite is perceived not only to deliver the news but to act as its curator. He is seen as both the most reliable conduit of the news *and* as the conscience of the news-gathering genus.

In his 25 years at CBS—virtually the entire life span of network television news itself—Cronkite has had the good luck, or the genius, to personify the prototypical Middle American. This persona is crucial to his success. Cronkite, without seeming to work at it, shares with the viewer a sense of being influenced by national and world events; a sense of curiosity, of reaction, of keen interest. None of the lofty cerebrations of Eric Sevareid in Cronkite; his is not a didactic nature. By the same token, none of the gratuitous kinetic showmanship that marks the modern local anchorman: no self-conscious tricky business or winking camaraderie. Walter Cronkite has found the Middle—not the innocuous Middle of uninvolved militant mediocrity, but a golden Middle of restraint, of suspended judgment, of an earnest, ingenuous news-hound passion, informed by experience and vulnerable to emotion.

Thus Cronkite, his voice breaking with emotion when he announced the news of President John F. Kennedy's assassination in November 1963. (One month before the assassination, Cronkite had inaugurated the half-hour nightly network newscast on CBS with an exclusive interview with the President.) Thus Cronkite "boning up" for space coverage, making himself an expert in aerodynamics so he could lucidly report the Apollo missions; thus Cronkite giving a yelp of "Oh boy!" as Apollo II blasted off. Thus Cronkite in Chicago in 1968, allowing himself a rare burst of anger upon seeing a CBS correspondent pummeled to the floor at the Democratic National Convention: "If this sort of thing continues, it makes us, in our anger, want to just turn off our cameras and pack up our microphones and our typewriters and get the devil out of this town and leave the Democrats to their agony."

There are those who believe that Walter Cronkite — that most un-hip of men, that most un-radical of citizens — may have expedited Lyndon Johnson's change in policy in Vietnam from a continuing test of force to a negotiated settlement. In 1968, Cronkite, who had until then scrupulously denied himself the indulgence of commentary on his TV newscasts, made a two-week visit to Vietnam. He returned shocked and indignant over what he had seen, and proceeded to conclude several newscasts with heartfelt assertions that the administration was wrong in its prosecution of the war. Johnson saw, and raged — but he knew a straw in the wind when it blew into his face. If the bearded, unkempt kids in the streets preached against the war, that was piecemeal agitation — containable. When Walter Cronkite said the same thing, in different language, it was as if the soul of America had opened up.

American news-watchers not only trust Cronkite, they prefer him to other anchormen. After trailing Chet Huntley and David Brinkley of NBC for a few seasons, he assumed a decisive lead in June 1967 and has held it, with sporadic exceptions, ever since. NBC has topped him occasionally, and gained overall strength when Brinkley resumed his co-anchor duties opposite John Chancellor, but the 52-week average of nightly viewers for August 1975 to August 1976 showed that Cronkite still led the field: he com-

manded an average audience of 9,326,000 Americans each evening, as compared with 8,560,000 for NBC and 6,470,000 for
ABC.

If Walter Cronkite symbolizes authenticity for men and
women on the receiving end of the television cameras, within the
industry itself he symbolizes that and more. Behind the scenes,
Cronkite has always been a stern, vigilant monitor of television
news's integrity and independence. When the Nixon Administration, at the peak of its power, was turning its cold eye toward the
irritant of network news, most network presidents, news directors,
and anchormen swallowed hard and looked the other way. A 1970
memo from Charles Colson to H. R. Haldeman gloated, in part:
"The networks are terribly nervous over the uncertain state of the
law, i.e., the recent FCC decisions and the pressures to grant Congress access to TV. They are also apprehensive about us. Although they tried to disguise this, it was obvious. The harder I
pressed them [CBS and NBC], the more accommodating, cordial,
and almost apologetic they became . . . Both CBS and ABC agreed
with me that on most occasions the President speaks as President
and that there is no obligation for presenting a contrasting point
of view under the Fairness Doctrine." Colson continued, paren-
thetically: "This, by the way, is not the law—the FCC has always
ruled that the Fairness Doctrine always applies—and either they
don't know that or they are willing to concede us the point."

In June 1973, well after Watergate revelations had begun to
shake the administration at its foundations, CBS voluntarily
dropped its "instant analysis" of administration speeches. (The
move prompted a dissenting radio script by an angry Roger
Mudd; the script never made it on the CBS airwaves.)

Virtually alone among the potentially influential voices in the
broadcast community, Walter Cronkite went to the barricades. In
May 1971, he publicly scolded the Nixon Administration for committing "a crime against the people" by trying to prevent television
from doing its job as the people's observer of the performance of
their elected representatives.

The June 1973 issue of *Playboy* magazine carried an interview
which I had conducted with Cronkite. At the time, Nixon's man
for "telecommunications policy," Clay T. Whitehead, was roaming
about the country to publicize a congressional bill that would place
a local station's license in jeopardy if the station couldn't demon-

strate "meaningful service to the community." One way to demonstrate such service, Whitehead was suggesting, was to eliminate reporting and analysis of the administration. The bill amounted to the Nixon Administration's swipe at television's jugular vein. In our interview, Cronkite asserted that this and other measures amounted to "a well-directed campaign against the press, agreed upon in secret by members of the administration . . . This administration has tried to bring, and may have succeeded in bringing, the press to heel."

I met Cronkite again, one spring morning in New York, to discuss with him the direction in which television news was going: having survived the Nixon Administration, could TV news survive itself? Specifically, I wanted to ask him, could it survive its consultant-induced snake-dance into trivia and softness?

The topic was tricky, I knew. Cronkite is hardly a chauvinist about his profession; indeed, he has often led his reluctant colleagues in self-criticism. Still, blanket doomspeak about the viability of TV news is something Cronkite does not suffer lightly. His is the pride of the newsman honed in covering police beats, the courthouse and World War II, and, given his considerable influence in the architecture of TV journalism, any suggestion that his profession is going to hell is subject to interpretation as a reflection on Cronkite himself.

The occasion of our interview provided a glimpse of the essential Cronkite, a character mix that combines the accumulated savvy of a highly cosmopolitan man with the residual self-delight of a country boy. One senses that he goes about his life in a perpetual state of bemusement and detached fascination that, of all the people in the world who might have been chosen for the role of Walter Cronkite, it turned out to be he.

We were to meet in the bar of the Sherry Netherlands Hotel at 11:00 A.M. The Sherry Netherlands bar is one of those darkly discreet Manhattan masculine enclaves, all right angles and polished brass and starched linen and waiters with blue jowls; its own coloration suggests Gucci. At 11:00 A.M., the bar is empty. Just the right combination of elegance and seclusion, I thought, for New York's most recognizable face. Walter Cronkite, perhaps to his own distress, is forever proscribed from Chock Full O' Nuts.

At 11:00 A.M. exactly, I took a stool at the Sherry Netherlands bar. I was the only customer. I tried to behave as though this was my natural environment. The blue-jowled waiter was not fooled; "You waitin' for Cronkite?" His reputation had preceded me.

At eleven-ten, I was paged for a telephone call from Cronkite's wife, Betsy. Walter would be a little late, she said—not to worry.

At eleven-twenty Cronkite entered the bar, looking very believable indeed in a black chalk-stripe business suit and carrying the reason for his tardiness—a duffel bag with the aluminum handle of a tennis racket protruding. Walter fights intermittent skirmishes with his middle; but I recalled a previous luncheon a couple of summers ago, when, having primed myself all morning on current events and political insights, I was guided by a felicitous Cronkite to the only restaurant in midtown Manhattan that featured a herring buffet. The conversation centered around the joys of going back for seconds.

We shook hands, and I indicated a corner booth with minimum exposure to the room; I was concerned for Cronkite's privacy. I had forgotten that Cronkite *likes* privacy, but he is not a *fanatic* about it. During the interview we were to be interrupted by, respectively, Steven Spielberg, the director of *Jaws;* by Richard Dreyfuss, the star of *Jaws,* who dropped by, wearing jeans and clutching a laundry bag, just to meet Cronkite; and by an angular actress whose name I failed to catch but who did not, I assumed out of charity, play the title role.

I brought up the question of news consultants and their effect on television journalism. Cronkite's brow furrowed and he chose his words carefully.

"In all honesty," he said, "I have not had personal dealings with them. There have not been consultants to the 'CBS Evening News,' as far as I know—as far as I know, not anywhere at the network level. I do know that there are managements who have surveys made, and their people never know about them. So a great deal of what I feel about the phenomenon is based on hearsay.

"Having said that, there is no doubt in my mind that, taken to its ultimate conclusion, consultancy can be a terrible evil. I am not considering at the moment the philosophy or content of any given recommendation. But the fact that a station management would abdicate responsibility to a consultant firm, in matters which are

so deeply concerned and rooted in what should be local judgment—to me, that is an unfortunate situation."

Cronkite continued to frown in concentration, rubbing his
hands together, elbows on the table. It was clear that he did not
relish the subject. It would be more pleasant if the news, which
Cronkite and his colleagues had worked so many years to nurture
and protect from threats on the outside, could be free from such
an embarassing form of self-destruction.

There may have been an added ingredient in Cronkite's dis-
comfort. Most criticism of television in general, and televison news
in particular, has come from the print press—which finds it easy
to adopt a posture of moral superiority by comparison. Cronkite,
who earned his spurs at United Press, seethes at the assumption
that newspaper journalism is, by definition, holier than the new
form he helped create. And here he was being asked by a print
journalist to acknowledge TV news's most conspicuous flaw.

But Cronkite proceeded with his thought. "I've seen some
recommendations that say no story should run longer than thirty
seconds, no film story longer than forty-five seconds. That you
must have three stories within the first two and one-half minutes
of the newscast, you know, and this sort of thing. This, of course,
is just ridiculous. You do not program news like that. It *cannot* be
programmed in that fashion.

"Of course," continued Cronkite, "it is when they deal with
content that I become most concerned—when they tell what kind
of stories attract the audience. When they show what the audience
wants to hear, not what they *need* to hear."

I asked Cronkite whether he believed that the new assumptions of television news amounted to a move away from the first
principles established in the early days of the form. Cronkite
looked thoughtful for several moments.

"Whether it amounts to a sea change," he said at last, "or
whether it is only a change of types of men at the stations is a question yet to be answered. I think that if such a change does take
place, then certainly the country is in an awfully poor position to
get its news. My feeling is that we in radio and television have to
be responsible for the balance in diversity of information, given
the trend toward newspaper monopolies in cities, and that sort of
thing.

"And if things continue the way we've been discussing, we will not be discharging that responsibility. It can't be done this way. You cannot edit by readership survey. You cannot edit television by a consultant's preconceived notion of programming. It simply can never work—I mean, never work in the sense that *people* will benefit. It will work by ratings, although I sometimes question whether that's true or not over a long period of time."

We talked for a few minutes more about news consultants, but it was clear that Cronkite found the subject uncongenial— whether out of defensiveness for his profession or out of lack of familiarity, I could not tell. His show-business guests arrived at the table, the subject changed, and I left the Sherry Netherland's bar with the impression that news consultancy was one barricade that Walter Cronkite did not wish to storm.

I was wrong. Less than a month later, Cronkite had loosed the full measure of his wrath against the trend toward pre-fabricated newscasts, the use of photogenic anchorpeople and the softening of substance in TV journalism. The occasion was the CBS-TV Network Affiliates Conference in New York. The conference occurred within days of Barbara Walters' multimillion-dollar contract-signing with ABC, and the event was paramount in Cronkite's thoughts. If any event of 1976 seemed to lend credence to the argument that TV news was drifting toward show business, it was Ms. Walters' contract sweepstakes.

But Cronkite may also have been motivated by more substantial factors: facing him in the audience were men who, as managers of CBS-owned and CBS-affiliated stations around the country, had plunged wholeheartedly into news consultancy as a panacea. In doing so, many of them had only exacerbated their stations' problems, had further embarrassed themselves and the network. The CBS Network. Walter Cronkite's CBS Network.

At any rate, Cronkite's language on the subject of news consultants was uncharacteristically blunt and acerb.

Cronkite began by acknowledging that most on-air news people shared in "show-business" salaries, and that the difference between Walters' new remuneration and that of the rest of the profession "is but a matter of degree."

Cronkite defended the higher salaries, noting that "what we do comprises a dimension beyond the skills required by the newspaper reporter, writer, and editor. If we do our jobs well, we do those things — reporting, writing, editing — as well as or better than the print journalist. But beyond that, we have to have the special skills — talents, if you please — to present our material through the spoken word and in a visual medium, frequently to think on our feet and to be right the first time, with no editor imposed as a protective buffer between us and the public."

Then Cronkite took off the gloves: "What I do have some problem understanding is why an anchorperson who does *not* have those qualifications still draws down such large compensation. In fact, I wonder if those stations that hire the young and beautiful, but inexperienced and callous, to front their news broadcasts, are not getting ripped off.

"Let me say right here, that I am not one who decries ratings. Those among us in the news end of the broadcasting business who do are simply naive. Of *course* ratings are important, and no one — newsman, program manager, salesman, or general manager — need hang his head in shame because that is the fact. We've been cowed into that position by a bunch of newspaper critics who conveniently forget their own history when they harp on our ratings battles.

". . . But it is *how* we get those ratings, what we do to make us competitive, that bothers me, for just as it is no good to put out a superior product if you can't sell it, it is far worse to peddle an inferior product solely through the razzle-dazzle of a promotion campaign.

"And aren't we guilty of that when we put the emphasis in our news broadcasts on performance and performers, rather than content? Isn't that really what we are looking for when we examine ourselves to see whether we are indulging in show business rather than journalism?

"There is no newsman worth his salt who does not know that advisors who dictate that no item should run more than 45 seconds, that there must be a film story within the first 30 seconds of the newscast and that it must have action in it (a barn burning or a jackknifed tractor-trailer truck will do), that call a 90-second film piece a 'mini-documentary,' that advise against covering City Hall because it is 'dull,' that say the anchorman or woman must do all voice-overs for 'identity' — any real newsman knows that sort of stuff is balderdash. It's cosmetics, pretty packaging — not substance.

"And I suspect that most station operators know that, too. But I think they've been sold a bill of goods; that they've been made suckers for a fad — *editing by consultancy*.

"Yes, suckers, because there is no evidence that this formula news broadcasting — the top-20 news items — works.

"It may — *may* — produce a temporary rating advantage, or an interesting set of demographics. But the evidence that it does not work is in the startling turnover of anchorpeople and news directors in our affiliated stations. Inexact, but indicatively approximate figures show that 50 per cent or so of these people change jobs every two years, and for many stations the roll-over is quicker than that.

"Now, that's no way to build a reliable, dependable news staff. For one thing, these fly-by-nights don't know the territory. They don't have the credibility of long-time residents, nor, what is worse, do they have any long-term interests in the community. And the unsettling fact must be these frequent comings and goings. These transient performers are simply using the broadcast manager as a stone in the quicksand to hold them up long enough to jump to the next rock.

"Let *me* play consultant for a moment. Permit me, if you will, to talk directly to those of you whose stations may have been caught up in this formula news presentation.

"The reason you are being taken is that the answer to your news problem probably is right under your nose.

"In the first place, why buy somebody else's idea of an ideal anchorperson or news editor for your market? Your anchorperson is the most intimate contact you have with your community. Don't you *know* what sort of person your neighbors like? Don't *you* know better than any outsider the tastes of your friends and acquaintances? If not, I suggest that maybe *you* ought to be the one to move along.

"Second, isn't a home-towner, or a long-time resident, or at least a young man or woman who has chosen your community and wants to make a career there — isn't he or she likely to give a great deal more in enthusiasm and dedication and interest — qualities, I might point out, that are easily detected across the airwaves — than the wanderer looking for the next big break in the next biggest town?

"And if you don't have those people immediately available,

have you thought about raiding your local newspaper? For what you pay those inexperienced announcers, you could hire the best — the *best* — newspaperman in your town as on-air broadcaster or news director, or possibly both: a fellow or gal who knows the city like a book, likes the city, warts and all, and plans to raise a family there.

"He very possibly has a little gray in his hair, may be bald, may wear horn-rimmed bifocals. Likely his collar is somewhat crumbled and his tie is done in an old-fashioned four-in-hand instead of a properly bulbous Windsor.

"But I'll guarantee you this: he knows more about your town and what makes it tick than will ever be learned by that young fellow from 500 or 1,000 or 2,000 miles away that some consultant tells you got good ratings there. And you know what? That slightly tousled codger is going to exude more authority and reliability and believability and integrity from the nail on the little finger of his left hand than that pompadoured, pampered announcer is ever going to muster. And isn't that really what our news departments are all about, isn't that really what you want to sell: authority, believability, credibility, integrity?"

Another CBS newsman keenly interested in news consultants is Mike Wallace, host of the network's showcase news-magazine program, "60 Minutes." When I interviewed Wallace in his office, he was even more circumspect than Cronkite had been in discussing consultants. Wallace refused any sort of general disparagement of their practice, suggesting that in certain areas they might prove helpful to a news department.

However, Wallace did provide me with transcripts of two revealing interviews he conducted for "60 Minutes": one with Phil McHugh of McHugh & Hoffman, and the other with Frank Magid.

Wallace conducted the interviews for a "60 Minute" program during the 1973–74 season, a look at local TV news in San Francisco. The McHugh and Magid interviews were ultimately edited out of the final program, but the show scathingly documented the results of the all-out ratings competition that consultants are retained to foster. The show focused on the ratings leader, ABC-owned KGO, served by McHugh & Hoffman, and its arch-rival, KRON, which had retained Magid to help it surmount a seven-year audience decline.

Following are some excerpts from Wallace's interviews with McHugh and with Magid:

WALLACE: You in particular, and news consultants in general, have been criticized by the former dean of the Columbia journalism school, Ed Barrett. He wrote about you in the *Columbia Journalism Review* as follows: He said, "The complaining news directors"—and by that, he means the fellows who complain about the news consultants—"see the consultants as trivializing the news. Placing palsy-walsy presentation above content. Leading, inevitably, to jazzed-up journalism." How do you plead?

McHUGH: Well, I answered him. I think he's wrong. I think that he, unfortunately, and I said so in the letter, doesn't really understand television journalism. Newspaper journalism and television journalism are very different. One is a visual art . . . and again, the mass communications problem. You have to be able to communicate to the 75 per cent of the people in the big, middle majority of this country or in your city. And you can't go over their head in the sense of using words that they don't understand. You can tell the same story, the same complex story, but you have to use words and visuals that make the story come off so they understand it.

WALLACE: I suppose you know that we went out there [to San Francisco] and taped every show on each of the three major stations for a week, every news show?

McHUGH: I knew you'd been out, I didn't know you'd done that.

WALLACE: We taped every one, and looked at the content and then computerized it and found out how much of whatever was on it.

We picked, at random, the eleven o'clock shows on Thursday night, January 24th, for each of the three stations—to see what they did.

KGO [McHugh's client] on that night had four minutes 25 seconds of sex. Two minutes 28 seconds of crime. Forty seconds of exorcism. A total of fire, crime, and sex: seven minutes 33 seconds. That's without murder, without violence, and they did virtually nothing of a local nature.

And when I say "of a local nature," nothing out of City Hall, nothing out of Scaramento [the state capital], nothing about Hunters Point. They didn't get into the story about Egil Krogh's sentencing. They didn't get into what Senator Jackson said to the oil people, the heads of oil companies. They didn't get into Mike Mansfield dressing down the Secretary of Defense. They had a gas-dealer story in Santa Clara for 55 seconds. They led with that. Then the truck driver business, for 25 seconds, then they had a 42-second film on a church break-in by five kids who stole two tape recorders, or something of that sort.

A brawl at San Quentin, 11 seconds. A woman who was hacked to death on the steps of her house in Florida, 16 seconds. Plane crash, murder, another murder, Rochelle McGee . . . That's before the commercial that they went into all of that stuff.

Then they did Egil Krogh in 28 seconds. The Maheu payoff to Nixon in 14 seconds. Rebozo to be called by the Ervin committee, 11 seconds. Another story about Nixon, 15 seconds.

Then 55 seconds showing the *Cosmopolitan* centerfold, nude photo of Jim Brown and John Davidson. A minute and 20 seconds. Twenty-seven seconds of the mother, the San Leandre mother of the *Playgirl*'s centerfold, another male nude. Then a story about nude sun-bathing. Then three minutes 45 seconds of the weather. Then a 30-second story about the Nashville Stomper, who got his gratification from stepping on the insteps of ladies on the streets of Nashville. The story of a Detroit policeman who got divorced. A VC bust story. And a "kicker," a minute and 47 seconds long, about Hornytown, North Carolina, a massage parlor. That's what I mean by tabloid.

McHUGH: What did they do on Wednesday?

WALLACE: The same — we computerized the whole thing for a week. KGO, 11:00 P.M. Percentage of news stories on all shows — hard news stories — 51 per cent. Only 46 per cent at 11:00 P.M. Less than half on hard news. Percentage of non-news, weather, sports, billboards, Happy Talk, and commercials, 54 per cent.

McHUGH: That would be pretty true of most stations.

WALLACE: Okay. Percentage of fire, crime, sex, tearjerker, disaster stories, of the total hard news stories — 55 per cent.

So what you really have on KGO — there's a girl who works there, I'll not use her name — who said that KGO stands for "Kickers, Guts, and Orgasms."

McHUGH: I wouldn't agree with that, I really wouldn't. You can't take any one night. In my experience, that was a very atypical week for that station. Nonrepresentative week.

WALLACE: You know, it's fascinating to hear you say that because KGO is famous in San Francisco for a tease they did once—you know how they "tease" what's coming up on the news—and it wasn't such a long time ago that a tease said, "Male Genitals Found on Railroad Track. Stay Tuned to the Eleven O'Clock News for Details." Now, you're saying that this is the station that doesn't indulge in that kind of thing.

McHUGH: Well, you're talking about things, you know, that are outside of my experience. I'm really not qualified to talk to you about them.

A bit later in the interview, Wallace returned to the subject of the weathercast.

WALLACE: Do you really need three minutes and 45 seconds of weather? You know and I know there isn't three minutes and 45 seconds worth of weather in San Francisco or New York or anyplace. It's a circulation builder. The weatherman is a kind of personality.

McHUGH: He is in that market. He isn't in a lot of markets, and they still do three minutes and 45 seconds of weather.

WALLACE: Why?

McHUGH: Because people are very much interested in weather. They plan their life. Again, please bear with me on this mass audience, the people who have to go to work for a living, and they have to get out and build the buildings that are going to be built, drive the buses that are going to be driven . . . all of the hard-working people are very much interested in weather because a lot of their livelihood . . . all of the mothers want to know how to dress their kids for school.

WALLACE: *Local* weather, out of that three minutes and 45 seconds, generally takes maybe a minute. Two to two and one-half minutes is the weather in the New England states; Fargo, North Dakota; Miami, Florida. . . .

McHUGH: Since we've become a tremendously transient society, almost everybody is interested in the weather from someplace else. A high percentage of people in San Francisco all came from somebody — someplace else, anyway.

WALLACE: That's what I've heard.

Wallace then interviewed Frank Magid, the consultant for KGO's competitor in San Francisco, KRON. Wallace encountered a certain obliqueness.

WALLACE: What was KRON doing wrong when you took over, and when did you take over as their consultant and researcher?

MAGID: I don't know that they were doing anything wrong.

WALLACE: Well, they were at the bottom of the heap.

MAGID: That doesn't mean that they're doing anything wrong. It means, really, what they were doing was not being viewed by the general public in San Francisco.

WALLACE: And you were hired because they wanted a bigger audience, and they thought they were doing something wrong, because Frank Magid doesn't come cheap.

MAGID: Well, again, I don't know that you would say they were doing anything wrong. They were desirous of serving the public in the most effective way that they could.

WALLACE: When did you take over?

MAGID: Well, in the first place, I don't know what you mean by "taking over." We've been retained . . . I don't know if a doctor "takes over," or an accountant "takes over". . . .

WALLACE: When were you retained by KRON-TV?

MAGID: I believe about a year and a half ago.

WALLACE: Eighteen months ago. And they were at the bottom of the heap then and they're still at the bottom of the heap. What have you done in 18 months?

MAGID: When you make the statement that we were third then and third now, please keep in mind that it was only on January 1 of this year that our new product aired. So it's only been on, at this sitting, less than four weeks.

WALLACE: Yes, but by the same token, your current promotional ads, which I understand you largely created, for KRON-TV, say that by February 18, "this will be your favorite news team." Now, that's only a couple of weeks away, Mr. Magid.

MAGID: Well, we're very hopeful that there are going to be some significant gains in terms of audience share in the intervening time . . . between January 1 and that particular time.

WALLACE: You say yourself that your new-look product took over on January 1?

MAGID: Correct.

WALLACE: And you largely created an ad that says, by February 18 this is going to be "your favorite news team"? Therefore, you expected miracles. You expected, in six or seven weeks, to turn the story around in San Francisco. What is happening?

MAGID: We feel that we do have a very good product, and we do feel that the response is going to be strong and that, to a lot of people, it will be their favorite news team by that date.

WALLACE: Is it just a coincidence that February 18 is in the middle of an important ratings sweep?

MAGID: I believe that it really is. As a matter of fact, someone asked us that after the fact, and it was not a planned thing, even though many people have accused us of setting it for that particular date. It just wasn't. And I can tell you that quite honestly.

*   *   *   *   *   *   *

The significance of Walter Cronkite's castigation of "editing by consultancy" before the CBS affiliate managers and the significance of Mike Wallace's relentless probing of McHugh's and Magid's motives, even though those interviews were not aired, were not trivial. For the first time, the assumptions of cybernetic news were being questioned not just by "outside" critics such as newspaper columnists and members of academia, but by the titans of broadcast journalism themselves.

SEND IN THE CLOWNS: THE ATHYN GROUP

By 1976, it was fashionable among TV station executives to insist that news consultancy (and its attendant perversions of journalism) had "peaked." In the orthodox view, the various consulting groups were something of a collective Elizabeth Ray, playing against the momentarily-indiscreet-but-contrite Wayne Hays that was the TV news establishment. Yes, the executives grinned wryly, scuffing their shoes in the dust, we went overboard on that cockamamie Happy Talk business a few years ago, but look at us now: we've come to our senses, we've stabilized, we're Responsible.

The fact was that a whole second-growth forest of news consultants began blooming by 1976. Suddenly, it seemed, everyone in television was a closet consultant. Former top-level network executives, former news directors, career broadcast hacks who had trouble pronouncing "subliminal"—all were stumbling over one another in their eagerness to pass out questionnaires and line up clients.

News consultancy was the phantom reform of 1976. The year had scarcely begun when the news department of a major-market station—KNXT in Los Angeles, owned by CBS, that proud standard-bearer of broadcast journalism—lay in shambles. KNXT's journalistic demise is a case study in TV news as a disposable commodity, in stations' competitive greed, in mismanagement fueled by opportunism. A neophyte news consulting organization, the Athyn Group of Philadelphia, figured prominently in KNXT's sad story.

In many ways, the Athyn Group brought into sharp and comic relief the inherent daffiness that underlay all the mock-academic posturing and theorizing of news consultants in general. A coterie of seven ambitious young paladins based in Philadelphia, the Athyn Group for a while threatened to become a sort of flying squadron of behaviorist Keystone Kops, ready to whisk off to an ailing news station anywhere in the country and administer on-the-spot first aid through what it termed "psychoeducational processes."

That the Athyn Group was taken seriously (that is, retained) by two CBS-owned stations—WCAU in Philadelphia and ill-fated KNXT in Los Angeles—is a testament to the level of hysteria surrounding cybernetic news in 1976. News consultancy had not "peaked." It had run amok.

The Athyn Group's methodology made Frank Magid's IBM 1130 computer appear, by comparison, a blunt instrument. Magid was the dinosaur; Athyn, the child of destiny.

In the group were one psychiatrist (Peter Brill), one ex-minister (L. Crosby Deaton), one advertising man (Allan Kalish), one lawyer (Dick Watson), two university professors (Rod Napier and Larry Krafft, both at Temple) and one aficionado of group dynamics and psychoeducation (William Wilkinsky). Brill doubled as squad doctor.

Wilkinsky, a plump, droll, and infectiously enthusiastic mensch of 32, was the leader of the band. A former public-school teacher and, later, an instructor in psychoeducational processes at Temple University, Wilkinsky speaks the suave argot of cybernetic theory; his conversation is laced with terms such as "role-model," "intervention" and the ever-popular "input."

At the time he met his present colleagues, Wilkinsky was kicking around at the fringes of group dynamics. He had done some community surveys, worked on a book exploring the public school "as a human system," and, with a friend, had completed an unpublished work titled "The Encounter Cookbook."

"We present ourselves as an eclectic group," Wilkinsky observed, just a shade unnecessarily, in his small, homey office in the

Western Savings Bank building in Philadelphia. "When we examine your TV station, we bring back data to our home base, and a lot of different kinds of people take a look at it."

Wilkinsky's spectacles flashed in late-afternoon sunlight from the window as he leaned back comfortably behind his desk and sipped coffee from a styrofoam cup. He and his colleagues (who have been together since 1973) were still regarding their new area of specialization — broadcast news — with a mixture of wonderment and bemused jubilation. (When I had telephoned Wilkinsky for an appointment, I reached him at his home, where he was dutifully poring over two books on TV news. "I'm not too much into TV journalism," he remarked at the time. This was several months *after* the assignments at WCAU and KNXT.)

The group began to materialize, Wilkinsky recalled, in 1972 at Temple University. "I was a student of Rod Napier's then," he said. "I was in a doctoral program in psychoeducational processes. Rod had started working with Allan Kalish, then an ad man in Philadelphia. Kalish was excited to bits over what Rod and I presented to him as an 'executive training model.' Rod had created a process he called 'role counseling,' and the training model employed it. Basically what it is, is a management training program for a key executive in a business that takes place *in the business*. We don't take them away to a retreat center and then come back. Those models have failed, because when you go away and come back very different and learned, you're rejected by your own organization. They haven't accommodated the changes.

"Allan agreed with us that our role-counseling process for an executive is a critically important one that exists nowhere else in the country. He thought it was a process we should market, as a firm. Allan said, 'Business. You guys should think business.' "

News consultancy was hardly a gleam in Athyn's eye when the group incorporated in August 1973 — their target-clients at the time were large industrial firms — but already they were developing a hypermethodical style that would later charm station managers. The story of how Athyn chose its name — a process that called forth every last measure of the group's collective behavioristic training and group-dynamics resources — is a priceless example of this style.

"What," I asked Wilkinsky, "does 'Athyn' mean, anyway?"

"Uh — we didn't know," was his reply. He elaborated: "We

called the phone company on a Friday after we opened the office. Said we'd like phones installed next week under 'Wilkinsky.'" They said, 'Well, gee, the White Pages go to the press on Monday. Don't you want your name in it?' 'We don't have a name.' So he said, 'Well, maybe you can pick one this weekend.'

"So we thought, well, it must be important to be in the White Pages. We worked all weekend. We categorized consulting names by different types.

"There is, for instance," Wilkinsky went on, leaning forward as he recalled the agony of this, the group's first major test of its decision-making prowess, "the category of major partners. We could have been Kalish & Napier.

"There were *abbreviations* of major partners. 'The Kal-Nap Co.' Sounded like dog food. We could have picked the letters 'K & N.' We could have picked 'Management Development, Inc.' Well, that tells what you do, but it's limited. We could have even been 'NBI'; just never tell 'em what the letters stand for until they ask. We didn't like *that*.

"Then," continued Wilkinsky, gazing at the ceiling, "there was a group of *future*-sounding names. And there was a group of names that meant nothing, or were geographic.

"We liked geographic names. We were a Philadelphia-based firm, so, for example, there's a famous square here called Rittenhouse Square. We wanted to be Rittenhouse Associates; that was our first choice. But we learned that that name was owned, and everything *like* it was owned in the state."

Wilkinsky puffed his cheeks and allowed a reflective sigh to escape. After a few moments, he continued. "We then made a list of all the things we liked. Words. We made *up* words, we *found* words—*Ross* Associates, from Betsy Ross. I mean, we had everything. We rounded up all the partners by conference telephone call—this was all in that 24-hour weekend period. And 'Athyn' was on our list. 'Athyn' is also a community around here; the full name is Bryn Athyn. Like Bryn Mawr, the college. Very old Welsh community outside of Philadelphia. A partner, Larry Krafft, wanted to name his *daughter* Bryn.

"We didn't like 'Bryn Associates,' but we liked 'Athyn.' So everybody got a vote. A 'plus' if you liked it, and a 'zero' if it was okay but you neither liked nor disliked it, and a 'minus' if you disliked it. The rules were that anything with one minus got kicked out. And at the end of the day, we had 'Athyn' left."

Wilkinsky stared at the ceiling for a long time, lost in retrospection. When he finally spoke again, his voice was filled with a quiet grandeur. "It had five zeros and a plus," he said.

Having thus successfully completed the first major group-dynamics assignment of its career — naming itself — the Athyn Group thereupon set out to look for new worlds to conquer.

"We did not go directly into broadcast consulting," said Wilkinsky. "We built up some experience in other sectors, in which we could practice the principles of psychoeducational processes. For a while, it was all serendipity and accident."

The first client to provide the Athyn Group with the "experience" it would later apply to network-owned television news departments in two of America's largest cities was the Pennsylvania Power & Light Company.

"They own coal mines," said Wilkinsky, "and we were hired to do some role counseling in some of them. Diagnosis and intervention, we call it. Conflict negotiation.

"I recall that at one of their mines, they had personnel problems involving two key people. Both of them were named Joe; I forget both their last names. The first guy was a mine foreman. He was responsible for everything that happened to the thousand men who worked there in the mine. And he was this warm, sweet, lovable human being. The kind of guy who, in the middle of a crisis, will be explaining to people how to do things properly — and meanwhile, the walls below are coming down. He's sort of like the guy on the football team, he's down 50 to nothing, and he's sitting there diagramming plays.

"The second guy was the head of management training for foremen. And you ought to see this guy run a training center for 30 new people. They have something called a Long Wall Miner; it's a piece of equipment valued at about $300,000. It goes into a wall, takes out a section 30 feet long, and moves on. And then the ceilings cascade down behind it. Intentionally, the mine collapses. Or something. I don't know how it works. And I don't want to watch.

"*Anyway*," continued Wilkinsky, turning back toward the point, "this guy is explaining the operation of this machine to the

new men. And he's like this." Here Wilkinsky stiffened his back
and raised his voice to an imitation storm-trooper pitch. " 'IT
VORKS DIS VAY UND DISS VAY UND YOU PRESS DISS
BUTTON *UND YOU DON'T DO ANYT'ING ELSE!' Then he says,*
'DO YOU HAFF ANY QUESTIONS?'

"Well," Wilkinsky said, his voice dropping back to normal,
"people were *terrified* to ask a question. The guy comes to us and
says, 'Well, I explained it to 'em. How, tell me how, in one week it
could break down *four times?* With them doing stupid things like
not oiling it?' "

Wilkinsky paused significantly. Then he spread his hands as
he revealed the Athyn Group's solution to Pennsylvania Power &
Light's personnel crisis at the mines.

"We switched the two Joes," he said, a conspiratorial smile
playing about his mouth. "That's the recommendation we made.
Well, maybe that's not a *brilliant* intervention, but they just sat
there and didn't — you know — didn't make a connection between
style and role. So we did a style-and-role analysis and said, 'Whose
style fits where?' "

After sharpening its style-and-role technique on a few other
medium-sized companies and industries, the Athyn Group turned
its attention toward the television industry.

The newsroom of KNXT, Los Angeles's CBS-owned station,
was a demoralized, disgruntled shop in the winter of 1975. Many
of the problems involved personality conflicts: the co-anchor team
of Sandy Hill (a former beauty queen from the state of Washington) and Pat Emory (a handsome cuss out of St. Louis) did not
care for one another. No one cared for the assignment editor. A
general sense of aimlessness pervaded the newsroom; there was a
lack of clear leadership, of news-related objectives.

But if part of KNXT's malaise could be attributed to personal
squabbles, the rest of it was a factor of the bizarre TV-news scene
in Los Angeles itself. The competitive picture was changing rapidly, and KNXT was threatened with sudden oblivion.

For years, television news in Los Angeles had been in a qui-
escent state, with venerable KNBC and its long-time anchorman,
Jeff Marlowe, the perennial ratings leader. (KNBC benefited from

the fact that it was something of an NBC News farm team. Tom Brokaw and Tom Snyder, among others, had done star turns at co-anchor there, and Los Angeles is one city that recognizes a star when it sees one.)

If there was any movement at all among L.A. news audiences, it was away from the news. The city's three network-owned stations competed with four powerful independents, none of whom evinced a deep civic commitment to public affairs. KTTV was devastating all three early-evening newscasts by counterprogramming reruns of "I Love Lucy" and "The Mickey Mouse Club." KTLA tempted viewers with "Bonanza," KCOP beckoned with "Adam 12," and KHJ did well with "Ironside."

In 1974, a bombshell exploded in L.A.'s midst. The bombshell was named John Severino. A *wunderkind* sales manager at stations in Detroit and Chicago, Severino advanced to the general manager's chair of Chicago's WLS in the late 1960's. There he presided over the refinement of that station's Happy Talk news team of Joel Daly, Fahey Flynn, John Coleman, and Bill Frink. For his brilliant service at WLS, Severino was rewarded with the KABC cloud in Television Heaven. AT KABC, Severino—a deceptively low-keyed, quiet-spoken managerial genius—lost no time in applying the same cybernetic formula that had made WLS America's most profitable station.

In July 1975, Severino raided KNXT for Jerry Dunphy, a popular and capable veteran anchorman. Severino then reached to Cleveland for a firebrand personality named John Hambrinck. Hambrinck is one of television news's premier showmen. He is, in the words of an envious competitor, "exhausting to watch." Late-breaking news flashes and apocalyptic developments seem to abound when Hambrinck is on the air. His delivery is frequently, laced with a breathless "Just in!"

At KABC, John Hambrinck joined his brother Judd, who then was anchoring one of Channel 7's newscasts. The fraternal market appeal of the Brothers Hambrinck—a third brother, Mike, is on the air in Rhode Island—was scarcely lost on KABC's ever-alert promotion department. "IT'S NOT LIKE WATCHING NEWS, IT'S LIKE WATCHING FAMILY!" crowed newspaper display ads and on-air promotions. There were filmed interviews with Papa Hambrinck, who recollected how it was when the three immortals were just little tykes. If KTTV had Lucy and

Mickey Mouse, KABC was going to do a variation on "My Three Sons."

Such promotional stunt-mongering paid off for the Los Angeles ABC outlet. Channel 7 climbed from third place to contention for the Number One ratings spot in less than a year. By autumn of 1976, the KABC research department was claiming ratings supremacy in all audience age groups. Most of that new audience came from KNXT.

KNXT's general manager at the time was a young, darkly handsome soldier of fortune named Russ Barry. Like Severino (and like most station managers), Barry had moved up through the ranks in TV sales. Affecting breezy leisure suits and open-collar floral shirts, Barry had roamed through several cities and jobs before blowing into L.A. In Chicago, he had been sales manager for CBS's owned station, WBBM-TV. After similar work at WCBS in New York, Barry got involved in CBS radio as an executive with the owned stations. He was next dispatched to KNXT.

It was the arrival of Barry, with his salesman's instinct for the quick solution, that eventually brought KNXT into the Athyn Group's orbit. Thus ensued a surrealistic interlude that began as theater-of-the-absurd and ended with the CBS station virtually out of the running in L.A. TV-news competition.

Just a few weeks after it was all over—after Athyn had packed its tenets and quietly stolen back to Philadelphia, after Barry himself had been ejected from KNXT's rapidly revolving door—Barry sat in Beverly Hills's exclusive Rangoon Racquet Club, sipped a fine Scotch, and reflected on the entire enterprise. He did not seem to consider the KNXT-Athyn episode, or its results, as in any way a departure from conventional TV news-department strategy.

"The station had done a market survey in late 1972, before I got there," he said. "I didn't find it particularly relevant or helpful. The suggestions they'd made were not unique to us. They were similar to those I had seen in other surveys.

"I hired the Athyn group, really, to repair a morale problem in my news department—not, primarily, to get the ratings up. Naturally, I hoped there'd be a cause-and-effect relationship there. I'd heard of Athyn because they'd done some work at WCAU in Philadelphia.

"I assigned them to my newsroom, as opposed to the whole station, because I felt I had the most organizational problems there. They were what you call 'organizational development' people," Barry said, relishing the phrase as though, despite all, it possessed aleatory powers. "They were not concerned with product.

"I wanted to use Athyn's findings as a data base to deal with our on-air talent and our producers. One of our failings, I felt, was that we in management were not giving enough feedback to people. There was no focus of leadership, no objectives and standards set. There was, generally, a lack of direction."

When Athyn arrived (at a total cost to CBS of $35,000) KNXT was clinging to second place in the Los Angeles news ratings. When Athyn left some weeks later, dismissed by CBS's parent-network hierarchy follwing a thorough purge of personnel at the station, the group had fulfilled at least one understanding with Barry. He had not hired them to "improve product," and they hadn't. KNXT was then third.

"Was Athyn useful to KNXT in any way?" I asked Barry.

He shrugged. "They codified a set of objectives," he said. "They pinpointed the fact that the assignment desk was one of the great areas of tension in the newsroom."

Sandy Hill, the blonde beauty queen who lost her co-anchor position not long after Athyn's visit, was somewhat more blunt in her appraisal. "It was so unbelievable," she said. "Suddenly there were these shrinks in the newsroom. Pat Emory and me spent time with this Rod Napier and his wife, Sandy Napier. We were told that we would be at their disposal. We had deadlines! We had things to do!

"They kept saying things like, 'How do you feel about this?' 'We can tell by your *body* language that you don't *communicate* with each other.' 'There are certain *moves* you make that show us you do not *relate* to one another.'

"I mean, it was incredible. There were shrinks constantly popping up and asking, 'How do you *feel* about that?' Their leader was this little Jewish dumpling with curly hair. He'd distribute questionnaires to all of us. They'd ask things like, 'Where do you go in your spare time?' Some of us put, 'To a massage parlor.' You know. Another question was, 'How do you relate to your spouses,' or something like that. One of our reporters wrote down that he liked to put whipped cream all over his wife. We couldn't deal with them in a straight way, you know?

"One shrink moved in with Jim Topping, who was then our news director. He used to be so goddamn glib—toward the end, he lost his verbal prowess.

"The assignment editor started going to meetings with little notebooks in his hand. They'd ask us things like, 'How would you pictorially depict your management system?' I mean it was *weird*.

"The effect of the whole experience," concluded Sandy Hill, "was that it did unite the newsroom—against the Athyn Group. We put up a united front against this albatross." She gave a bitter little smile. "It got our backs up—which, in a way, was what they were supposed to do, I guess."

* * * * * * *

In Philadelphia, I asked Bill Wilkinsky to give me his version of Athyn's "intervention" at KNXT. He consented, but prefaced his account with this lofty explanation of his group's *raison d' être:* "We have forgotten," he said, "that the reason TV is where it is today is because of *technical* advances—*not* the human-potential process. TV is where it is right now because of engineers. They have created enormous advances that have improved reception in the home, created color—all that.

"But without trying to hurt people's feelings, I guess I'd say that the people in the television news business are *not* communications experts, and in many cases, are not even communications-knowledgeable."

Wilkinsky folded his hands behind his head and gazed at the ceiling. "I think," he said reflectively, "that if I asked this question of the TV industry, 99 per cent of the people could not answer it: 'Would you describe for me the dynamic process that occurs between a sender of information and a receiver of information, and how that information is integrated by the receiver related to how it is administered by the sender?' "

I asked Wilkinsky how *he* would answer that question.

He took his gaze from the ceiling abruptly and blinked at me. An uncertain smile formed on his lips. "Now, that is a sneaky thing to do," he said after a second or two, "but I will be glad to try: The communication process between any two individuals has several variables related to it. One, it involves our two psychological states: Are you ready to receive a message? If I'm about to have a salary negotiation with you and you're angry with me, then I'm foolish because I haven't taken into account your readiness to deal with that specific topic—"

I interrupted Wilkinsky to assure him I agreed with his estimate that not one person in one hundred could answer his question—but that I'd like to hear about his experiences at KNXT.

Wilkinsky took a deep breath and began. "Russ Barry hired us for a large intervention into his system. A heavy involvement in his organization. I went out there in December 1975 for a few days, came back, and our team went out in January of 1976 for seven weeks. I took an apartment, took my wife and baby—my wife has a master's in secondary education and has advanced training in group dynamics and organizational behavior. She was part of the team that did the videotape analysis.

"We did Management Training, we did Management-Effectiveness Analysis, we did Team Effectiveness, we did Critiquing Programs. We have this 70-item questionnaire that we distribute to almost all the employees of a system; it has open-ended items about their product. Why it is where it is; what would *they* do?

"Secondly," said Wilkinsky, although it was difficult to recall at the moment what was "first," "we did Observational Diagnosis. That involves a skilled person walking around in a system and getting a feel for what happens in it. I use a lot of schemas to do that: a Verbal Inventory System, a Structural Analysis of the furniture position in relationship to the people."

I was not sure I had heard Wilkinsky correctly. "Furniture position?" I repeated.

"Sure," said Wilkinsky. "You look at the studio set and get a sense of what they are trying to do on a news presentation. What are they saying about their style? Where are their systems?"

I told Wilkinsky I understood, and asked him to please continue.

"We looked at management decisions and management effectiveness," said Wilkinsky, "by sitting in on meetings. I tried to apply my knowledge of the TV world to their systems. I've spent over 150 days at stations. That's a goodly time.

"We asked for ten to 15 hours of videotapes of recent news

programming so we could do our Transactional Analysis Audit.
We did our SAVI analysis. SAVI means System for Analyzing
Verbal Interaction. Do you know that, during one 30-minute pe-
riod at WCAU, we counted the use of the word 'okay' *48 times?*
'Okay, Jim.' 'okay, Bob' 'Okay, Bill.'

"At KNXT, the word was 'well.' That was their transition
phrase. We tried to get them to stop saying that.

"I created a category called 'noise.' I described 'noise' as anything that interferes with the communication process. KNXT did
its newscast in a live newsroom. We counted, in one half-hour, 33
times when a person would move, in camera range, out of focus.
Each time, subliminally, that is an interruption. Occasionally,"
Wilkinsky went on, warming briskly to this subject, "people are on
the air, they don't *know* they're on the air, and they're playing with
each other. TADOOOOM! A paper flies across the screen! Absolutely no system. No preparation."

I wanted to question Wilkinsky more closely on the matter of
reporters playing with each other on screen, throwing paper wads
and whatnot, but he was plowing enthusiastically ahead.

"We tried to get at the subconscious identification level of the
audience. That's where Transactional Analysis comes in so well.
In Transactional Analysis there is a Parent, an Adult, and a Child.
Three very basic ego-states. Within each one of those states there
are subdivisions: there's a *problem* Child, there's a *spunky* Child,
there's a *playful* Child. Now, the anchorperson always corresponds
to one of those states. He or she may be a punishing Parent. May
be a *curing* Parent. One who loves. And in return for the love,
places no demands on it. Just says, 'I accept and love you. I care
about you.'

"In that way, the anchorperson mimics the family system.
Walter Cronkite, for instance—I'd say Walter Cronkite mimics,
and in a lot of ways becomes, a *caring* Parent. Tom Snyder is an
alive, vibrant Child. *Spunky* Child. *Angry* Child. Not a *punishing*
Child; the one Child we don't want to deal with is the Child who
punishes. And makes us feel guilty. And Snyder doesn't do that.
He just says, '*I'm* angry. You want to get angry with me? Join in.
It's fun. Come play with me.' "

As Wilkinsky was explaining all this, I was searching for a
way to direct the conversation back to the subject of his work at
KNXT in Los Angeles. Finally I pressed the matter on him, gently

but insistently, perhaps like a curious Adult. "What eventually happened to your project?" I asked him.

For the first time in the interview, Wilkinsky looked somewhat crestfallen. He sighed, as though considering a painful memory. Then he said, "Our best guess was that we had five months to prove something. I say, 'we,' because when we get into a relationship, it's a partnership between the client system and us. And it becomes a 'we-identity,' not *us* telling *them* what to do, not *them* telling *us* what—"

"The end result," I coaxed.

"We spent 10 days," Wilkinsky said, a bit sadly, "every night, every morning, during the day, weekends—planning. We developed a Four-Week Action Plan to change things around.

"On the second day of the Action Plan, I was scheduled to take a five-day break. I went to San Francisco. That was on a Wednesday. I got a call Saturday night. The new management team had arrived and taken over. That was the end."

Wilkinsky gazed ruefully down at his hands, which were now in his lap. He was silent for quite a long time. "The new team didn't know what the hell we were doing there," he said finally. "They asked us not to return to their station." He turned his head and gazed out the window, pondering the capriciousness of it all. When he turned back to stare at me, his voice was incredulous. "They didn't even know what a Four-Week Action Plan was," he said.

For KNXT, the aftershocks continued well after the dismissal of Barry. Several weeks later, widespread personnel changes swept the station. Sandy Hill and Pat Emory were among the casualties, as were several other reporters, anchor people, and management personnel.

But those changes were not the crowning blow. In the spring of 1976, KNXT abandoned an entire hour of early-evening local news in favor of Dinah Shore's show. The station moved Walter Cronkite's network feed to six o'clock from seven o'clock, and slotted "Dinah!" from six-thirty to eight. Cronkite, the very personification of TV journalism, was thus being used as a lead-in to an entertainment show.

It would be a severe mistake to cite the Athyn Group as the cause of KNXT's descent into journalistic oblivion in 1976. The fault, clearly, lies with the station's own management and with the competitive priorities of the parent CBS network, which manifestly cared less about stablizing KNXT's news identity than about reaching for a stopgap audience device.

Athyn's role in the affair was, however, symptomatic. Russ Barry (and, by tacit consent, those who hired him) had tried to pass off, as "journalism," a pastiche made of beauty queens, handsome faces, and the hocus-pocus of questionnaries, body language, Observational Diagnosis, Transactional Analysis Audits, and Systems for Analyzing Verbal Interaction. The audience saw through it all and opted for the real thing: Mickey Mouse.

END OF AN ERA?

The Athyn Group used "Psychoeducational Processes" in its tin-kerings with television newscasts.

ERA uses electrodes.

ERA stands for Entertainment Response Analysts, and by 1976 ERA had pushed its way into big-time TV news consultancy as a major competitor to Magid and McHugh & Hoffman. Appar-ently, the word "entertainment" in its title did not throw up too many red flags in the minds of station managers and news direc-tors: ERA's "Television News Client Market List" showed ac-counts in New York, Chicago, Los Angeles, San Francisco, St. Louis, Philadelphia, Dallas, Washington, and Boston. Among them were the five CBS-owned stations.

If Athyn is a collection of youthful, self-important but ulti-mately well-meaning intellectuals, the men of ERA are their per-fect shadow image: older, worldly-wise, hale fellows well met, ca-reer broadcast pros rather than scholars—and profoundly on the make.

An ERA "memo" distributed to visiting TV executives at the 1976 National Association of Broadcasters Convention in Chicago is illustrative of the group's breezy, sales-pitch celebration of cy-bernetic news:

Research has come a long way in the last three years.

And it's about time.

The challenge of producing successful television news programs is a complex mix of journalism, practical sociology . . . and Show Biz.

The old idea that you could do meaningful TV news research with only one technique is just that . . . an old idea.

223

ERA research approaches the problem with *five* state-of-the-art techniques. When we answer a basic question like "Is my anchorperson any good?", we build our answer from several, overlapping data sources.

We do much of our research into viewer responses to tapes of actual news programs . . . your and your competition's. The result? No more vague generalities, speculation and inferences based on what viewers *think* they *remember*. We get down to hard facts about what works . . . and what doesn't.

What communicates? What irritates? Who is effective? What kind of writing, film editing, sequencing and pace works best? Production, sets, format, specials, reporter involvement, supers, scores, radar, minicam . . . we test *whatever you want to know about,* the way you do it and the way your competition does it. We tell you how strong your programs are with the everyday news viewers, both in terms of the competitive situation, and with ERA national norms.

Every News Director we know, who's in a competitive situation, wants and needs credible information about every element of the program.

ERA can build a reliable, ongoing feedback loop from your audience . . . channeling information to you . . . that you can *believe* and *act on.*

So when research is on your mind, we're on the other end of a phone. Call us . . . Collect.

The three principal partners of ERA, which operates out of San Francisco, are Willis Duff, Sebastian Stone, and David Crane. All are career broadcasters, with no particular training in the "research" that is so blithely bandied about in their promotional literature. Duff, a bearded, bearish, affable man of 40, has been a disc jockey, station manager, general manager—and salesman. He describes his colleague Stone as "a long-time radio programmer" and former disc jockey, and Crane as having been with "a number of stations."

The names of Duff, Stone, and Crane appear on all of ERA's letterheads and promotional pamphlets. The name Tom Turicchi does not. All Tom Turicchi did for ERA was to provide the group with its competitive warhead: an audience-testing system known as "psychographics," built around an $8,000 hospital machine, the Physiograph Six-B.

The Physiograph Six-B measures, by the use of electrodes,

the galvanic skin responses of human beings listening to music or watching images on a television screen. It can detect boredom, enthusiasm, arousal, dislike, and other emotions by the subtle changes in bodily functions. With the arrival of Tom Turicchi and his galvanic-skin machine in the news-consultancy field, the term "cybernetic news" attained literal validity: no longer would it be necessary for consultants to take the primitive route of asking test groups what their informational preferences were. Now the consultants could simply plug in the human bodies themselves for the answer.

Psychographics had not been designed for anything as Orwellian as probing the adult central nervous system for responses to news items, of course. Turicchi devised the method in order to wire up adolescent girls and find out what sort of rock music they were willing to buy.

Dr. Thomas Turicchi is a 37-year-old Ph.D. in music and psychology who also has an undergraduate degree in mathematics. A native of Providence, Rhode Island, Turicchi stumbled onto the psychographic system while teaching music literature at Texas Woman's University in Denton, a Dallas suburb, in the late 1960's.

"I was looking for some way to turn my students on to classical music," he told Chicago *Sun-Times* rock writer Dick Saunders in a 1975 interview, "and I decided to try the 'greatest hits' approach—to make a kind of classical Top 40 list. I applied everything I knew about attitudinal research. But I found out that just *asking* them what they liked was the weakest method. People tell you what they think you want to hear. The next stop was tapping their subconscious responses."

Fortunately for Turicchi, Texas Woman's University happened to be stocked with some $13,000 worth of physiographic equipment: hospital-related machines used to take electrocardiograms, measure blood pressure, respiration, muscular tension, and galvanic skin response. Turicchi began to fiddle around with this arsenal of the Aesculapian art in his spare time. His initial approach, he admitted to Saunders, was somewhat unpolished: "I'd grab students out of the hall and tie them to a chair."

As Turicchi proceeded with his experiments on the human guinea pigs of Texas Woman's, he winnowed out the less effective items in the school's inventory. Eventually, he had things narrowed down to the galvanic skin response as the key to the human subconscious. "The other tests," he said, "would show some difference in reaction if you played two pieces that were really far apart—one stimulative and one sedative. But if you had three strong pieces, galvanic skin response could tell you which was strongest."

Perhaps Turicchi's initial dabblings into the alchemy of psychographics were, indeed, unsullied by thought of personal gain: the eternal inquiry of academia. However, like the Sorcerer's Apprentice, Turicchi was to find that he could not contain the handiwork of his tinkerings. By 1974, Turicchi had forsaken the ivy halls and refined young spirits of Texas Woman's University for rock 'n' roll.

The agent of Turicchi's entree to worldliness was a Chicago rock-radio-station manager named Lew Witz. Witz visited Dallas in 1973 to negotiate some business with a company that produced the jingles for Witz's station, WCFL. Witz learned of Turicchi through the jingle firm; the professor *had* done a bit of remunerative work here and there. Within a few months, Witz was compiling WCFL's playlist based on Turicchi's test findings.

At about the same time, Sebastian Stone, then a radio programming director in San Francisco, had also wandered into Dallas and discovered the galvanic academic. (Rumor has its own psychographic network in the wired-in world of rock music.) Stone and Turicchi worked out a four-month agreement whereby the programmer would send new record releases to the professor, who would skin-test them on his students and report the results by mail. On the first batch of tests, Turicchi was accurate in his predictions more than 90 per cent of the time.

It was then only a matter of months before Dr. Thomas Turicchi, the good don of classical-music appreciation, had become Tom Turicchi, the modish, bearded, leisure-suited profit-prophet of Top 40 rock, given to such utterances as, "We don't just tell the company if a record will sell. We tell them whether it will be superstrong, a mid-charter or a stiff." He got around Dallas in a Grand Prix.

Turicchi set up a laboratory in the Dallas suburb of Richardson and began an extravagantly profitable business of weekly reports on new pop records for radio-affiliated clients across the country—program directors, record-company presidents and publicists.

On a given day, a visitor to Turicchi's lab could look through a one-way mirror and observe six to eight subjects, usually teen-aged girls, slumped in their chairs and listening to new pop recordings by Paul Anka, Tony Orlando, Donny Osmond, or Barry Manilow. Electrodes attached to the subjects' fingers would send their bodily reactions to an adjoining room, where the Physiograph Six-B would chart their boredom or brio on graph paper.

"Tom developed a Coca-Cola formula," Paul Gentry, Turicchi's assistant and brother-in-law, proudly told Michael Gross in *New Times* magazine, "and he sells it." Of the test subjects, Gentry observed, "their heads may say they hate [a song], but their belly-buttons tell the tale."

Test subjects are found in the schools, colleges, and shopping centers around Dallas. Wrote Michael Gross:

> The average person is what Turicchi wants, and average is universal in Big D. They aren't told what the tests are, or that they'll be paid. Only after screening, when they've fit neatly into Turicchi's middle-class heavy test sample, do they find out what he does. Average is average, whether it's in Dallas or Duluth, and, according to Gentry, "A stiff in New York is a stiff in Dallas. A hit is a hit."

Gentry confided to *New Times* that his brother-in-law has little trouble recruiting test subjects. "The kids enjoy coming in," he said. "It's the best thing since masturbation."

Thus the background of Entertainment Response Analysts' methodology for researching television news.

It was Sebastian Stone who recognized the potential of psychographics for radio programmers (Witz having directed Turicchi's expertise toward the record companies themselves, forming Research Consultants Incorporated). Stone organized Entertainment Research Associates, which later became Entertainment Response Analysts, and which, beginning in 1973, applied the science of predicting rock-record hits to television news departments.

Turicchi is not a visible exponent of ERA. Willis Duff does most of the group's promoting, having apparently graduated from an informal course in Turicchese, the language of psychographics. Duff lacks what one would call a keen scientific grasp of behaviorist theory, but he does have the salesman's knack of breaking things down into dollars-and-cents terms for TV station managers.

I interviewed Duff in Chicago in the spring of 1976, during the National Association of Broadcasters convention there (Duff was in town to recruit clients.) We launched at the Barclay Club as guests of a current client, Neil Derrough, the general manager of CBS-owned WBBM. Duff sipped a vodka-and-grapefruit juice as he explained ERA's particular endowment for broadcast journalism.

"The trick," Duff said, "is to figure out how to communicate what our client wants to communicate." Duff is a walking treasure trove of pithy maxims like that one, and delivers each with great deliberation and a furrowed brow, as though he has weighed every word carefully beforehand.

I observed to Duff that a number of news consultants were seemingly onto that trick already, and asked him how his techniques differed from those of the titans in the field.

"Our principal departure from somebody like Magid," he said, "is on the theory that no single technique of research such as that used by the traditional researchers is enough. I mean the long interview, show you a tape and let you fill out a questionnaire, simple discussion group." These single techniques, Duff explained, were inadequate because of "the subtleties and complexities" involved. He did not make clear exactly which "subtleties and complexities," but forged briskly ahead with a hint of how ERA manages to avoid their tentacles: "Attitudinal research, which we use extensively, which we balance off with a variety of other types of research, tends to give you answers that dig into someone's opinions further than they've articulated."

Articulation, it was turning out, was something that Willis Duff regarded with the gravest suspicion: "Fact is that verbal devices are so inconsistent. Someone tells you something is terrific. Someone else tells you it's okay. And they mean exactly the same thing; it relates to their degree of hyperbole and their normal conversation."

The remark was pure Turicchi; it recalled his "People will tell you what they think you want to hear." I was eager to hear Duff's version of ERA's breakthroughs in research technique (the phrase "So when research is on your mind . . ." kept running through my brain like the lyrics of a catchy floor-wax commercial), but first I wanted him to define his conception of "research." Duff was only too glad to oblige. He had, as it turned out, given the matter some thought.

"Research," he said, "is gatherin' a lot of data and then goin' into the inferential process in terms of what in heaven's name does all this stuff mean."

I nodded. Linus Pauling could not have put it any better. But Willis Duff was not through. ". . . And the more you have," he was saying, "the more likely you are to make a rational conclusion."

With this epistemological framework in mind, Willis Duff proceeded to outline ERA's news-consultancy approach. "What we try to do," he said, "is just simply build a general hypothesis about the problem, whatever the problem is. Basically," he conceded after a moment's thought, "there's only one problem: Why are we not reaching a sizable group of people?

"We do what we call 'Limited Attitudinal Research.' We interview a thousand people in the client's market area. They'll all be representative of some predefined group. They'll all be 25-to-49, or 35-to-64, or whatever it is you're looking at as a target audience.

"And we will, in our questioning device, and our technique of how we find these people, achieve the result of all those things we think we can get out of attitudinal research."

Without actually having left the Barclay Club luncheon table or strayed more than an elbow's length from his vodka-and-grapefruit juice, Willis Duff seemed to have just completed a perfect circle. The reasons for his distrust of articulation were becoming apparent.

To get things down to brass tacks, I suggested to Duff that 1,000 interviews constituted an exceptionally large sample.

"We only interview some of 'em for 20 minutes," he said, "because we think that elaborations beyond that start getting cloudy." "Like a ten-second news item?" I almost asked, but didn't. "Then," went on Duff, "we put them through a lot of *panel testing*. Panel testing involves a group of techniques. We pick out 80 people from the 1,000 and put them through these techniques.

"The first group of techniques they run into are Personality

Perception Tests. Where they describe to us the *best* personality they've ever seen. The best anchorman, the best weatherman, the best sportscaster, the best reporter. We do a great deal, by the way," he emphasized, "to overcome the problems of research by giving the people a sense of their own anonymity. We want to reduce peer-group pressure as much as possible. They don't put their names on the papers they fill out. We never know who's going what within the test group.

"Then," Duff went on, "we show them tapes. Videotapes of clients' newscasts, competition's newscasts, guys from out of town, whatever it is we want to bounce off these people. While they are observing these tapes, they are giving us a conscious reaction to what they see as they see it. They do this by pushing buttons.

"The use of the buttons is explained in detail to the people. They are always pushing a particular button to tell us how good, how interesting, how authoritative, how revealing, whatever it is they expect out of a newscast. There are four buttons: one for Superior, one for Good, one for Poor, and one for Tune-Out.

"Then," said Duff, "we divide everybody up into four groups of 20. Twenty young women, 20 young men, 20 old women, 20 old men. Internal to each group there will be a socioeconomic spread, an ethnic spread, and a geographic spread—to make it representative of, uh, the people. The groups of 20 are to be a model of the original 1,000.

"So they view these tapes we've put together. And while they're viewing them, they're pressing these buttons, and we have the Turicchi speciality, the electrodes on their other hand, which, while they're watching, generates two lines of data: the conscious line and the unconscious.

"So," said Duff, sitting back in his luncheon chair with the indulgent, self-deprecatory smile of the dedicated scientist, "we go back to our ivory tower with an enormous amount of data. And we're looking at: how do you communicate, with a linear medium, an audiovisual medium, to do whatever your journalistic objectives are?" The smile broadened; another fatherly maxim was coming on. "I think," Duff said, "that the best description of what we do is 'research in communication.' "

Beyond his obvious tendency to parrot jargon without fully comprehending its meaning (twice in the interview Duff referred to television as a "linear" medium, unaware that he was exactly reversing McLuhan's most celebrated characterization), Duff raises more questions about ERA's involvement with TV news than he answers.

What, for instance, do galvanic skin responses have to do with the quality of journalism? If a news story or a film clip makes a sample audience's pulse jump, is that an index of the story's intellectual worth? News film that depicts bloodstains on a sidewalk following a murder, or an amateur striptease night in a suburban nightclub, or a patient swathed in bandages in a hospital, might well cause an emotional "spike" on a graph-paper readout. (Indeed, such stories did exactly that in tests for WBBM.) Does that mean that they are newsworthy—that they qualify, on their own merits, to occupy the limited time span of a television broadcast?

Conversely, stories about economic trends, about environmental debate, about developments in the detection of influenza strains—these and countless other "abstract" themes undoubtedly make little discernible impact on a psychographic scale. Does that rule them out of a newscast's agenda, or relegate them to the second-class status of "items," to be mentioned quickly and then passed over for something juicier? The logic of psychographics would seem to dictate that this is so. Psychographics was not invented as a journalistic yardstick, but as a measure of what "sells."

Paul Gentry, Turicchi's loquacious assistant, made one further, and highly revealing, remark to *New Time*'s Michael Gross. Sex, death, and money, he said, "get people off." It is perhaps no accident that soon after retaining ERA, WBBM, which had been building a prestigious image as Chicago's most dedicated TV news shop, began running "mini-documentaries" on runaway wives, pornographic movies, Chicago's richest bachelors, and suburbia's most elegant mansions, and began showing reporters doing hospital-related stories while standing beside the beds of patients swathed in bandages.

"The idea is insidious," said WBBM co-anchorman Bill Kurtis, "of anybody interfering with judgment that should be left to free men to make, of their own free choice, by experience and education. Anything like that is a danger. And it presents a trend that I don't like in the business."

Kurtis did not denounce the ERA research at WBBM out of

hand. However, he echoed the caveat of other newsmen and more sophisticated station managers that the danger of such material is its susceptibility of being misunderstood.

"When I read ERA's results," he told me, "I interpreted the material much differently than the sales department would interpret it. Someone without the journalism base might look at it and say, 'This galvanic skin response indicates an emotional reaction to this particular story, so let's emphasize *this,* and that.' When I read it, I interpreted most of the reaction as being very similar to the judgments that we had been making as newspeople all along. I was surprised that people reacted to content and information. Believe it or not, they really watched the news to get the news."

Kurtis suggested a further, more subtle danger inherent in the ERA approach to judging news content.

"We always lead with something sensational," he acknowledged. "A fire, a murder, the Patty Hearst story last year. There is always something like that. The *real* rub comes in those marginal stories. When it comes to choosing between, say, a mild political development and a softer educational-medicine kind of story, the tendency is to go with the political story. And I think that, a lot of times, more people will be helped by medical information than by one more political development. But research tells us to keep hitting those peaks, to insure audience interest. We're not expanding our definition of what is really news."

Not too many weeks after Willis Duff sat pontificating in the Barclay Club, with WBBM's general manager Neil Derrough part of his admiring audience, WBBM was to learn a painful and embarrassing lesson in the difference between "hitting peaks" in a cybernetic screening room and communicating with total human beings.

On the basis of an ERA "Personality Preference Test," WBBM demoted its long-time weatherman, a gentle and kindly broadcast professional named John Coughlin, to the position of staff announcer. ERA's testing program had discovered that Coughlin "generated little excitement."

Coughlin's replacement was a kinetic and fast-talking actor-comedian named Tom Alderman, who had most recently served as the public-relations aide to Illinois Governor Dan Walker. Alderman, who in fact had genuine gifts in comic acting and dazzling repartee, "hit peaks," all right. The negative outcry from

Channel 2 viewers was without precedent in Chicago broadcast history. In a four-week period, more than, 6,000 angry letters deluged WBBM.

Sun-Times television critic Bill Granger, reporting that the management of Channel 2 was "simply stunned" by the outpouring of protest, went on to observe:

> Channel 2 insiders tell me that Alderman's patronizing way of "relating" dry weather facts to viewers was suggested by an outside consulting firm. In fact, the whole Alderman performance has largely been a triumph of consultation-for-a-fee over common sense.
>
> Did Channel 2 seek more excitement in weather news? It got it.

* * * * * *

Thus far, ERA, Athyn, and other "second-growth" consultant firms have penetrated only the local-station level of television news. But the news-as-show-biz ethic itself has already reached the networks, where it is an inescapable fact of life for some of the most honored names in electronic journalism.

A MODEST PROPOSAL

When a consultant group can sell itself to television news departments in nine of the country's largest cities, the CBS-owned outlets among them, by promising "a mix of journalism, practical sociology . . . and Show Biz," something has gone wrong with America's informational system.

When TV news directors allow "galvanic skin responses" to determine even a fraction of their news programs' content, the public interest is being manipulated, and the protections implied in the Communications Act are being subverted.

When a TV station manager (the de facto "managing editor" of his station's newscast) hires an outside company of para-behaviorist scientists to smooth over the symptoms of deteriorating morale—instead of applying his own managerial skills to attack the root of the problem—he is delegating responsibility for his journalistic product and blurring the distinctions between its illusions and its reality.

When local stations create and choreograph entire news programs along guidelines supplied by researchers—toward the end of gratifying the audience's surface whims, not supplying its deeper informational needs—an insidious and corrosive hoax is being perpetrated on American viewers through a system that implicitly asks, and has been granted, their trust. The hoax is made more insidious by the fact that very few TV news-watchers are aware of what information is *left out* of a newscast in order to make room for the audience-building gimmicks and pleasant repartee.

When evidence of these and similar intrusions into the conventional journalistic process is presented to television audiences, two things could happen:

(1) The audiences could, by their indifference, indicate an

endorsement of developments — and, by extension, indicate that their traditional requirements of American journalism have broken down under the imperatives of technology, marketplace primacy, and the inertia of public will that is a factor of sheer population size. It is the fundamental aim of journalism to intellectually arm the citizen to make decisions about how to protect his well-being. If the citizen feels powerless, in a mass society, to exercise personal control over his well-being in the first place, then perhaps cybernetic news, news as nonfiction entertainment, is the wave of the future, an index of human evolution. The diminishing percentage of active voters among eligible voters is a statistic that lends credence to this possibility.

(2) A minority of citizens within the mass audiences — a minority that perhaps may not be persuasive on the scale of TV's competitive viewing requirements, but which nonetheless contributes leadership to neighborhoods, communities, cities, and the nation — could assert its proprietorship over the airwaves and demand reform. This minority has already been effective, on a grassroots level, in several areas of broadcast policy-making. The most notable example is the success of Action for Children's Television, a Boston-based group of concerned parents who have raised the standards of Saturday-morning programs and commercials aimed at young children. Other citizen-interest groups with effective watchdog credentials include the communications office of the United Church of Christ (whose director, Dr. Everett C. Parker, is described in the DuPont-Columbia survey as "the nation's leading license challenger") and the Washington-based National Citizens Committee on Broadcasting, headed by the former citizens'-advocate commissioner of the FCC, Nicholas Johnson.

Such organizations are of interest not only as referral sources for those interested in protesting cybernetic news, but also as prototypes for new groups that could be formed specifically for that purpose. Earlier I mentioned the monitoring project undertaken for the DuPont-Columbia survey by the American Association of University Women, which analyzed the news content of half-hour news programs of 262 local TV stations across the country. Similar monitoring projects could be organized within a given community by church, PTA, or other civic groups. The newscasts of a certain station could be taped and transcribed over a given period — a week or a month — and the content could then be collated and compared to that of the local newspapers, or to the group's own personal knowledge of what is (and is not) happening within the community.

What would these groups do with the results of their surveys?

Representative Lionel Van Deerlin, a Democrat from California, is the chairman of the communications subcommittee of the House Interstate and Foreign Commerce Committee. This subcommittee could be called upon to open an investigation of the news-gathering and reportorial practices of local television stations.

It should be clearly understood that the aim of any congressional hearings on TV news would not be to prescribe standards of broadcast journalism. Government-imposed standards would be as inimical to the integrity of TV news as are the standards suggested by consultants and researchers — more so, as they would carry the censoring force of a totalitarian stamp.

Short of suggesting standards, however, the hearings would offer for public scrutiny the organization and administration of television news. If, as Dr. David LeRoy suggests, there is widespread delegation of programming responsibility, in direct opposition to the provisions of the Communications Act of 1934, the public has a right to know of it — toward the end of challenging station licenses. If it is now to the economic advantage of station managers to *hire* news consultants, perhaps it should be a matter of even greater advantage *not* to hire them.

And what, after all, does constitute the ideal newscast?

The answer is not easy.

Throughout this book, I have implied a somewhat narrow function of "news": to monitor and report on the conduct of public officials and others who exercise power over private citizens, toward the goal of assuring openness, accountability, and the intelligent administration of community life. This sort of information, the traditional wisdom has it, assures people of a clearer basis on which to make their political choices.

Obviously, this definition doesn't begin to encompass the full range of subjects and interests that "news" media in America have always presented. Nor should it. Human beings are curious — randomly curious, illogically curious, morbidly curious. The news apparatus of a community should reflect that curiosity; in fact, it always has. Even the New York *Times* has its "People" column, and the *Wall Street Journal* is not above an occasional tidbit of juicy gossip.

The determining factor in the quality of a news-gathering agency, then, is its shared relationship with the community it serves. American newspapers—the predominant news form until 25 years ago—have always been parochial in outlook: published, edited, and written by people who have made long-term commitments to the city they cover, and who have a stake in its viability. The modular, transient nature of American business in the last 20 years has cut into this parochial tradition, to be sure; newspapermen move from city to city, as do middle-management executives and professional engineers. And the enticing economics of collectivism, in the form of burgeoning wire-service use and the use of "packaged" features, have added to the standardization of the local daily.

Nevertheless, the American newspaper, augmented by the rise of the suburban press and even by "alternative" weeklies, remains a voice of its environment: idiosyncratic, steeped in the complex history of local controversies and concerns, familiar with the performance patterns of civic leaders. Its faults are several and familiar. It is too responsible to "official" versions of controversial events, slow to accept social change as its host community is slow to accept social change, boosterish, encrusted with its own anachronistic biases. But through it all, the daily paper often manages to be a benign intervener, a flawed but reliable curator of the ongoing processes of a city's life.

The television news department, by contrast, has seldom been able to escape a colonial persona. It is an emissary to a community, not an indigenous product of it. Its reference point is time present; unlike the newspapers, the TV stations seldom bother to accumulate a reference library in which reporters can check the past coverage of an ongoing issue. Often (as is the case with the 15 network-owned stations and the dozens of other "group" stations) the TV news staff responds to the pure marketing priorities of absentee ownership. The on-air men and women look and sound less like their fellow citizens than like some idealized product of genetic breeding. This may be good for viewers' sexual fantasies; it does not do much for a station's credibility.

The anchor-gods and -goddesses seldom remain long in a given "market"; they are nomads on the move, their aspirations fixed on New York whence their loyalty often derives.

Television stations reap enormous profits from the communities they are licensed to serve. Annual pre-tax profits of between $2 million and $10 million, depending on market size, are not uncommon among stations. Average rates of return on sales are consistently between 30 and 50 per cent—robust figures indeed in the American industrial community.

Until local television news ceases to exploit the entertainment bias that is conditioned by its host medium, and shares some of the profit with its "market" in the form of comprehensive, compact newscasts, it is engaging in a pollution of the worst sort: a pollution of ideas. Its options should be the same as those of any polluter: clean up the mess or pay the consequences.

INDEX